Personal Meanings of Death

SERIES IN DEATH EDUCATION, AGING, AND HEALTH CARE

HANNELORE WASS, CONSULTING EDITOR

ADVISORY BOARD

Herman Feifel, Ph.D.
Jeanne Quint Benoliel, R.N., Ph.D.
Balfour Mount, M.D.

Benoliel	Death Education for the Health Professional
Davidson	The Hospice: Development and Administration
Epting, Neimeyer	Personal Meanings of Death: Applications of Personal Construct Theory to Clinical Practice
Wass	Dying: Facing the Facts
Wass, Corr	Helping Children Cope with Death: Guidelines and Resources
Wass, Corr, Pacholski, Sanders	Death Education: An Annotated Resource Guide

IN PREPARATION

Davidson	The Hospice: Development and Administration, Second Edition
Degner, Beaton	Life–Death Decision Making in Health Care
Doty	Effective Communication and Assertion for Older Persons
Stillion	Death and the Sexes: A Differential Examination of Longevity, Attitudes, Behavior, and Coping Skills
Turnbull	Terminal Care
Vachon	Occupational Stress in the Care of the Critically Ill, the Dying, and the Bereaved
Wass, Corr	Childhood and Death
Wass, Corr, Pacholski, Forfar	Death Education: An Annotated Resource Guide, II

Personal Meanings
of Death

Applications of Personal
Construct Theory to Clinical Practice

Edited by

FRANZ R. EPTING
University of Florida

and

ROBERT A. NEIMEYER
Memphis State University

HEMISPHERE PUBLISHING CORPORATION
Washington   New York   London

DISTRIBUTION OUTSIDE THE UNITED STATES
McGRAW-HILL INTERNATIONAL BOOK COMPANY

Auckland	Bogotá	Guatemala	Hamburg
Johannesburg	Lisbon	London	Madrid	Mexico
Montreal	New Delhi	Panama	Paris	San Juan
São Paulo	Singapore	Sydney	Tokyo	Toronto

NOTICE

Because this volume is appearing as an issue of *Death Education: An International Quarterly*, as well as a hardbound book, it was necessary to use a numbering system that would incorporate both the continuous journal page numbers and the book page numbers. The pages are double-numbered as follows: page 1 of the book is equivalent to page 87 of the journal. The numbers appear on the pages as journal page number followed by book page number in brackets.

This book was set in Baskerville by Hemisphere Publishing Corporation.
The editors were Christine Flint and Judy Cameron; and the typesetter
was Shirley J. McNett.
Edwards Brothers, Inc., was printer and binder.

Library of Congress Cataloging in Publication Data
Main entry under title:

Personal meanings of death.

(Series in death education, aging, and health care)
Bibliography: p.
Includes index.
1. Death—Psychological aspects. 2. Personal
construct theory. I. Epting, Franz R., date.
II. Neimeyer, Robert A., date. III. Series.

BF789.D4P47   1983   155.9'37   83-8529

ISBN 0-89116-363-8
ISSN 0275-3511

CONTENTS

Death Education

Resources for Further Research

PREFACE

Attendants at a recent workshop on hospice care for the dying participated in a rather unconventional opening exercise. They were first presented with a list of contrasting adjectives (e.g., open versus closed, good versus bad, free versus restricted) and then were asked to select those that seemed especially important or relevant to them in conceptualizing death. Participants were instructed to use the dimensions to rate themselves and their own death, thinking about the latter as if it were to occur in the near future. Next, these hospice workers were asked to consider those instances in which they placed self and death in opposition to one another on dimensions high in personal significance— as when the self was aligned with "purposeful" and death with "purposeless." Finally, participants were paired into dyads and were invited to discuss with their partners their experience of their own mortality, with the self/death "splits" on personally important dimensions serving to focus their attention on areas in which their deaths seemed threatening or inimical to the meaning of their lives. Some lively and revealing conversations followed.

The above exercise used an adaptation of the Threat Index, an instrument for assessing death concern, which is in turn rooted in George Kelly's psychology of personal constructs. The hallmark of Kelly's theory and methodology is a concern with the personal meanings that events carry for individuals, whether social relationships, their lives more generally, or their deaths in particular. The last decade has seen a proliferation of personal construct work in thanatology, addressed as much to the death counselor or educator as to the research psychologist. The goal of this volume is to present for the first time in one place a broad sampling of original work in this area, written by construct theorists from throughout the English-speaking world. Despite the diversity of these international contributions, each reflects the central theme of this volume by elucidating the personal meaning that death carries for individuals in a variety of psychotherapeutic, medical, and educational contexts.

In the opening selection, Robert Neimeyer, Franz Epting, and Seth Krieger introduce the personal construct approach that characterizes this volume and provide a bibliography of basic source books in the theory, as well as references to published thanatological work deriving from or discussing construct theory concepts or methodology. In the next paper Dorothy Rowe explores the way in which certain of her psychotherapy clients conceptualize death and loss; she concludes with a discussion of how the personal meanings attached to death also determine the purpose of people's lives. The following paper by Jerome Tobacyk empirically examines the relationship between various classes of "paranormal" belief and death orientation. His results suggest that certain types of metaphysical belief may play a role in reducing death threat and death concern.

In the second section three papers deal with issues directly relevant to clinical psychology and psychotherapy. Robert Neimeyer reviews the burgeoning cognitively oriented literature on depression and self-destruction and then outlines a personal construct conceptualization of the two processes that accommodates the present empirical findings. The second article, written by Alice Hoagland, similarly details how construct theory can be used to understand more deeply the "emotional" processes entailed in grieving. Finally, Michael Rigdon concludes the section with an intensive clinical case study of a suicidal individual, drawing on a range of personal construct methodologies to illustrate the relationship between death concern and cognitive structure.

The third section collects together three empirical investigations of death concern in medical contexts. The utility of the Threat Index is demonstrated in the paper by Paul Robinson and Keith Wood. These authors employ a measure of self-ideal discrepancy derived from the index to assess the self-actualization of physically ill respondents and find that such actualization predicts level of death anxiety, whereas seriousness of physical illness does not. The second paper, by Linda Viney, also explores the relationship of death concern to illness but does so through content analyses of open-ended interviews conducted with nearly 500 seriously ill patients. Finally, Greg Neimeyer, Marylou Behnke, and John Reiss derive measures of both death threat and death anxiety from the Threat Index and explore the relationship of these death orientation variables to the cognitive and behavioral strategies that physicians use to cope with patient death.

The next section focuses on the implications of personal construct theory for death education. W. G. Warren's opening statement argues that a serious consideration of construct theory and existential philosophy would lead to a conceptualization of education that would break radically with the more instrumental, technical approach now current in the field. Lawrence Rainey follows this with a discussion of the specific utility of personal construct concepts in conducting death and dying programs for medical caregivers.

Finally, materials intended to encourage further research into thanatological issues from a personal construct perspective are provided. The first of these is a manual for analyzing the content of death-relevant constructs, a previously neglected area of investigation. The second is a procedure manual for the Threat Index that gives explicit instructions on administering and scoring each of the instrument's most commonly used modifications.

In sum, the papers collected here illustrate the diversity and vitality of personal construct theory's application to thanatology. It is our hope that they will stimulate a more widespread consideration of the theory's potential contribution to this young and exciting field of study.

Franz R. Epting
Robert A. Neimeyer

PERSONAL CONSTRUCTS IN THANATOLOGY: AN INTRODUCTION AND RESEARCH BIBLIOGRAPHY

ROBERT A. NEIMEYER

Memphis State University

FRANZ R. EPTING

University of Florida

SETH R. KRIEGER

Pembroke Pines, Florida

In spite of the proliferation of clinical and empirical work in the psychology of death and dying over the last two decades, this literature still lacks a unifying psychological theory that could help integrate disparate observations. George Kelly's theory of personal constructs is well situated to provide this much-needed conceptual grounding. The paper sketches the methodological and substantive contributions that construct theory can make to thanatology and provides a bibliography of relevant materials for the interested researcher and clinician.

In a broad sense, each of us gives his life for something, something noble or ignoble, though mostly something in between. Some do it decisively in one abrupt and frightening gesture. Some do it slowly and unobtrusively, sacrificing themselves little by little. Some face death outright; others stumble in its general direction. To seek to die well is an object of the full life, and those who fail to live well never succeed in finding anything worth dying for. Thus life and death can be made to fit together, each as the validator of the other. (12, p. 259)

In 1963, Herman Feifel (2) wrote of death as a taboo topic, as the new pornography. Even as he was writing, however, numerous articles and studies were beginning to appear in the literature, written by philosophers, psychologists, psychiatrists, sociologists, and nurses. Since the early sixties the previously scant body of literature has grown to formidable proportions. Recent years have even seen the publication of extensive bibliographies concerned solely with material related to death and dying (e.g., 3, 4, 5).

Nevertheless, in spite of the abundance of reading material that might be collected beneath the rubric of "the psychology of death," the field is still clearly in its infancy. Reflecting on the burgeoning literature in thanatology, or the study of death, Edgar N. Jackson recently wrote:

> When more and more people focus on an area of research it often follows that the preoccupation with smaller and smaller aspects of the subject leads to fragmentation . . . . This tends to lead the research into small pockets of interest, and the large view of the human condition may be lost in this fracturing process. (6, pp. 275-276)

An examination of the thanatological literature suggests that this topical fragmentation is indeed taking place. Such an overview of research in the field reveals not a systematic, progressive discussion and investigation of a topic area, but rather a chaotic mosaic cluttered with duplication of effort, unconfirmed opinion, questionable research methodologies and paradigms, and a striking absence of anything approaching a coherent unifying base of psychological theory.

The psychological study of death has proceeded along two routes. Clinicians have reflected on their experiences with death and dying and have catalogued and drawn patterns out of their observations in retrospect. Empirical researchers have brought techniques and methodologies from sociology, social psychology, and personality research to test individual, isolated hypotheses. Neither approach has made a very substantial contribution to our understanding of human beings' relation to their mortality.

Certainly, much of the diffusion in the existing literature can be attributed to the variety of disciplines that legitimately contribute to it. The study of death goes far beyond psychology into the domains of medicine, sociology, philosophy, and religion. Indeed, each of these disciplines has potentially valuable and unique contributions to make. The question facing psychologists is the nature of their own special contribution. What special talent and knowledge do psychologists have that can aid in the quest for an understanding of the last and most profound of human mysteries?

Historically, psychology has grown within a theoretical framework, and has progressed through the successive formulation, testing, and revision of theory. Even in its present divided state, the various camps within the psychological community are identified most easily by their theoretical allegiances. This inclination toward theory building is what makes the discipline a science and what separates it from more applied fields.

It is our contention that meaningful strides toward a coherent psychology of death can and will be made only within the context of a continuous cycle of formulation, testing, and revision of a unified psychological theory that treats the psychology of death as a specific of a more general psychology of human life. It is time for psychologists to begin grounding their investigations in an explicit theory that can be shown to offer a satisfactory interpretation of existing data and that suggests significant avenues for future exploration.

The present volume was conceived with the assumption that a unified framework for thanatological research could be provided by George Kelly's theory of personal constructs (1). Essentially, construct theory posits that the sine qua non of human existence is our tendency to attribute unique meanings to the data of our experience. These meanings, termed "personal constructs," serve not only as interpretations of past events, but also as hypotheses about events yet to be encountered. For example, if an individual has construed many previous transition points in life as offering "chances for growth," it is likely that such a person will anticipate further life changes as additional opportunities for personal enhancement. It is in this sense that Kelly (7, p. 28) once defined life as "a way of using the present to link the future with the past in some original fashion." Our current construing of events grants significance to our past and direction to our future.

According to Kelly (1), the process of construing entails comparing and contrasting particular classes of people, things or events: some causes are perceived to be worthy and others unworthy; some people are seen as kind whereas others are cruel. In general, then, a construct can be defined as "a way in which some things are seen as being alike and yet different from others" (8, p. 25). Each individual characteristically evolves, over the course of his or her life, a complex and often idiosyncratic system of constructs. This system is organized hierarchically, with relationships of superordination and subordination among the interconnected constructs that comprise it.

Superordinate constructs tend to be more abstract. They are more permanent and play a more central role in the process of construing. The core constructs are among the most super-ordinate structures in the system. They are particularly important in that they "govern a person's maintenance pro-cesses; they enable him to maintain his identity and sense of continuing existence . . . they cannot be changed in any way without disturbing the very roots of a person's existence" (8, p. 30).

Construct theory views each person's understanding of the world as a direct function of the organization and content of his or her unique system of personal constructs. The whole of experience is filtered through this matrix of meaning that extends into the outside world through its channeling effects on perception at one end and its provision of a finite number of behavioral alternatives at the other.

When an individual's most fundamental understandings are called into question, he or she is said to experience threat. In more theoretical terms, threat can be defined as "the awareness of imminent comprehensive change in one's core structures" (1, p. 489). Threat, then, occurs with a person's recognition that his or her most basic constructions of the world are seriously flawed and in need of extensive revision. Because a person's whole construct system depends on the validity of certain comprehen-sive core constructs, their invalidation disrupts the organization of the large majority of the remaining constructs within the system, and transforms the person's previously well-ordered, meaningful world into a chaotic abyss.

Kelly recognized that death represented the paradigmatic threatening event to most people. As he noted,

We describe it as threatening to them because they perceive it both as likely to happen to them and likely to bring about drastic changes in their core constructs. Death is not so threatening when it does not seem so imminent. It is not as threatening to those who see either their souls or the fundamental meaning of their lives as being unaffected by it. In such persons the core structures are not so likely to be affected by the prospect of death. (1, p. 490)

Historically, the thantological interests of construct theorists have grown outward from their attempts to measure the degree of death threat experienced by the individual. Thus, although an occasional research report examining death and dying appeared in the personal construct literature prior to 1970, such as Ryle's 1967 case study of a suicide attempt (9), explicitly thanatological research was inaugurated with the development of the Threat Index (TI) by Krieger, Epting, and Leitner in 1974 (10). Operationally, the TI measures death threat by assessing the person's reluctance to construe "self" and "death" on the same pole of a sample of bipolar constructs. It is assumed that persons who describe themselves and their deaths in similar terms are cognitively organizing their worlds in such a way as to be able to see death as a personal reality, as an event compatible with their lives. Individuals who place themselves and death on opposite poles of the majority of their constructs, however, would have to reorganize their systems in a radical way in order to construe self and death together.

Since its development in the mid-1970s, the TI has been used in more than a dozen published studies (see 11 for a review of this literature through 1979). Much of this work has focused on establishing the psychometric soundness of the instrument itself (i.e., its convergent, discriminant, and construct validity, as well as its internal consistency and test-retest reliability). At this point, it is fair to conclude that the TI is the most carefully validated measure of death orientation in the literature to date.

In the past few years the production of personal construct research into death has increased exponentially. Not only has the number of articles appearing annually grown at a steady rate, but the publication outlets for this material and the nationality of its authors have become more varied as well. This proliferation in the field suggests the need for a comprehensive research bibliography to organize the work that has been completed up to this time. The present bibliography contains two sections: the first includes basic references in construct theory for thanatologists working in other areas, and the second presents genuinely thanatological work incorporating personal construct concepts or methodologies.

Basic References in Personal Construct Theory

Adams-Webber, J. *Personal construct theory: Concepts and applications.* New York: Wiley, 1979.

Bannister, D., & Fransella, F. *Inquiring man.* New York: Penguin, 1971.

Bannister, D., & Mair, J. M. M. *The evaluation of personal constructs.* London and New York: Academic, 1968.

Bonarius, H., Holland, R., & Rosenberg, S. *Personal construct psychology: Recent advances in theory and practice.* London: Macmillan, 1981.

Epting, F. R. *Personal construct theory psychotherapy.* London and New York: Wiley, in press.

Fransella, F., & Bannister, D. *A manual for repertory grid technique.* New York: Academic, 1977.

Kelly, G. A. *Personal construct theory* (2 vols.). New York: Norton, 1955.

Landfield, A. W., & Leitner, L. (Eds.). *Personal construct approaches to psychotherapy and personality.* New York: Wiley, 1980.

Maher, B. (Ed.). *Clinical psychology and personality: The selected papers of George Kelly.* New York: Wiley, 1969.

Neimeyer, G. J., & Neimeyer, R. A. Personal construct perspectives on cognitive assessment. In T. Merluzzi, C. Glass, & M. Genest (Eds.), *Cognitive assessment.* New York: Guildford, 1981.

Thanatological References in Personal Construct Theory

Durlak, J. A., & Kass, R. A. Clarifying the measurement of death attitudes: A factor analytic evaluation of fifteen self-report death scales. *Omega,* 1981, *12*, 129–141.

Epting, F. R., Rainey, L. C., & Weiss, M. Constructions of death and levels of death fear. *Death Education,* 1979, *3*, 21–30.

Hays, C. *A methodological evaluation of the Threat Index and the introduction of a short form.* Unpublished thesis, University of Florida, 1974.

Hays, C. H., & Neimeyer, R. A. *Self-reported usefulness, importance, and meaningfulness of provided and elicited constructs.* Unpublished manuscript, University of Florida, 1974.

Kastenbaum, R., & Costa, P. Psychological perspectives on death. *Annual Review of Psychology,* 1977, *28,* 225–249.

Krieger, S. R. *Personal constructs, threat, and attitude toward death.* Unpublished master's thesis, University of Florida, 1972.

Krieger, S. R. Death orientation and the specialty choice and training of physicians. *Dissertation Abstracts International,* 1977, *37,* 3616B. (University Microfilms No. 77-95).

Krieger, S. R., Epting, F. R., & Hays, C. H. Validity and reliability of provided constructs in assessing death threat: A self-administered form. *Omega,* 1979, *10,* 87–95.

Krieger, S. R., Epting, F. R., & Leitner, L. M. Personal constructs, threat, and attitudes toward death. *Omega,* 1974, *5,* 299–310.

Landfield, A. A personal construct approach to suicidal behavior. In P. Slater (Ed.), *Explorations of intrapersonal space.* New York: Wiley, 1976.

MacInnes, W. D., & Neimeyer, R. A. Internal consistency of the Threat Index. *Death Education,* 1980, *4,* 193–194.

Neimeyer, R. A. Death anxiety and the Threat Index: An addendum. *Death Education,* 1978, *1,* 464–467.

Neimeyer, R. A., & Chapman, K. M. Self/ideal discrepancy and fear of death: The test of an existential hypothesis. *Omega,* 1980, *11,* 233–240.

Neimeyer, R. A., & Dingemans, P. M. Death orientation in the suicide intervention worker. *Omega,* 1980, *11,* 15–23.

Neimeyer, R. A., Dingemans, P. M., & Epting, F. R. Covergent validity, situational stability and meaningfulness of the Threat Index. *Omega,* 1977, *8,* 251–265.

Rainey, L. C. *Validity studies of the Threat Index.* Unpublished master's thesis, University of Florida, 1976.

Rainey, L. C., & Epting, F. R. Death threat constructions in the student and the prudent. *Omega,* 1977, *8,* 19–28.

Rigdon, M. A., Epting, F. R., Neimeyer, R. A., & Krieger, S. R. The Threat Index: A research report. *Death Education,* 1979, *3,* 245–270.

Robinson, P. J., & Wood, K. *The Threat Index: An additive approach.* Manuscript submitted for publication, 1982.

Rowe, D. *The experience of depression.* Chichester (England): Wiley, 1978.

Rowe, D. *The construction of life and death.* Chicester (England): Wiley, 1982.

Rowe, D. *Depression: The way out of the prison.* London: Routledge, 1983.

Ryle, A. A repertory grid study of the meaning and consequences of a suicidal act. *British Journal of Psychiatry,* 1967, *113,* 1393–1403.

Tobacyk, J., & Eckstein, D. Death threat and death concerns in the college student. *Omega,* 1980, *11,* 139–155.

Viney, L. L. *Experiencing chronic illness: A personal construct commen-*

tary. Paper presented at the Fourth International Congress on Personal Construct Theory, Brock University, St. Catharines (Ontario), 1981.

Viney, L. L., & Westbrook, M. T. Psychosocial reactions to heart disease: An application of content analysis methodology. *Proceedings of the Geigy Symposium on Behavioral Medicine.* Melbourne, 1980.

Warren, W. G. Personal construction of death and death education. *Death Education,* 1982, *6,* 17–28.

Warren, W. G., & Parry, G. Personal constructs and death: Some clinical refinements. In H. Bonarius, R. Holland, & S. Rosenberg (Eds.), *Personal construct psychology: Recent advances in theory and practice.* London: Macmillan, 1981.

Wood, K., & Robinson, P. J. Actualization and the fear of death: Retesting an existential hypothesis. *Essence,* in press.

Woodfield, R. L., & Viney, L. L. A personal construct approach to bereavement. *Omega,* in press.

References

1. Kelly, G. A. *The psychology of personal constructs* (2 vols.). New York: Norton, 1955.
2. Feifel, H. The taboo on death. *American Behavioral Scientist,* 1963, *6,* 66–67.
3. Pearson, L. (Ed.), *Death and dying.* Cleveland: Case Western Reserve Press, 1969.
4. Kalish, R. A. Death and dying: A briefly annotated bibliography. In O. G. Brim, Jr., Freeman, Levine & Scotch (Eds.), *The dying patient.* New York: Russell Sage Foundation, 1970.
5. Kastenbaum, R., & Costa, P. Psychological perspectives on death. *Annual Review of Psychology,* 1977, *28,* 225–249.
6. Jackson, E. N. Bereavement and grief. In H. Wass (Ed.), *Dying: Facing the facts.* New York: McGraw-Hill, 1979.
7. Kelly, G. A. A psychology of the optimal man. In A. W. Landfield & L. M. Leitner (Eds.), *Personal construct psychology: Psychotherapy and personality.* New York: Wiley, 1980.
8. Bannister, D., & Mair, J. *The evaluation of personal constructs.* London: Academic, 1968.
9. Ryle, A. A repertory grid study of the meaning and consequences of a suicidal act. *British Journal of Psychiatry,* 1967, *113,* 1393–1403.
10. Krieger, S. R., Epting, F. R., & Leitner, L. M. Personal constructs, threat, and attitudes toward death. *Omega,* 1974, *5,* 229–310.
11. Rigdon, M. A., Epting, F. R., Neimeyer, R. A., & Krieger, S. R. The Threat Index: A research report. *Death Education,* 1979, *3,* 245–270.
12. Kelly, G. A. Suicide: The personal construct point of view. In N. Farberow and E. Shneidman (Eds.), *The cry for help.* New York: McGraw-Hill, 1961.

DEATH ORIENTATION

∞∞

CONSTRUCTING LIFE AND DEATH

∞∞

DOROTHY ROWE

Lincolnshire Area Department of Clinical Psychology, England

Grief can be understood as the attempt to maintain the continuity of the construct system that death has interrupted, and the end of grief as reconstruing to form a new continuity. How death is construed is central to the construct system because it determines how the purpose of life is construed.

"My sister's son is not a bit like my father." An ordinary statement, but said to me with that mixture of anxiety, jealousy, doubt, and certainty that suggests that what is being stated is also being passionately denied. Why? Family resemblances are hardly matters to arouse strong feelings. But it was not just family resemblances that we were discussing. We were discussing how she saw death, her death and her father's death, and in the way she construed death family resemblances were very important.

Nora had been referred to me by her physician, who was concerned that she was unable to take off the weight that she had steadily put on over the last two years. The doctor connected this increase in weight with the death of her father, but she did not. Indeed, the whole business of putting on weight and not getting any thinner even though she kept, so she said, to her diet was a mystery to her. It did not sound like a mystery that bothered her much. She was hurt by the cruel remarks made by her husband and two young sons, and she did miss not feeling comfortable and attractive when she wore trousers, but there was a certain blandness in her assurances to the doctor, the dietician, and me that she ate very, very little. She saw no reason to consult me, but she accepted her doctor's direction and was content to have an interested audience for her stories about her family. And they were interesting stories. She was one of a large family; she had travelled abroad with her husband; and she had worked in all kinds of strange jobs. As she talked some common themes emerged. There was the theme of her mother, who had still not pulled herself together after being widowed and who had disgraced the whole family by sobbing and wailing at the funeral. Nora had dealt with her by forcibly removing her to her bedroom and quietening her with a large does of the sedatives the family doctor had had the good sense to provide. Nora's father, so she said, would have been very angry that his wife had behaved so disgracefully. People, he always said, should control themselves. Nora's father, as she described him, was a wonderful man. A Yorkshire John Wayne if ever there was one. Big, strong, handsome, ruling his family with firm, loving kindness. Setting standards. Never complained, even when a bad accident made him give up work. No complaint when he was dying. He told the family the pills he was taking were for indigestion. Then he got up one morning, lit the kitchen fire as he always did, and dropped down dead. His head hit the fender as he fell and there was blood everywhere when his wife and daughter found him. Nora sat beside her father's body for two hours alone waiting for the doctor to come to certify him dead, while her mother was being cared for in a neighbor's house.

As Nora told me this tears came to her eyes. Quickly she mopped them away. "It's so silly to cry," she said, "and after all this time."

"Two years isn't long when you've lost someone you love," I said, adding that crying in grief is a good, sensible thing to do.

Nora disagreed. Crying is stupid, babyish, wrong. She should not allow herself to cry. I thought, but did not say, if you really did not allow yourself to cry you would be much more depressed than you are, and if you ate as little as you say you do, you would be a lot thinner than you are. I suspect that you often weep in private and also in private you comfort yourself with cream cakes and chocolates. But in public you want to be the daughter your father loved and admired. You cannot afford to be seen as self-indulgent and lacking in self-control.

There was, however, more to her predicament than trying to live up to her dead father's standards. This became clear as she answered the question that I ask all my clients. "How do you see your death? Do you see it as the end of your existence or as a doorway to another life?"

Nora did not answer directly. She said, "Dad and I sometimes talked about that—not seriously, just a joke. He always said that if there was something over there, if he was still around, he would come back and tell me."

Nora's father had encouraged her to be strong, but had always been there not just to advise and protect her but because he wanted her to be a part of his life (the most important part, she liked to think). When she left school and got a job he insisted she still live at home, and when she married she moved into a house across the streeet. When her husband was posted abroad her father came to visit ("the best holiday we ever had"), and when she returned to England her father visited her every Friday morning ("our special time together"). He always kept his promises to her. If he said he would arrive at 10 o'clock he arrived at 10 o'clock. If he said he would come back and visit her after he died he would do that.

Or would he? She had sat beside his body for two hours, and he had not come. She had waited for two years, and he had not come. Did it mean that there was no other side, that when he died he disappeared from her life forever and she had lost the best friend she had ever had, would ever have, the only person who loved her for herself alone and not for waht she could give? Or did it mean that he had not kept his promise, that he had gone, forgotten her, left her to fend for herself in a world where all the brightness had drained away and all the joy had fled?

She clutched at straws. Someone told her how people were reincarnated as their grandchildren. Not a common belief in England, although in Bali the words for great-grandfather and great-grandson are the same since it is believed that life is cyclical and so after death a man returns as his great-grandson. Nora's sons were presumably too old to be a reincarnation of their grandfather, so perhaps her sister's son, born a few months after her father's death, was he. But how could he go to her sister's house when he knew how much she needed him? She could have no more children. She peered at her nephew, and when she saw a family likeness she was jealous. She tried to dismiss the reincarnation idea as rubbish.

To say she was still grieving over her father is all too simple. "Grieving over the death of a loved one" sounds like the person is engaged in a sad but uncomplicated action of sorrowing and feeling lonely. Nora was doing this of course, but she was also engaged in the problem of finding a meaning for this death with which she could live. Alternative meanings presented themselves to her, but none was completely acceptable because all had implications that caused her great pain. Her doctor was right when he saw her bereavement as the cause of her obesity. Thanks to the work of Dr. Murray Parkes and others, many doctors nowadays can see a relationship between grief and physical illnesses and compalints, but in the way that the person trained in scientific method tends to oversimplify, many doctors think of grief as some sort of unified effect and cause. Someone dies and we feel grief. Grief causes us to become ill. What is needed is a cure for grief. But grief is not a thing, like a stone in the kidney. Grief is pain, fear, sorrow, and anger. It is also the desperate attempts to mend the rifts that have been made in one's world of meaning.

Grief and Continuity

The individual world of meaning is a complicated, intercon- nected network of meanings that encompasses not only present relationships with people and things but past and future and the projects on which one is engaged. When someone who is close and important dies one asks, "Why did this happen?" The physical reasons for the person's death are relatively easy to find—the car's wheel went over his chest, a blood clot blocked an artery, the lungs filled with fluid. Such reasons do not capture the bereaved person's interest for long because they do not answer the questions really being asked. Why should a small child die? Why should such a good person be punished like this? Why should people be robbed of the best years of their lives? Why should this happen to me? The death of someone close cuts across the continuity of meaning that one calls life. In grief people search for an answer to their question "Why did this person die?" that will re-establish the continuity of their lives.

In the early stages of bereavement people try to re-establish continuity by denying that the person has died. Even though they go through the procedures of the funeral, the exchanges of condolences, the practical tasks disposing of the personal effects and carrying out all the legal requirements, all this seems like play-acting or a dream. They expect to waken any moment or to see their loved one walk through the door. Then one day the play-acting ends, the dream vanishes. They know that the person is dead. They ask "Why?" and there is no answer. They are in grief, which James Carse described in the following way:

> It is in grief that we feel most acutely the discontinuity, the meaninglessness, of life ... death need not confront us [just] in the loss of a person with whom we have shared much life—*death confronts us whenever we experience a radical threat to the continuity of our existence.* Anything that causes us to see that our lives come to nothing, and are essentially meaningless, has the power of death, since it has thrown across our path an impenetrable boundary, a terminus to all the lines of meaningfulness that extend outward from our vitality .... *We are in grief whenever the continuity of our lives has been destroyed.* The concept of grief appears prominently in all great systems of thought, although it does not always go by that name. We find it discussed under such categories as ignorance, despair, karma, yearning, neurosis, or the abandonment to history. Whatever the term, each of these shares the universal characteristics of grief: lack of effective speech, isolation from others, no interest in the future, abnegation of freedom—in sum, the contradictory state of living in a way that resembled death. Grief is our refusal to recognize the fact that death has not taken away our freedom to reconstitute the continuities it has destroyed. (1)

In grief individuals ask "Why?" and get no satisfactory answer. They try out different answers: "Because it was bad luck." "Because God wished it so." "Because it was part of the cycle of life." But none is satisfactory because none re-establishes the old continuity. Then one day they realize that they have to find a new continuity, a new meaning, and that in fact they have been constructing this new meaning all through the work of mourning when they have been reviewing, reassessing and reconstructing. Instead of saying, "I refuse to accept that he died," one says, "I accept his death." Instead of saying, "I cannot give up being young," one says, "Being middle-aged certainly has some advantages." Instead of saying, "If I can't work, I'm useless and valueless," one says, "I've worked hard all my life. It's time I had a rest and someone looked after me."

In the process of mourning people examine, each in their own way, the metaphysical questions of the nature of death and the purpose of life. They work on the problems that have exercised the minds of philosophers and theologians through the ages. They try to find a meaning for death that allows them to establish a continuity to life so that they can say, "Death is, but is not." James Carse in his book *Death and Existence* looked at 10 major religions and 13 philosophical systems "to learn what the *agency of death* is for each of these traditions and thinkers; that is, how they describe the way we are threatened by discontinuity. This in turn brings us to the way they conceive *grief,* and its subsequent cure by the achievement of new life, a greater *freedom* to establish an inclusive continuity" (1).

Thus in Judaism death is seen as inevitable and continuity in history. Victory over death lies in the history of the Jewish people, which is not simply the story of the lives of one group of people but a continuing creative discourse with God. The teaching of the Talmud is that evil comes from within us, our sins are punished by suffering and death, and so we must repent. This focuses attention on life, on the present, and not on life after death. This was the theme of Jesus's teaching as reported in the synoptic Gospels. He mentioned death and a place of punishment, but what concerned Him was how we related to one another and to God. God, He said, "is not the God of the dead, but the God of the living" (Mark 12:27). The first commandment was "Thou shalt love the Lord thy God with all thy heart, and with all thy soul, and with all thy mind, and with all they strength." The second commandment was "Thou shalt love they neighbour as thyself. There is none other command-ment greater than these" (Mark 12:29, 30). The living should take precedence over the dead. "Follow me and let the dead bury the dead" (Matthew 8:22). The Gospel of St. John, however, includes the distinctive Christian view of death as transformation and continuity by faith. Jesus said to Martha, "I am the resurrection, and the life: he that believeth in me, though he were dead, yet shall he live. And whosoever liveth and believeth in me shall never die" (John 11:25, 26). This was the theme of Paul's teaching: "Behold, I shew you a mystery. We shall not all sleep, but we shall all be changed. In a moment, in the twinkling of an eye, at the last trumpet: for the trumpet shall sound, and the dead shall be raised incorruptible, and we shall be all changed.... O death, where is thy sting? O grave, where is thy victory?" (I Corinthians 15:51, 52, 55).

Thus Jews in grief must ask themselves and their God how this particular death fits into the story of the Jewish people. A Christian can seek an end to grief in the hope of a reunion in heaven or in the hope of some kind of enhancement of life through the love of his God and his creatures. Sometimes it is fairly easy to see the continuity in these terms—when the person who had died has made a contribution to Jewish life or has deserved peace from suffering or, through example and actions, inspired others or brought them closer together. But when the deaths are of innocent people in circumstances of great suffering then people who would at other times describe themselves as firm believers have difficulty in finding the continuity that their faith promises.

But what of those people who have no religious faith, who see life in terms of the philosophy of modern science? In this philosophy, says Carse, death is regarded as dispersion, and continuity is established by disregarding death. Life is a continuity of continuous change. Nothing comes to an end but simply changes its form. In death consciousness disappears and the atoms that comprise the body disperse into other forms, but a person's continuity continues through the effects of his or her actions. So when those dear to me die they continue on in the memory of the living, in the influences that their existence had, in their children, in the memory of their friends, in the things that they created; and all memories, influences, and creations take their place in the causal chain of effects. Thus can the person who sees life and death in this way come to terms with grief. But suppose the loved one has died before leaving a mark on the world, before achieving a particular purpose in life, before gaining the sought-after rewards, recognition, and satisfaction of life. Suppose this person was cut down by childhood leukemia, an avalanche, or a ricocheting bullet, what causal pattern can be found to bring comfort and continuity?

Carse's study of death and grief as an account of the formation and change of constructs is within the framework of personal construct theory, although Carse does not mention the theory as such. He draws a parallel between mysticism and psychoanalysis, in that in death is seen as both separation and continuity in love. Were he to include personal construct theory the appropriate parallel would be Buddhism. For Buddhists

> death is the force that causes reality to be a *fiction*. What death reveals, what the Buddhist experiences in a first encounter with suffering and death, is that life and the world are not what we thought they were. They are falsehoods, inventions, fabrications . . . . The response of grief to death in this form is . . . the craving to find something real, a truth, being . . . in grief the impulse of the mind was to leap off the wheel of ceaseless change in the desperate attempt to find something immovable. It is this desperation that gives rise to suffering. This is what Buddhists call attachment. Attachment leads inevitably to suffering because nothing is exempt from change and to think that something is, that one is oneself, is to be in profound contradiction to one's own samsaric (completely relative) existence . . . the only true release from pain comes when one *freely* moves with the wheel [that is, when one accepts the discontinuity of death].

To put this in personal construct theory terms, onto the "complicated tissue of events" (2), which is the reality that can never be known, individuals impose their system of constructions (constructs), which they then assume *is* reality. The system of constructs that they have created has a continuity that links them to others and that projects their lives into the future. Death, or a loss that has the force of death, disrupts the continuity and reveals the construct system to be a fiction and not reality. In grief they try to deny this and assert, first, that the death has not occurred and, second, that the construct system is not a fiction but a reality that does not change. An end to grief is found only when they accept that the continuity of their system has been disrupted, that the system of constructs is a fiction, and that, as it is a fiction, something they have made, now that it is broken they can build something else. By building something else they can establish another continuity.

Thus a young child might grow up believing that he is being watched over by a loving God who will protect him from all evil so long as he strives to be good. He builds the project of his life on this central construct. As a child he is a credit to his parents; as an adult he works hard and looks after his family; and nothing bad befalls him. His reality is, "If you are good, God looks after you." Then one day his youngest child playing in the yard is killed by a car driven by an hallucinating drug addict. How can he explain this death? Can it be explained within the continuity of his construct system? There are only two possible explanations. Either the child was so wicked that God would not protect him or that he himself was so wicked that God refused to protect his child. A loving father might be reluctant to draw such a conclusion about his innocent child. To preserve his construct system he can compound his grief with guilt, but if he rejects the notion that his wickedness demanded the sacrifice of his child his construct system is thrown into doubt. He has to consider the possibility that his belief that God protects good people is a fiction and that the truth is something else. Once he allows the possibility that his belief is something he has constructed and that he is free to construct something else, then he can change his construct system to recreate another continuity. He may abandon his belief in God altogether, or he may decide that God is wicked and malicious, or he may decide that his relationship with his God is more complicated than he knew and that he should consider St. Augustine's teaching that faith comes before understanding. Each belief has different implications for his construct system because each belief would establish a different kind of continuity.

Another child might grow up believing, not in a loving, protecting God, but in a world of natural justice where merit is rewarded. If, as a small child, she discovers that her family values boys more than girls, she might resolve to be so outstanding in her chosen field that her family will be chastened and her achievements secure her fame forever. Her adult life takes her well along this path, but then changes in the world economy or betrayal by the person on whom she depends cut across the continuity of her life's project with all the force of death. To maintain her construct system she would have to believe that in the application of natural justice she did not merit reward, and so she can never obtain her family's approbation and be remembered forever. Such a conclusion could lead only to despair. If, however, she comes to see her belief in natural justice as a construct and not a universal law existing in nature, then she can avoid despair by explaining her loss as the result of random bad luck and therefore as simply an obstacle to be overcome or as the result of the stupid or malicious actions of others that she must in the future take into account. Each change of belief has different implications.

Neither of these accounts of how the discontinuity of death can be overcome by reconstruing gives any hint of how profound and deeply emotional such changes are. Constructs are not just ideas in our heads. They are human beings in action, experiencing, living the life that they have constructed.

The Construction of Life and Death

Some parents try to protect their children from learning about death. They never refer to death in the hearing of the child. They monitor what the child reads or sees on television. Yet every time they warn the child "Be careful crossing the road" or "Don't go near the water," the child knows what the unspoken reason is. I once gave the Binet Intelligence Test to a child who I knew was greatly cherished and protected by her parents. To the question, "Why should you obey your parents?" she replied, "Because if you don't you will die." Children who are less protected learn of death more directly.

Learning that "I shall die" poses the immediate question of what dying, one's own dying, means. There are, in fact, only two meanings that people can give to death. Either death is the end of their identity or it is the doorway to another life. They can interpret "another life" in many different ways—rejoicing in heaven, suffering in hell, returning to the world to live another life, or wandering the earth in some spiritual form. They can think of their identity as disappearing totally, like a burst bubble, or they can think of their identity disappearing but not its effects in the lives of their children and friends and in the things that they have created. The construction that people choose determine what they see as the purpose of their lives. If they see death as the end then they have to make their lives in some way satisfactory; if they see death as a doorway to another life they have to live this life in terms of the next. They may define "satisfactory" in ways that are difficult to fill; or they may define the "next life" as having rules that are very difficult to follow in this life. On the other hand, they can choose to be satisfied with little in this life or decide that Heaven's gates are wide. Whatever choice they make that choice determines how they try to live their lives and how they measure their failures.

When I first began studying the construct systems of people who were depressed I had not realized that the way that people construe death is central to the entire structure of their system. Awareness of death is not merely feeling a chilling shock as one narrowly misses being mown down by a bus. It also informs, however silently, every decision that one makes.

Carol, who is described in my book (3), spent most of her life either nearly immobile in depression or in hectic activity. Rarely she was in between, because she was always in a temper.

> I'm striving to be different, to be calm, placid, all the things I'm not. But, as fast as I try to shake things off, something seems to pop up to hold me back or to hinder me. It seems to be all these frustrating things that make me irritable and worked up.... These things, they're only drops in the ocean, really, but to me they seem like mountains.... I never get over one mountain and think, "I'm here" because looming up in the distance there's something else. There's never a clear view in front. If ever I've thought to myself "Things are going quite well. We seem to be on a quite level plain," lo and behold something happens and there it is again, a great big mountain.

Life then was a series of mountains to climb, in the endeavor to get everything right, to find a clear and open plain. When Carol described her image of mountains and valleys it seemed obvious that she was using the name of a geographical feature when she said "plain." However, when she told me of how she envisaged heaven, it seemed that this "plain" also incorporated its homonym "plane," with its meaning of a grade of development. The reason she had to get everything "ship-shape and Bristol fashion" in this world, on this plane, was

> if I pop off everything will be in order. There won't be any mistakes or muddles. In the next world I'll look back on what I've done wrong. Then I would try and do my best to help them get shipshape. I'd feel I still had a job to do. I feel we're on this earth for a purpose. I don't think we die and that's it. It is the Christian religion, life after death, and I feel when you go on to the next world you are there and you are helping those in this world. I think that by helping those in this world you are then getting yourself on a higher plane possibly in the next world. I don't believe that one goes straight up to God. But I feel that one even in the next world has to work one's way. It's in stages. What one does in this world helps towards the next and then what you do in the next, helping down in this world, helps you towards greater things. There is no end of worlds. "In my Father's house there are many mansions."

D. Rowe: "So you're working on what you're doing here in thie world with a view to what's to be done inthe next world."

Carol: "Yes, I'm trying to."

D. Rowe: "That's why, today, on the first day of the summer holidays, you're making a list of the clothes the boys will need next term?"

Carol: "Yes . . . I think I shall wake up in heaven and someone will say, 'Look down and see what you can do to help'."

D. Rowe: "How do you think your family will feel when you die?"

Carol: "Very sorry. I think it would cut Bob to pieces. I've got the feeling that Bob will get to the age his father died and he'll go. When Bob's father died, Bob's mother said 'They're not a long-lived family.' All I want is that I shouldn't be left. I have a terrible fear of that. I've never been right since his dad died."

D. Rowe: "Do you see yourself joining Bob in heaven?"

Carol: "Definitely. In time. I don't think it happens straight away. Probably I would have to do a little work because he'd be on a higher plane if he went first. Sort of find him by working. I feel that what you sow here you reap in the next and what you sow in the next you reap in the one after that."

No wonder Carol was so frantically active, only to collapse into a depression when she overreached herself.

Conversations like this with others of my clients convinced me of the importance of understanding how we construe life and death. One striking fact about my clients who come to me in a distressed state and usually depressed was that although the meanings they gave to life and death covered a wide range of possibilities, the implications of their beliefs were the same, in that they created in the client a state of fear and hopelessness. Carol was a Christian, but the way she interpreted her religion trapped her in a frantic, endless quest for perfection and an equally frantic running away from the fear of being isolated from her loved ones. The peace of God was not for her. When I suggested to her that not everyone saw heaven in this way she replied, "I can't see anybody else's point of view. I have got my set idea of what it is." Clients who believed in God described to me a God even more wrathful and vengeful than that of the Old Testament. Some clients saw their depression as a punishment for sins, a punishment that had to be accepted to obtain God's forgiveness. Some saw their depression as karma, the result of sins committed in an earlier life. Interpreting depression in these ways means that all attempts by others to remove the depression must be resisted. People who saw the world inhabited by the spirits of the dead saw these spirits as lonely and as inspiring fear. Those people who saw death as the end of their identity saw their lives as failures and knew that they would be forgotten or remembered only in ways that brought them no joy to contemplate. By contrast, I found that people who cope with their lives have just as wide a range of beliefs but these beliefs inspire them with courage and optimism. If they believe in God, they see God as a good friend, and if they believe in heaven, then they see themselves as meeting the requirements of entry. Believers in reincarnation rejoice in good karma while believers in spirits feel strengthened by the presence of their dead loved ones. Those who look to satisfaction in this life are modestly assured of their success and know that they will be lovingly remembered (4).

Indeed, having a philosophy of life or religious beliefs that lead to pessimism and fear is one of the six basic assumptions that one must have to enter the prison of depression. (The other five are "No matter how good and nice I appear to be. I am really bad, evil, valueless, unacceptable to myself and other people," "Other people are such that I must fear, hate, and envy them," "Only bad things have happened to me in the past and only bad things will happen to me in the future," "It is wrong to get angry" and "I must never forgive anyone, least of all myself") (5). Holding metaphysical beliefs that render individuals pessimistic and fearful makes it more difficult for them to bring grief to an end by reconstruing. If they believe in a loving God then a bereavement may make them question His love or even His existence, but they can reconstrue in terms of trusting where they do not understand, or in terms of increased trust in themselves. If people believe in a God of wrath and vengeance then a bereavement serves only to confirm this belief. If they believe in their ability to secure a satisfaction in the term of their life, then a loss can be interpreted as a temporary setback or a challenge to be mastered and overcome. If they believe that they lack the ability to secure a satisfactory life or that there are people conspiring to prevent or injure them, then a loss confirms these beliefs.

In saying that some metaphysical beliefs promote optimism and courage while others engender pessimism and fear is not to say that there are certain beliefs that overcome all problems and make life secure and death welcome. Some people are horrified by the promise of eternal life, whereas others are equally horrified by the prospect of oblivion. The scientific attitude can make existence seem meaningless, and the existence of suffering poses a continuing question of the benevolence and omnipotence of God. There is no set of metaphysical beliefs that will bring joy and peace to everyone. Every individual in the course of life becomes aware of the questions and has to find his or her own answers.

Nick had spent the 12 years of his life in the tropics, so on his first winter visit to England he was fascinated by the snow. As we searched for suitable toboggan runs Nick and I discussed politics and religion. He was against religion, and he gave political reasons to support his views. I felt that his atheistic beliefs had deeper roots than politics. I had known Nick's father when he was a young man, and I well remember the passionate scorn he poured on all things religious. He even took the ringing of church bells on Sunday as a personal affront. I gathered from Nick that his father had not changed. Nick, loving his father, had espoused his views. But one can be an atheist only if one can view with some measure of equanimity the end of one's identity. This Nick could not do. As Nick talked he revealed a profound fear of ceasing to exist. He questioned me about my beliefs and shivered in dread when I said that I quite liked the idea that one day my total existence would end. He was unimpressed by my explanation that I felt secure as being a changing part of a changing cosmos. He had worked out another solution. Because he feared the loss of his identity and was precluded from religious belief, his solution was to believe in ghosts. He liked the idea of the freedom and activity a ghost might enjoy, but he still had to consider the questions of certainty of belief and of the rules governing the behavior of ghosts. The existence of ghosts, he told me, had been proved, and he cited in evidence a book called *True Ghost Stories*. As well as giving proof, this book gave some of the rules. As he talked about the rules Nick grew troubled. The word "rules" is mine; the book did not set out rules but made oblique references to standards or outcomes of certain events. To have a pleasant life as a ghost a person needed to have a proper death (not a violent death brought on by one's evil deeds) and a proper funeral. Even if he did manage to have a proper death could he be sure that his family would give him a proper

funeral, whatever that was. There were other worrying outcomes. Once properly buried he would be free to roam, but if it
so happened that he was the first person to be buried in a
graveyard then he would have to stay in the graveyard to guard
over it and the other ghosts. As Nick lived in a town that had
been destroyed by a hurricane and then rebuilt and that is now
increasing in population, he could see a strong chance that he
would be the first person buried in a new graveyard and so
become a watch-ghost—not a pleasing prospect to an active boy.

It is easy to smile at Nick's metaphysical perplexities, but
one can see that crisis and loss, sickness and death, could turn
these perplexities into fearful confusion that robbed him of all
hope. To find his way out of his confusion he would need either
to dare to believe in something that his father despised (this
includes spiritualism) or to learn to accept with equanimity the
end of his identity.

Many therapists, not just personal construct therapists, talk
of learning their clients' language, coming to understand how
clients construe themselves and their world. To do this one has
to come to understand what meaning clients give to death and
what implications this meaning has for the way they live. To do
this the therapist must respect the philosophical and religious
beliefs of clients, no matter how odd and unfamiliar they may
seem, and the therapist must try to find a common language in
which to discuss the implications of clients' beliefs. The therapist must also remember the one great difference between
rational and metaphysical beliefs (bearing in mind that believing
that life ends in death is just as metaphysical a belief as
believing that death is a doorway to heaven). Rational beliefs are
capable of proof; metaphysical beliefs are not. One does not
help clients by urging them to give up their beliefs and to accept
one's own. What a therapist can do is to help clients construe
the objects of their beliefs in a more hopeful, less fearful
way—to see God as loving or one's life as acceptable. In such an
endeavor the therapist is not the expert directing ignorant clients
along the right path. On the questions of the meaning of death
and the purpose of life all people are confused and ignorant.
Some may have a modicum more of hope and courage than

others, and so may be able to offer a helping hand, but on the long search, all are pilgrims.

References

1. Carse, J. P. *Death and existence: A conceptual history of human morality.* New York, Wiley, 1980.
2. Heisenberg, W. *Physics and philosophy.* London: George Allen and Unwin, 1971.
3. Rowe, D. *The experience of depression.* Chichester (England): Wiley, 1978.
4. Rowe, D. *The construction of life and death.* Chichester (England): Wiley, 1982.
5. Rowe, D. *Depression: The way out of your prison.* London: Routledge and Kegan Paul, 1983.

∞∞

DEATH THREAT, DEATH CONCERNS,
AND PARANORMAL BELIEF

∞∞

JEROME TOBACYK
Louisiana Tech University

Relationships among death threat, death concerns, and paranormal beliefs were investigated in a personal construct theory framework. First, the Threat Index measure of death threat and the Paranormal Belief Scale, which provides a measure of degree of belief in each of seven paranormal dimensions, were administered to 78 college students. As hypothesized, one paranormal belief dimension (traditional religious belief) was significantly associated with decreased death threat. In addition, the Death Concern Scale measure of conscious concerns about death and the Paranormal Scale were administered to 73 college students. As hypothesized, significant positive correlations were obtained between six of the seven paranormal belief dimensions (all except for traditional religious beliefs) and Death Concern Scale scores. Thus, greater beliefs in these six paranormal dimensions were associated with greater death concerns. Findings are discussed in terms of the notion that paranormal beliefs may play a role in reducing fear and threat of death. Further, results indicate that death threat and death concerns are separate death orientation constructs.

According to George Kelly's personal construct theory, each person interprets or construes the world through a system of personal constructs (1). A construct is a bipolar meaning dimension that can indicate how some events are similar to, but different from other events. The person's personal construct system develops and is modified through experience. A personal construct system is hierarchical, with superordinate constructs subsuming subordinate constructs. Perhaps the most existentially significant superordinate constructs are the core constructs, which provide individuals with their sense of identity and fundamental meanings.

According to personal construct theory, when a person's core constructs are challenged, implying that comprehensive change is imminent in the construct system, the person experiences threat. Bannister and Mair (2) contend that "Death is an exemplary threatening event for most persons, since it is viewed as likely to happen and as likely to cause drastic changes in one's core constructs. Death is less threatening when construed as far away or when fundamental meaning of life is not affected by it (e.g., one believes in an afterlife)" (p. 32).

The Threat Index, a measure of death threat derived from Kelly's personal construct theory, is thought to assess "the extent to which a person's construct system is structured to anticipate death" (3, 4). In using the provided construct form of the Threat Index, the participants are requested to first rate "self" and then to rate "your own death" on each of 40 provided bipolar constructs. The Threat Index is scored by summing the number of "splits," defined as a placement of "self" and "your own death" on different poles of a bipolar construct. Death is considered threatening in proportion to the amount of construct system reorganization needed to construe death as a personal possibility. Thus the greater the number of splits, the greater the construct system reorganization necessary to construe self and one's own death similarly, and therefore the greater the presumed death threat. Considerable evidence supports the reliability and validity of the Threat Index as a measure of death threat (4).

Existential philosophers, including Heidegger and Sartre, have argued that the ultimate encounter with Nothingness for humans is their personal death, which is inescapable. According to Becker (5), "the idea of death, the fear of it, haunts the human animal like nothing else; it is the mainspring of human activity— activity designed largely to avoid the fatality of death, to overcome it by denying, in some way, that it is the final destiny for man" (p. ix). Becker further contends that the fundamental function of religious and other paranormal beliefs is to decrease the fear or threat of death by positing (directly or indirectly) an afterlife of personal survival. Indeed, how can life be meaningful if humans simply cease to exist on death?

Many paranormal beliefs, directly or indirectly, concern personal survival of physical death. By "paranormal" is meant belief that (*a*) is counter to normative beliefs, expectations, or perceptions about reality, (*b*) would require considerable revision in current scientific theory to achieve explainability, and/or (*c*) is unexplainable by current scientific principles. Religious beliefs are considered paranormal because they appear to share similar origins and characteristics with other paranormal beliefs (6, 7). These similar characteristics include (*a*) methods of communication outside of typical, normal ways, (*b*) a unity or basic principle as the foundation of the universe, (*c*) a view of the human being as both a body and a mind, soul, or spirit, (*d*) the notion of an afterlife, and (*e*) the idea that the reality typically experienced is not the true reality. Thus, this definition of paranormal includes a wide range of beliefs or experiences concerning religion, psi, ESP, witchcraft, superstition, the supernatural, and extraordinary and extraterrestial life forms.

In a study of the structure of paranormal beliefs, Tobacyk and Milford (8) found seven independent paranormal belief dimensions. Their conclusions were based on factor analytic results from 391 college students, who rated their degree of belief in 61 items selected to sample as wide a range of paranormal beliefs as possible. Each item was rated on a 5-point scale ranging from 1, corresponding to a rating of "strongly disagree," through 5, referring to a rating of "strongly agree." A 25-item Paranormal Belief Scale[1] was constructed on the basis of these findings. The scale in turn consisted of seven paranormal belief subscales: (*a*) traditional religious beliefs (concerning beliefs in heaven, hell, god, afterlife), (*b*) psi beliefs (concerning psychokinesis, clairvoyance, and telepathy), (*c*) witchcraft (concerning black magic, witchcraft, and voodoo), (*d*) less common paranormal beliefs (concerning communication with the dead, astral projection, reincarnation), (*e*) superstition (concerning black cats,

---

[1] Copies of the Paranormal Belief Scale and scoring instructions are available from the author.

the number "13," and the like), (*f*) extraordinary creatures (concerning Loch Ness Monster, Abominable Snowman, Bigfoot), and (*g*) predicting the future (concerning precognition). Each subscale was constructed by selecting the three or four items that had the strongest loadings on the factor defining that subscale. Considerable evidence supports the reliability and validity of this Paranormal Scale and its subscales as a measure of degree and type of paranormal beliefs (8).

Traditional Religious Beliefs

Although many paranormal beliefs concern or imply personal survival after death, most of these beliefs are not as socially accepted and institutionalized as traditional religious beliefs. It appears that traditional religious beliefs, as a consequence of their accompanying institutionalized social support system concerning afterlife, enable individuals to more readily construe death as a personal reality and therefore to not be as threatened by it. Thus, it was hypothesized that the greater the score on the traditional religious beliefs subscale, the more that death would be construed as a personal reality and therefore the lower the death threat, as measured by the Threat Index. Other paranormal belief dimensions that directly reflect the notion of survival of death, such as witchcraft and less common paranormal beliefs, may not be as strongly related to less death threat, because these beliefs lack the institutionalized social system characterizing traditional religious beliefs. Indeed, Krieger, Epting, and Leitner (9) reported a trend indicating that those who believed in an afterlife tended to have lower Threat Index scores, $t_{36} = 1.41$, $p < .10$, one tailed. Moreover, Neimeyer, Dingemans, and Epting (10) reported that those who more frequently attended church tended to report less death threat on the Threat Index, $F(2, 35) = 3.43$, $p < .05$. These findings support the hypothesis that greater traditional religious belief may be associated with decreased death threat.

Method and Results

The Threat Index (40-construct-provided form) and the Paranormal Belief Scale were administered to 78 introductory psychology students. As hypothesized, traditional religious belief subscale scores showed a significant negative correlation with Threat Index scores, $r = -.23$, $p < .05$. As indicated in Table 1, neither the full Paranormal Scale score nor any of the six remaining paranormal subscale scores were significantly correlated with Threat Index scores. Correlations ranged from $-.13$ to .13, which is low.

If a major function of paranormal beliefs is to reduce death threat, these findings suggest that only traditional religious beliefs may be effective in this regard. Further, the magnitude of the correlation between traditional religious beliefs scores and Threat Index scores, although significant, is modest. Traditional religious beliefs, although perhaps important in decreasing death threat, are clearly not the critical factor. Even this interpretation must be qualified because the evidence is from a correlational study, with scores on both the traditional religious beliefs subscale and the Threat Index being naturally occurring variables. Thus, self-selection of subjects with regard to these or other variables is a possible confounding factor.

To speculate further, if among the seven paranormal belief dimensions only traditional religious beliefs are effective in decreasing death threat, then perhaps traditional religious beliefs also would be associated with fewer conscious death concerns, which constitute a more affective component of death orientation than death threat. Further, if the other paranormal belief dimensions are perhaps less effective in decreasing death threat, might they not be associated with greater conscious death concerns? These issues are examined next.

Death Concerns

There is evidence for the independence of death threat, as measured by the Threat Index, and other death-related constructs, such as death anxiety and death concerns (4). Krieger, Epting, and Leitner (9) present evidence indicating "that the Threat Index might assess a person's conceptual understanding of the way death relates to other aspects of his/her life," whereas death anxiety "might concern affective arousal concern-

TABLE 1 Descriptive Statistics and Correlations for the Threat Index, Paranormal Scale, and Subscales ($n = 78$)

	Full paranormal scale $\bar{X} = 77.1$ $SD = 12.2$	Traditional religious beliefs $\bar{X} = 4.2$ $SD = 0.9$	Psi beliefs $\bar{X} = 3.2$ $SD = 0.8$	Witchcraft $\bar{X} = 2.8$ $SD = 0.9$	Less common paranormal beliefs $\bar{X} = 2.1$ $SD = 0.8$	Superstitions $\bar{X} = 2.6$ $SD = 0.8$	Extraordinary features $\bar{X} = 2.8$ $SD = 0.8$	Predicting the future $\bar{X} = 3.5$ $SD = 0.9$
Threat Index $\bar{X} = 7.5$ $SD = 5.8$	.11	−.23 $p < .05$	−.01	.01	−.01	.13	−.13	−.09

ing death." Neimeyer, Dingemans, and Epting (10) concluded that the Threat Index may be a more stable measure of cognitive orientation regarding death than other death orientation assessment instruments.

The Death Concern Scale (11, 12, 13) is thought to provide a measure of "the degree to which one consciously confronts death and is disturbed by its implications." Tobacyk and Eckstein (14) reported a correlation of .30, $n = 108$, $p < .002$, between Death Concern Scale and Threat Index scores. Although statistically significant, the magnitude of this correlation indicated that the two instruments share only 9 percent common variance, implying that they are probably assessing different death-related constructs.

On the basis of theoretical and empirical evidence, the Threat Index may be construed as providing a deeper, more stable, core-level, cognitive assessment of death orientation, while the Death Concern Scale may be viewed as providing an assessment of death orientation at a more conscious, affective level. This distinction is consistent with Kelly's personal construct theory, in which threat is conceptualized as a process occurring at the core of the personal construct system, whereas fear and anxiety are viewed as processes occurring at more peripheral levels of the construct system.

If the Threat Index assesses a deeper, more stable, core orientation toward death and the Death Concern Scale assesses a conscious, more affective level of death orientation, then death threat may be a more fundamental process (perhaps an antecedent condition) in death concerns (which may reflect conscious anxiety or fear about death). Further, if Becker is correct in contending that the fundamental human life motive is to reduce death threat and if paranormal beliefs (directly or indirectly) have this function, then the findings from the first part of this study indicate that only traditional religious beliefs may be effective in reducing death threat. The other six paranormal belief dimensions were not significantly associated with decreased death threat. If these assumptions are correct and if death threat is an antecedent condition in conscious death concerns, it is expected that most paranormal beliefs, except for traditional religious beliefs, would be associated with greater death concerns. Although many of these other paranormal beliefs imply personal survival of death, none of them appears to significantly reduce death threat, which may be antecedent condition for decreased death concerns. Thus, it was hypothesized that increased traditional religious beliefs was associated with decreased death concerns. Further, it was hypothesized that greater belief in the other paranormal belief dimensions was associated with greater death concerns.

Method and Results

The Paranormal Belief Scale and the Death Concern Scale were administered to 73 introductory psychology college students. Descriptive statistics for these measures are provided in Table 2. As indicated in Table 2, consistent with hypotheses, significant positive correlations were obtained between the full Paranormal Scale scores and Death Concern Scale scores, as well as between six of the seven paranormal subscales and Death Concern Scale scores.

The only paranormal subscale not significantly and positively correlated with Death Concern Scale scores was the traditional religious beliefs subscale, $r = .01$, not significant. The traditional religious beliefs subscale was unrelated to Death Concern Scale scores rather than inversely related as hypothesized.

It is interesting to note that each of the six paranormal subscales that were nonsignificantly related to death threat in the first part of this study had significant positive correlations with the Death Concern Scale. Further, the traditional religious beliefs subscale, showing a significant negative relationship to death threat, was the only subscale not significantly related to the Death Concern Scale.

From the pattern of findings presented, it appears that death threat and death concerns are separate death-related constructs. These two constructs have very different relationships with paranormal beliefs. Further, there is some support for the notion that death threat reflects a deeper, core-level, cognitive component of death orientation, while death concerns reflect a more conscious, peripheral, affective component of death orientation. Moreover, it may be that among the seven types of paranormal

TABLE 2 Descriptive Statistics and Correlations for the Death Concern Scale, Paranormal Scale, and Subscales ($n = 73$)

	Full Paranormal scale $\bar{X} = 76.1$ $SD = 13.5$	Traditional religious beliefs $\bar{X} = 4.3$ $SD = 0.9$	Psi beliefs $\bar{X} = 3.2$ $SD = 1.0$	Witchcraft $\bar{X} = 2.7$ $SD = 0.9$	Less common paranormal beliefs $\bar{X} = 2.1$ $SD = 0.9$	Superstitions $\bar{X} = 2.6$ $SD = 0.9$	Extraordinary creatures $\bar{X} = 2.7$ $SD = 0.8$	Predicting the future $\bar{X} = 3.6$ $SD = 0.9$
Death Concern Scale $\bar{X} = 69.5$ $SD = 11.0$	.40 $p < .001$	.01	.29 $p < .02$	.25 $p < .04$	.31 $p < .01$	.38 $p < .002$	.28 $p < .02$	.29 $p < .02$

beliefs studied here, only traditional religious beliefs have the institutionalized social support system needed to decrease death threat. The other types of paranormal beliefs may be more often adopted by those for whom traditional religious beliefs do not effectively reduce death threat. These other paranormal beliefs have perhaps not yet evolved the institutionalized social support systems needed to reduce death threat, as have the traditional religious belief systems. Because these other beliefs are not associated with decreased death threat (perhaps an antecedent condition in lessening death concerns), the result may be greater conscious death concerns.

References

1. Kelly, G. *The psychology of personal constructs* (2 vols.). New York: Norton, 1955.
2. Bannister, D., & Mair, J. *The evaluation of personal constructs* (2 vols.). New York: Norton, 1955.
3. Krieger, S. R., Epting, F. R., & Hays, C. H. Validity and reliability of provided constructs in assessing death threat: A self-administered form. *Omega*, 1979, *10*, 87-95.
4. Ridgon, M., Epting, F., Neimeyer, R., & Krieger, S. The threat index: A research report. *Death Education*, 1979, *3*, 245-270.
5. Becker, E. *The denial of death*. New York: Free Press, 1973.
6. Clark, W. Parapsychology and religion. In B. Wolman (Ed.), *Handbook of parapsychology*. New York: Van Nostrand, 1977.
7. Leshan, L. *The medium, the mystic, and the physicist*. New York: Viking, 1966.
8. Tobacyk, J., & Milford, G. Beliefs in paranormal phenomena: Assessment instrument developed and implications for personality functioning. *Journal of Personality and Social Psychology*, 1983, *44*, 1029-1037.
9. Krieger, S., Epting, F., & Leitner, L. Personal construct, threat, and attitudes toward death. *Omega*, 1974, *15*, 299-310.
10. Neimeyer, G., Dingemans, P., & Epting, F. Convergent validity, situational stability, and meaningfulness of the threat index. *Omega*, 1977, *8*, 251-265.
11. Dickstein, L. Death concern: Measurement and correlates. *Psychological Reports*, 1972, *30*, 563-571.
12. Dickstein, L. Self report and fantasy correlates of death concern. *Psychological Reports*, 1975, *37*, 147-158.
13. Dickstein, L. Attitudes toward death, anxiety, and social desirability. *Omega*, 1978, *8*, 369-378.
14. Tobacyk, J., & Eckstein, D. Death threat and death concerns in the college student. *Omega*, 1981, *11*, 139-155.

∞∞∞

CLINICAL ISSUES AND PSYCHOTHERAPY

∞∞∞

∞∞

TOWARD A PERSONAL CONSTRUCT CONCEPTUALIZATION
OF DEPRESSION AND SUICIDE

∞∞

ROBERT A. NEIMEYER

Memphis State University

Research is examined that is relevant to a conceptualization of depression and suicide from the viewpoint of personal construct theory. This review highlights the role played by the following cognitive processes in the two disorders: (a) constriction in construct content and application, (b) construct system disorganization, (c) a breakdown in anticipation of the future, (d) negative self-construing, (e) polarized or dichotomous construing, and (f) perceived interpersonal isolation. Similarities and differences in the construct systems of depressed and suicidal individuals are explored and testable implications of the personal construct model are detailed. The paper concludes by noting construct theory's potential conceptual, methodological, and therapeutic contributions to further work in this area.

The phenomena of depression and suicide are among the most pervasive forms of serious psychological disturbance. Studies in Europe and the United States indicate that 18 to 23 percent of adult women and 8 to 11 percent of adult men have experienced a major depressive episode at some point in their lives (1) and that depression may account for as much as 75 percent of all psychiatric hospitalizations (2). Similarly, the incidence of suicide is far greater than is commonly assumed, claiming 25,000 to 50,000 lives annually in the United States alone (3). Yet despite the prevalence of depressive and suicidal behaviors, clinicians and theorists remain divided among themselves concerning both their etiology and treatment. The goal of the present paper is to order at least some of the disparate research

127[41]

findings in these areas within a single theoretical framework—the psychology of personal constructs.

Depression and Suicide

Before undertaking this task, the relation between suicide and depression needs to be clarified. Traditionally, self-destructive fantasies and behavior have been considered symptomatic of major depression. In fact, of the 13 sources reviewed by Levitt and Lubin (4), the presence of suicidal thoughts was the only symptom consistently associated with the syndrome by all the authors, placing it above such symptoms as dejected mood, pessimism, and sleep disturbance. The common co-occurrence of depression and self-injury in clinical populations has led some theorists (e.g., 5, 6) to suggest that "partial death" in the form of a reduced life may be a psychological substitute for overt self-destruction. This opens the intriguing possibility that similar cognitive factors may play a role in both suicide and depression, a premise that is examined in greater detail below.

But it would be a mistake to assume too strong a correlation between depressive and suicidal behavior. The findings of Vandivort and Locke (7) underscore this caution. Interviewing nearly 4,000 adults regarding their experience of depression and suicide ideation, these authors found that, on the average, acknowledged suicide ideators reported greater depression than did their non-suicidal counterparts. Fully 77 percent of the "depressed" sample (as gauged by direct questioning) reported no thoughts of suicide, however, and 53 percent of the ideators indicated little depressive symptomatology. Beck's report (8) that 26 percent of severely depressed psychiatric patients deny any thoughts of killing themselves further demonstrates that suicide and depression, though related, cannot be regarded adequately as a single psychological process (c.f. 9). It therefore appears that to be maximally useful, a conceptualization of these two phenomena would need to take into account both their unique and common features.

Traditional Theories and the Cognitive Trend

Traditional psychiatric theories of depression can be classed roughly into two categories, the psychodynamic and the bio-chemical. The view that the depressive syndrome reflects a basic biological dysfunction gained impetus in the 1950s when re-searchers demonstrated that depression could be pharmacologic-ally induced in normal subjects with reserpine, an agent found to reduce levels of certain biogenic amines, such as norepineph-rine and serotonin (10). Becuse these amines function as neuro-transmitters in the brain, and are implicated in the mediation of various motivational processes, a number of biologically oriented theorists (e.g., 11, 12, 13) have suggested that the depletion of these amines is associated with the development of clinical depression. The reversibility of depressive symptoms with medi-cation also has been interpreted as evidence for the viability of such theories. For example, Goodwin and Potter (14) make the following argument:

> Careful comparative studies of pharmacotherapy with and without psychotherapy consistently demonstrate the effectiveness of anti-depressant drugs; it is this fact, above all others, which points to an involvement of biology in depression. (p. 14)

Despite the promise of these biological theories, the present evidence for them is less than compelling. For example, Mendels and Frazier (15) point out that reserpine induces depression in only 10-15 percent of the subjects to whom it is administered and then chiefly to those with histories of affective disorder. In addition, as Hollon and Beck (16) reason, "evidence that an intervention (e.g., drug treatment) reduces an existing phenome-non does not in any way support the theory of induction from which it may have been derived" (p. 161). Finally, from the standpoint of the present paper, a third shortcoming of the biochemical approaches may be mentioned, namely, that they fail to account for the phenomenon of suicide in some, but by no means all, depressives. This failure does not seem to represent

a limitation that can easily be overcome by additional physiological research, so much as an inherent limitation imposed by
the biochemical perspective. Suicide, by definition a behavior
resulting from intentional self-injury, may remain poorly understood by an approach that restricts from study the cognitive
processes that eventuate in the self-destructive act.

In contrast to the biochemical approaches, psychodynamic
theories offer a single framework within which both depressive
and suicidal behaviors can be interpreted. Freud (17) set the
style for much subsequent analytic writing on the topic by
emphasizing the role of self-reproach and aggression in the
melancholic's predicament. Having lost (actually or symbolically)
some important love object, the depressive individual withdraws
the emotion that once had been invested in the cathected
object and reinvests it in the self. This establishes the lost other
as a permanent part of the self, expressed as the "ego-ideal."
This identification with the love object renders the victim
vulnerable to his or her own criticism and aggressive impulses,
because the largely nonconscious resentment and anger that
might more properly be directed toward the lost love object are
turned inward toward its only remaining representation: the
ideal self. In committing suicide, therefore, the individual is
irrationally seeking the destruction of the loved-and-hated other
(18). With certain revisions and extensions (e.g., 19, 20, 21), this
dynamic analysis of the meaning of depression and suicide has
been the predominant one in psychology for three quarters of a
century (22).

Although this traditional formulation has been enormously
influential, it also has been the target of much criticism. For
authors outside the analytic perspective, the "retroflected anger"
hypothesis appears "mysterious" and "alchemistic" (c.f. 16), out
of line with both intuition and clinical experience. Even writers
within the psychodynamic camp who are persuaded of the
model's essential validity nonetheless question its comprehensive-
ness. Thus, Isenberg and Schatzberg (23) admit that the Freud-
ian prototype of melancholy and most of its contemporary
variants "do not take into account precipitants other than loss
and their significance in the individual's psychological makeup"
(p. 159). A more serious failure of the dynamic orientation has

been its inability to generate empirical support for its theoretical propositions. In fact, such studies as have been conducted frequently adduce evidence that contradicts key aspects of the psychodynamic formulation (e.g., 24, 25, 26).

Motivated in part by the shortcomings of psychodynamic and biochemical theories, investigators recently have begun to focus on the cognitive processes that both predispose the individual to depression and mediate between environmental stress and the suicidal act. Two major models of clinical depression have evolved from these efforts, one having its roots in experimental comparative psychology, the other originating in psychotherapeutic practice.

The first of these models was derived from Seligman's (27) learned helplessness theory, which drew attention to the parallels between the behavior of laboratory animals exposed to uncontrollable noxious stimuli and the symptoms of human depression. Seligman contended that the common element in both was the organism's expectation that important environmental events or outcomes could not be controlled. He further hypothesized that it was this experience of helplessness that produced the passivity and retardation of new learning typical in both situations. Abramson, Seligman, and Teasdale's (28) attributional reformulation of this theory sharpened its cognitive implications. Although lack of control over one's environment was still seen as depressogenic, the reformulated theory stressed that the generality and duration of the depression and its implications for self-esteem were contingent on the globality, stability, and internality of the attributions regarding the helplessness. For example, a student who attributed his failing a final exam to his low IQ (global, stable, internal) would be predicted to show reduced motivation in more academic areas, be depressed for a longer period, and be more self-critical than another student who attributed her failure to more specific, unstable, and external factors (e.g., to the fact that noisy construction work was being done outside her usually quiet classroom on exam day). Despite its recency, this attributional model of depression is already gaining empirical support (e.g., 29), and has generated therapeutic implications (30).

The second model of depression to gain ascendancy in recent

years is associated with Beck's (31, 32) "cognitive therapy" approach to the disorder. Like Kelly (33), Beck (32) postulated that individuals interpose a framework of interpretations or "schemas" between themselves and the events they experience. In depression, such schemas comprise a "cognitive triad" consisting of a negative interpretation of the self, the world, and the future (34). These negative assumptions are supported by cognitive processes (e.g., overgeneralization, assuming excessive responsibility) that systematically distort experiences to reinforce the schemas' apparent validity. Therapy consists of conveying to the patient that (a) perceptions of reality are not identical to reality itself, (b) interpretations depend on fallible cognitive processes, and (c) beliefs are hypotheses that are subject to disconfirmation and modification (35). Various behavioral self-monitoring tasks and homework assignments then are employed to help patients recognize and challenge the "automatic thoughts" that determine their emotional responses to situations. Preliminary research (e.g., 36, 37) has demonstrated the presence of cognitive distortions in depression, and available evidence supports the superiority of cognitive therapy relative to traditional psychotherapeutic (16, 34) and perhaps even pharmacological treatments (38) for the disorder.

In spite of the fact that neither the learned helplessness nor cognitive therapy model was formulated to account principally for suicide, both seem capable of explaining self-destructive behavior within their more general theoretical frameworks. From the former perspective, suicidal depressives might be assumed to make more stable and especially internal attributions for their helplessness than their nonsuicidal counterparts. Cognitive therapists have dealt with suicide more explicitly, seeing it as the result of hopelessness (35) and the inability to conceive of alternatives to the self-destructive act (39).

The personal construct conceptualization of depression and suicide that is outlined below shares certain fundamentals with both of these cognitive models, particularly with that deriving from Beck's work (32). This similarity notwithstanding, the unique epistemological and methodological commitments of construct theorists could enable them to make a fresh contribution to this area of research, as I attempt to demonstrate.

The Original Kellian Formulation

In his *Psychology of Personal Constructs* (33), Kelly attempted to formulate a comprehensive theory of personality that he envisioned as an alternative to the then-dominant psychoanalytic and behavioral positions. At the core of his theory was the metaphor of "man-as-scientist." He assumed that all persons, like scientists, hypothesize about the meanings of events, and assess, refine and elaborate these hypotheses on the basis of their subsequent experience. Kelly contended that the basic "unit of meaning" in the personal theories that individuals evolve is the *construct,* defined as a way in which two things are seen as related to one another and distinct from a third. For example, a client in psychotherapy may construe her husband and employer as "self-serving" and contrast them to the therapist, whom she construes as "concerned about others." For this client, the construct "self-serving versus concerned about others" might be used to evaluate a great many persons in her past, present, and future, including herself.

Depression, for Kelly, was linked most closely with the gradual constriction of one's awareness in an attempt to minimize the disruptive implications of events that seem foreign and uninterpretable (33, p. 477). Because Kelly (33) defined anxiety as "the recognition that the events with which one is confronted lie outside the range of convenience of one's construct system" (p. 495), constriction can be seen as an attempt to avoid anxiety-arousing situations. For example, a depressive woman may tend to deal with life's uncertainties by progressively, over a period of years, placing further limits on her range of activities. Eventually, she may restrict her interests solely to her home and the care of her family, a strategy that may leave her vulnerable to an acute sense of loss at the point that her children leave home (33, pp. 904–905). Thus, although constriction temporarily may serve a useful psychological function, it seldom provides a workable long-term solution to life's problems (40).

Kelly's interpretation of depression was elaborated in his treatment of suicide. Acknowledging that self-destruction could sometimes represent an attempt to validate life's personal significance (as in the death of Socrates), Kelly (41) nonetheless contended that

> there are two conditions of personal construction under which the actual abandonment of one's life seems like the sensible thing to do. The first is when the course of events seems so obvious that there is no point in waiting around for the outcome. The score has become so lopsided that there is no reason to stay through until the end of the game. The other is when everything seems so utterly unpredictable that the only definite thing to do is abandon the scene altogether. It has ceased to be a game with perceptible rules. (p. 260)

The former condition Kelly identifies with depressive "fatalism," the sense that the future offers no prospect of change in a hoped-for direction. The latter condition he identifies with "total anxiety," and sees the ensuing suicide attempt as "a desperate bid for some kind, any kind, of certainty." In both cases, suicide can be seen as an essentially constrictive act, one that preserves the apparent validity of the suicide's interpretation of reality by eliminating all incompatible evidence "in one abrupt and frightening gesture."

Theoretically, Kelly (41) notes that,

> It is indeed striking that these should be the two limiting conditions for the sustenance of life; on the one hand, the sense of knowing everything worth knowing and, on the other, knowing nothing worth knowing. Yet, since the very essence of life is the use of the present to bridge the past with the future, any construction that makes such an undertaking futile serves psychologically to destroy life. Once this destruction has taken place, the question of whether the person keeps on breathing or not becomes a side issue. Psychologically he is alread dead. (p. 260)

In brief, Kelly theorizes that the individual may become suicidal at the point that events appear to invest his or her construction with inexorable validity, or alternatively, threaten its utter collapse. In the depressive suicide, self-destruction merely represents the end point in a long process of constriction. Having evolved a construct system that can adequately interpret and predict only a very restricted range of experience, the depressed individual may be unable to anticipate a future that differs importantly from the present. This condition gives rise to the sense of hopelessness that Beck and his colleagues also see as mediating the suicidal choice. Acts of self-injury committed in this state tend to be deliberate, well planned, and often lethal.

In the anxious suicide, on the other hand, self-destruction represents an immediate and dramatic constrictive movement. The act is preceded by an increasing disorganization in the construct system, a process that may signal the imminent breakdown in the individual's entire cognitive framework. In this condition, suicide may represent an attempt to avoid additional life experiences that could further undermine the system's validity. Self-injury in this case tends to be impulsive, poorly planned, and less often lethal.

Recent work confirms and extends Kelly's conceptualization (33, 41) of depression and self-destruction in personal construct terms. The subsections below selectively review theoretical and empirical work consistent with his original formulation. For convenience, this material is organized according to the three processes most emphasized by Kelly: constriction, construct disorganization, and anticipatory failure.

Constriction

Theorists outside the personal construct camp lend support to Kelly's interpretation of suicide and depression as essentially constrictive processes. Ringel (42), for example, regards constriction—"the feeling of being ever more tightly squeezed into a steadily tightening space"—as one of three components of the "presuicidal syndrome." As an analyst, Ringel believes that "aggression turned inward" and suicidal fantasies constitute the other two necessary components. His remark that constriction entails "rigidity in apperception and association" and "fixed patterns of behavior" clearly converges with Kelly's earlier theorizing. Similarly, "increased constriction of intellectual focus" and "tunneling or narrowing of the mind's content" are key features of Shneidman's (43) psychological theory of suicide.

More important than the convergent support provided by other theorists is the existence of empirical research that implicates constriction in the cognitive processes of the suicidal individual. In an explicit test of Kelly's argument, Landfield (44) studied the personal construct systems of several student groups varying in their levels of suicidality. As a means of assessing each respondent's unique cognitive framework, Landfield employed a grid form of Kelly's (33) Role Construct Repertory Test, or Reptest for short (45, 46). Essentially, the Reptest asks the respondent to compare and contrast various "elements" (e.g., relatives, friends, and acquaintances), thereby eliciting certain bipolar descriptions of significance to the respondent in organizing his or her perceptual world. These descriptions, or constructs, then can be used to rate each of the several elements in the grid.

Translated into Reptest methodology, constriction can be evaluated in two ways. Constriction in the application of one's constructs can be measured by the number of instances in which the respondent is unable to apply either pole of the dimension to a figure being rated, whereas constriction in the content of the constructs can be inferred from the presence of excessively concrete descriptions, which emphasize a factual or relatively superficial interpretation of the elements under consideration.[1]

---

[1] Strictly speaking, the overuse of constructs having concrete content does not represent constriction so much as a restricted range of convenience in the conceptual templates the person has at his or her disposal. Thus, in discussing a particular psychotherapy client who was unable to role play the part of his therapist and whose constructs on the Repgrid were predominantly concrete, Kelly (40) remarked: "The *concretistic* nature of his concepts is such that he cannot lift them and apply them to an interpersonal situation where he plays the part of the therapist. In other words, his constructs do not have sufficient *ranges of convenience* to be used when he gets away from certain concrete, particular situations. Thus, by limiting his range of convenience of his constructs and constriction (meaning limiting the realm of things with which he deals, limiting the realm of elements), he has kept himself reasonably safe. The task of therapy now, of course, is to start moving out away from these prison walls by extending the ranges of convenience of his constructs so that he can apply the thinking he already has to new and unfamiliar materials" (p. 91). Stated differently, constriction represents a stimulus set in which the individual selectively refuses to construe persons or events having disruptive implications for the construct system. Employing constructs with narrow ranges of convenience, on the other hand, can be seen as a response set in which the construer's encoding schemes are irrelevant for processing much potentially important information. In either case, the result may be the same: many elements of experience are left only minimally and inadequately interpreted within the existing construct system.

Both cases exemplify system failure, in that the individual seems incapable of including numerous important personal realities in an interpretive framework that could render them meaningful.

In order to test his proposition that these indices of construct system failure would provide the cognitive context for a serious suicide attempt, Landfield (44) examined a Reptest of a young woman who had ingested what she considered to be a lethal dose of tranquilizers the day following her testing. Both of the expected features of system constriction were found: the presence of such descriptions as "drinks" and "likes long-hair music" pointed to some degree of concreteness in thinking, and a very high percentage of instances in which she could not interpret the persons on her Reptest under either alternative of her bipolar dimensions suggested a great deal of uncertainty as to how to apply her constructs to others. Landfield concluded that the incipient constriction of her interpersonal construct system may well have precipitated her suicidal crisis.

Exploring the generality of his hypothesis, Landfield (44) subsequently compared the degree of constriction in the Reptests of six different student groups differing in their degree of maladjustment: serious suicide attempters, suicide gesturers, suicide ideators, long-term therapy clients, premature terminators from long-term treatment, and better adjusted students. As predicted, the serious attempters had a higher average score on both measures of constriction than did members of other groups, although a few specific comparisons were marginally insignificant (e.g., $p = .07$) perhaps as a result of the small number of attempters (five) in the sample.

Two additional studies conducted by researchers outside personal construct theory also reinforce Landfield's conclusions. Shneidman and Farberow (47) compared 33 genuine suicide notes with 33 simulated suicide notes written by nonsuicidal controls matched for age, sex, and occupation with the attempters. As hypothesized, content analyses of the two samples disclosed a significantly greater "concern with minor details, trivia, and neutral statements" in the actual notes than in the faked ones. The inestigators interpreted this finding as an indication that suicidal persons behave as if they will be psychologically present following their deaths, because only in

that case would their greater preoccupation with trivial instructions to the survivors, and so on, make sense. Similarly, Osgood
and Walker (48) reported that genuine suicide notes "reflect
greater concreteness" in content than matched simulations,
although they failed to account for this difference in terms of
their Hullian theoretical rationale. From the standpoint of the
present paper, both findings might be interpreted more consistently (and more parsimoniously) as reflecting content constriction in the personal construct systems of seriously suicidal
individuals.

Taken together, these findings provide some evidence for the
presence of constriction (particularly content constriction) in the
construing of self-destructive individuals. Moreover, it is worth
emphasizing that this restricted awareness preceeds the attempt,
instead of occurring as a result of it. This is in line with Kelly's
(41) discussion of the depressive suicide, for whom self-injury
follows a gradual course of cognitive constriction over time.
Unfortunately, direct evidence for the presence of constriction
in depression per se (as opposed to suicidal depression) is not
available. Landfield's data (44) reflect on this issue only
obliquely: there is some indication that "more maladjusted"
(but nonsuicidal) psychotherapy clients are more constricted in
the content and application of their constructs than "better
adjusted" controls, but the diagnostic heterogeneity of the
clinical samples makes definitive statements concerning depressives impossible at this time.

Construct Disorganization

Kelly (41) argued that in at least some suicides, the abandon-
ment of life may represent an attempt to avoid the intolerable
uncertainty associated with the collapse of the personal construct system. In such cases, this collapse should be fore-
shadowed by the incipient disorganization of the system.
Landfield (44) sought to test this hypothesis. He operationalized
construct disorganization in terms of the Functionally Independent Construction (FIC) score, which essentially reflects the
degree of conceptual differentiation in the individual's cognitive
framework (46, 49). The measure is derived by comparing the

ratings of all role figures or elements on all of the constructs used on the Reptest. Constructs that are used similarly to sort elements are termed "functionally dependent" and are grouped into a single cluster; the FIC score represents the total number of such clusters that are independent of one another.

In moderation, "functional differentiation among independently organized subsystems can increase the level of overall efficiency in information processing" (50, p. 61) and is therefore adaptive. But in the extreme case, differentiation could lead to a "total absence of connections between a person's constructs rendering organized thought an impossibility" (50, p. 60). Landfield (44) contended that if "the imminence of a breakdown in one's construct system is the *instigating context* of suicidal behavior" (p. 95), then serious suicide attempters should display more extreme degrees of construct differentiation (disorganization) on the Reptests than should less self-destructive individuals.

As he had predicted, Landfield found that attempters had a higher average disorganization score than a variety of other pathological and nonpathological groups (see above section), although again the small sample sizes limited the statistical significance of some of the comparisons. Interestingly, when he combined the disorganization score with the two indices of constriction (in construct content and application), the suicide attempters had a higher total on this multiple-sign score than the other groups and the differences were significant in every comparison. It is particularly impressive that this contextual approach to scoring discriminated attempters from gesturers and ideators, that is, from other suicidal groups differing in their degree of self-destructive intent.

Three other studies have employed personal construct measures to assess the conceptual differentiation of suicidal or depressed persons. Lester (51) compared the "cognitive complexity" (differentiation) of 14 students "who had threatened or attempted suicide" with that of 15 "neurotic" but nonsuicidal controls. Although suicidal respondents tended to have higher scores, the difference between the groups was statistically insignificant. Lester's calculation of cognitive complexity, however, was based on a factor analysis of Kelly's (33) Situational

Resources Repertory Test rather than a conventional Reptest. Because the former instrument simply requires the respondent to designate which of several role figures (e.g., father, minister), might provide help with different kinds of problems (e.g., financial, emotional), no personal constructs per se are elicited by the procedure. This makes inferences about the differentiation of the construct system highly questionable, and it is not surprising that there is no precedent for such an analysis in the literature.

Space and Cromwell (52) have compared the cognitive complexity of 19 hospitalized depressed patients (chiefly unipolar reactive) with equal numbers of normal and non-depressed psychiatric controls. They found no differences among the groups on any of three indices of cognitive differentiation derived from principal components factor analyses of standard Reptests. This negative finding can be accepted with some degree of confidence given the authors' care in ensuring that their depressed subjects met Feighner's (53) diagnostic criteria for the disorder. Moreover, Beck Depression Inventories (BDIs) administered to the three groups confirmed the presence of severe depression in the indexed group and the absence of significant depression among controls.

Finally, Neimeyer, Klein, Gurman, and Griest (37) have investigated the relationship of cognitive structure to level of depressive symptomatology. Subjects consisted of 68 non-hospitalized adults, all of whom met Research Diagnostic Criteria for unipolar depressive illness. Although the sample scored as clinically depressed on the Derogatis (54) Symptom Check List (SCL-90), imminently suicidal individuals were excluded from the study. Unlike previous investigators, who had employed instruments focusing on the construing of significant others in the respondent's life, Neimeyer and his co-workers (37) administered a specially constructed Reptest assessing construing of the self in a variety of social contexts. Disorganization of self-construing was represented by the FIC score. They discovered that although a number of cognitive variables correlated positively with the level of depression on the SCL-90, construct differentiation did not.

Perhaps the clearest conclusion to be drawn from these four

studies is that more depressed individuals, as a group, do not seem to display greater construct disorganization than less depressed individuals. Space and Cromwell (52) and Neimeyer and co-workers (37), sampling different populations of carefully diagnosed depressives (hospitalized versus nonhospitalized) and using different measures of both cognitive complexity (factor analysis versus FIC) and depression (BDI versus SCL-90), reported similar zero-order correlations between differentiation and level of depressive symptomatology. Moreover, the fact that these authors evaluated the complexity of different cognitive domains (construing of others versus self) further reinforces the generality of this conclusion. Landfield's finding (44) of elevated FIC among serious suicide attempters, however, leaves open the possibility that construct system disorganization provides a unique "instigating context" for high-risk self-destructive behavior. At this point it is not known whether such disorganization characterizes a suicidal subgroup of depressives per se or whether it is more closely related to other clinical phenomena (e.g., anxiety). In either case, the hypothesis that imminent breakdown in the construct system presages self-destructive behavior deserves further empirical attention.

Anticipatory Failure

In formulating his theory of personality, Kelly (33) explicitly resisted positing broad motivational principles such as "drive reduction" or "instinctual energy" to explain the obvious—that human beings are inherently active. Instead, he took it for granted that "man is a form of motion" and regarded as the proper task of psychological study the charting of that course of movement. Kelly's approach to that task, of course, was to study the unique way in which each individual charts his or her own course of movement, via the constructions that he or she places on life events. Yet there is implicit in this emphasis a motivational principle that Kelly presumed was basic to human functioning:

> (Man's) structured network of pathways leads toward the future so that he may anticipate it. This is the function it serves. Anticipa-

tion is both the push and the pull of the psychology of personal constructs. (33, p. 49)

Kelly (55) believed that this posture of anticipation was so quintessentially human that he equated "experience" with the cycle of framing hypotheses about upcoming events based on past occurrences, having them confirmed or disconfirmed as the present extends forward to meet them, and finally revising or extending one's predictive framework based on the outcome. It is in this sense that Kelly (41) wrote that "the very essence of life is the use of the present to bridge the past with the future." Any psychological stance that disrupts this anticipatory process would be considered inimical to life itself.

From a personal construct viewpoint, the sine qua non of depression is precisely this sort of anticipatory failure. Rather than extending forward toward a horizon that remains ultimately unknowable and challenging, the depressive perceives a future so devoid of possibilities, so utterly determined, that the whole purpose in living out the present in order to experience it is called into question. As Kelly (41) notes, this depressive fatalism can become so extreme that "whether the person keeps breathing or not becomes a side issue. Psychologically he is already dead" (p. 260).

Support for this view of depression comes from a variety of sources. Bakan's (56) qualitative research into the phenomenology of suicide is one example. After extensive discussion with a psychologist who had attempted to take his life many times, Bakan sought to make the imaginary leap into the life-world of the other-in-distress. A background for this effort was provided by his reading much of the literature on suicide, attempting to absorb the mood or feeling tone of the self-destructive personality, and by his going over the case notes of colleagues who had dealt with suicidal clients. In seeking to recreate in himself the suicidal outlook, he encountered and tried to surmount his own considerable resistances to taking up this despairing outlook. As a result of his immersion in the suicidal perspective, Bakan (56) concluded:

Living seems to entail a sense of openness of the durational dimension . . . . For the suicide the sense of duration is somehow

blocked of . . . the sense of time as the matrix of possibility seems
to be stultified . . . . In the imaginary leap the author picked up
the feeling of being "blocked," as in a game of chess in which
every move that one thinks of making is blocked . . . . Perhaps one
of the things about the future which is lacking in the suicide is the
hope and excitement of the unrevealed. (p. 118)

The results of several more traditional studies reinforce these
general conclusions. Dilling and Rabin (57) have investigated the
temporal experience of 20 schizophrenics, 20 depressives (6 of
whom were diagnosed as psychotic), and 20 normal controls. In
an attempt to control extraneous variables that could be related
to the experience of time, they equated the subgroups on sex,
age, education, and intelligence, and accepted into the study
only psychiatric patients who were early in their first hospitalization. Measures of time extension (amount of future time
conceptualized), coherence (logical order imposed on events),
perception (accuracy in judging the length of brief time
intervals), and orientation (preoccupation with past, present, or
future) were derived from semiprojective tests administered to
each subject individually. They reported that of the three
groups, the depressives were least able to extend themselves into
the distant future and were intermediate in organizing future life
events in a logical fashion.[2] Moreover, relative to normals,
depressives were less future-oriented and less accurate in their
estimation of 31-minute, but not 14-minute, intervals (tending
to overestimate the amount of time that had passed). It is
interesting that the "severely limited future time span" of the
depressives emerged most clearly in storytelling tasks that dealt
"mostly with the hero's thought." It may be that such tasks
permitted the subjects to project their own temporally truncated
cognitive frameworks onto the imaginary characters they
invented.

Yufit, Benzies, Fonte, and Fawcett (58) have examined
similar variables with specific reference to suicide potential. By
administering a questionnaire that required respondents to select
a year "in the future" and then answer a series of questions "as

[2] This latter tendency apparently reflected the greater lack of coherence in the time
experience of the subsample of psychotic depressives.

if it were that future year now," they were able to obtain measures of the extent to which respndents could project into the future and then elaborate their fantasies. Parallel questions permitted an assessment of preoccupation with the past. They discovered, as they had predicted, that a "diagnostically heterogeneous" group of 70 depressed patients displayed less future extension and elaboration than did 92 nonclinical controls. Moreover, when the clinical sample was subdivided into a more severely depressed hospitalized group ($n = 44$) and a generally less depressed outpatient group ($n = 26$), the former was found to have lower scores on both variables than the latter. Both clinical groups also showed greater preoccupation with past events than did normal controls.

In order to focus more clearly on the relation between time perspective and suicidality, the authors then divided the inpatient group into high-risk and low-risk subgroups on the basis of each patient's clinical history. As hypothesized, the future time perspectives of the more self-destructive patients were both more immediate and more impoverished than those of their less suicidal counterparts.

Wyrick and Wyrick (59) have reported results that corroborate and extend these findings. They tested 30 hospitalized patients who scored as severely depressed on the Multiple Affect Adjective Check List (MAACL) and compared them with 30 normal college students who were similar in age. As predicted, the depressed group showed less future extension on an incomplete sentences test than controls and consistently overestimated a number of time intervals ranging from 160 seconds to 30 minutes. In line with this tendency, the depressives indicated on a verbal report measure that they experienced time as passing slowly during the experiment, that they generally overestimated the passage of time, and that prior to their depression, time did not seem to pass so slowly.

A somewhat different approach to the assessment of future orientation in depression follows from the work of Beck and his colleagues. According to cognitive theory (34), one hallmark of depression is a characteristically negative view of the future. In the extreme case, this negativity can take the form of utter hopelessness, the conviction that the future offers no chance for real satisfaction or gratification. Because clinical experience suggested that both level of depression and hopelessness covary with suicidality, Kovacs, Beck, and Weissman (60) explored the interrelationships among the three variables in a sample of 87 patients who had been hospitalized for suicide attempts. Each patient was administered a 20-item Hopelessness Scale (HS) consisting of short statements (e.g., "The future seems dark to me") to be answered simply "true" or "false." In addition, each respondent filled out the Beck Depression Inventory (BDI) and underwent an interview-based assessment of suicidal intent. All data were collected within 48 hours of admission. Results indicated that although all three variables were positively correlated, hopelessness showed a significantly stronger relationship to suicide risk than did depression. Furthermore, when degree of hopelessness was statistically controlled, the correlation between the BDI and suicidality was insignificant; the relationship between HS and suicide intent remained significant even when the BDI was partialled out. In other words, the relationship between suicide risk and depression was due primarily to a common source of variance—hopelessness.

Finally, Neimeyer and his colleagues (37) examined several dimensions of self-construing in a group of 68 unipolar, non-hospitalized depressives (see above section). Respondents were administered the SCL-90 depression scale along with a modified form of the Reptest that required them to rate themselves in various situations (e.g., "Me as a spouse," "Me one year in the future") on a set of 10 personal construct scales coded for valence (positive versus negative). Several cognitive structural variables (e.g., self-negativity, hierarchical organization of the system) were computed based on these ratings. Of these variables, negative construing of the self in the future was selected by multiple regression to be the single best predictor of symptomatic distress (as gauged by the SCL-90) among these depressed, but nonsuicidal subjects.

In summary, the findings of several studies are compatible with Kelly's implication that depression entails an impairment in the individual's anticipation of the future. Relative both to normal controls and other psychiatric groups, depressives seem less able to extend themselves into the future and less able to conceptualize it in very elaborated terms (57, 58, 59). It is noteworthy that the extent of this anticipatory failure differentiates more symptomatic depressives from those who are less distressed and distinguishes suicidal individuals from depressives in general.

When such persons do orient themselves toward the future, it appears not as the "matrix of possibility," but as something preordained and determined (56). The subjective reaction that accompanies this perception is hopelessness, a reaction that is linked with higher-risk suicide attempts (60). Even in relatively severe but nonsuicidal depressions, this hopelessness is manifest in the negative construing of the self in the future (37).

In spite of the convergence between these studies and Kelly's (41) theorizing, it should be recognized that his is not the only theory that can accommodate these findings. Wyrick and Wyrick (59), for example, note that a sharply limited future orientation could be explained by Seligman's (27) learned helplessness model, because the depressed individual comes to believe that future outcomes are controllable and reacts by withdrawing interest in them. Only Neimeyer and his co-workers (37) conducted their study explicitly from a personal construct perspective, and it can be seen as at least as congruent with Beck's cognitive model (32) as with Kelly's own. Thus, predictions regarding temporal experience in depression that are unique to personal construct theory remain to be formulated.

A final point that deserves mention concerns the explanatory status of some of these temporal variables. For instance, is the subjective sense of "time passing slowly" (59) a cause, correlate, or result of the depression itself? Such issues can be clarified only by longitudinal experimental or quasiexperimental designs (61), designs that are a rarity in the clinical literature.

Elaborating the Personal Construct Model

In formulating the psychology of personal constructs, Kelly was aware that his work represented only a starting point, not an end point, for psychological inquiry. This was reflected in his observations on the process of theorizing in science:

A scientist formulates a theory—a body of constructs with a focus and range of convenience. If he is a good scientist, he immediately starts putting it to test. It is almost certain that, as soon as he starts testing, he will also have to start changing it in light of the outcomes. Any theory, then, tends to be transient. And the more practical it is and the more useful it appears to be, the more vulnerable it is to new evidence. Our own theory, particularly if it proves to be practical, will also have to be considered expendable in light of tomorrow's outlooks and discoveries. At best it is an ad interim theory. (33, p. 14)

Kelly clearly believed, then, that scientific formulations were necessarily provisional and modifiable and recognized that his own theory was no exception. In fact, one sign of a theory's vitality is the extent to which it is carried further by subsequent investigators.

Several recent studies conducted by construct theorists and other cognitively oriented researchers have set the stage for an elaboration of Kelly's original model of depression and suicide. These studies focus on three additional cognitive processes not specifically discussed by Kelly: negative self-construing, polarized construing, and interpersonal isolation. Research bearing on each of these areas is reviewed below.

Negative Self-construing

One of the most striking features of depression in relation to other psychological disturbances is the sense of self-deprecation that it entails. In fact, "feelings of worthlessness, self-reproach, or excessive or inappropriate guilt" occur with such regularity in the disorder that they are listed among the eight defining criteria for major depression (1). From the standpoint of cognitive therapy (34), viewing oneself negatively assumes even greater importance, because theoretically it plays an etiological role in inducing depressive affect. In personal construct terms, this suggests that the self-construing of depressives should be significantly more negative than that of nondepressed controls. Ross (62) attempted to test this hypothesis.

Subjects in the Ross study consisted of 47 undergraduate students who completed the BDI; those who scored 9 or more

($n = 14$) were designated as "depressed." Each subject completed a form of repertory grid that elicited his or her self-evaluations on a sample of 15 personal construct dimensions, as well as a set of self-report scales reflecting mood and stress management skills. As predicted, negative self-ratings on the grid correlated significantly with the Likert scale assessing extent of current depression. The depressed and nondepressed respondents, however, were not found to differ on any of several additional measures of personal construct content, organization, or application. Ross (62) offered various explanations for these negative findings, including the absence of serious depression in the sample, the exclusive reliance on self-report, and the failure to measure changes in self-construing over time.

Working with a more stringently diagnosed sample of 68 unipolar depressives, Neimeyer and his co-workers (37) found clear evidence for a positive correlation between negative self-construing and degree of depressive symptomatology on the SCL-90. The fact that these authors employed a form of the Reptest virtually identical to that used by Ross (62) suggests that the equivocal findings of the earlier study may in fact have been due to the very mild levels of depression assessed in the Ross sample.

The role of self-negativity in depression and suicide also has been documented in a number of single case studies. Rowe (63), for example, administered a Reptest to a melancholic woman whom she was seeing in therapy. Principal components analysis of the instrument disclosed the "separation of self and ideal self often found with depressed people, with self being associated with negative feelings and ideal self with unattainable attributes" (63, p. 10). Norris and Makhlouf-Norris (64) have reported similar self-ideal discrepancy in the case study of a suicide.

A particularly valuable illustration of the link between negative self-construing and self-injury comes from the work of Rigdon (65). As part of a study of personal death orientation, Rigdon had administered the Threat Index (TI) to a large sample of college students twice over a period of seven weeks. Based on rationale derived from construct theory, the TI elicits ratings of oneself and one's death on a sample of 40 bipolar constructs and yields a measure of self-death splits reflecting the respondent's level of death threat or anxiety (66). It was discovered retrospectively that one of the subjects had made a serious suicide attempt only a few days prior to the second TI administration, thereby permitting an evaluation of cognitive changes associated with the act. A comparison of data from the two TI's showed that the self/death split score of this respondent fell from 21 to 7 over the seven weeks, indicating that he perceived death as far less threatening around the time of his attempt than he had previously. A closer analysis disclosed that this lessening in death threat resulted not from a reconstruing of death in more positive terms, but from a sweeping reconstruing of the self in more negative terms (from 3 negative self-ratings at pretest to 27 at posttest). This leads to the speculation that the dramatic increase in negative self-construing may have had a role in precipitating the suicidal crisis.

Additional well-controlled studies lend qualification to the general statement that depressives are characterized by a high degree of self-negativity. The work of Space and Cromwell (52) is a case in point. Using a traditional Reptest including elements for self and significant others, they compared 19 major depressives to comparable numbers of psychiatric and normal controls. Depressives scored highest on all three measures of negative self-construing: self-ideal discrepancy, nonpositive self-ratings, and the proportion of variance in the grid accounted for by negative, as opposed to positive, self-descriptions. These findings were corroborated by the substantial correlations that were obtained between each of these variables and the BDI.

A factor analysis of the grid ratings, however, suggested a somewhat more complex interpretation of these findings. The authors examined the frequency with which depressives described themselves as both positive and negative within the same factors of the varimax solution, and they discovered that the percentage of variance accounted for by consistently negative self-valence was surprisingly small. Instead, subjects showed a "mixed self-valence," that is, they tended to construe themselves positively on some construct dimensions and negatively on others within the same cluster. The prevalence of this pattern of contradictory self-construing in the depressed sample led Space and Cromwell (52) to the following formulation:

> The mixed self-valence relationship within a factor produces a disequilibrium so that recent events of relatively low importance, whether viewed favorably or unfavorably by the individual, may cause slot movement, i.e., the shifting of attribution of self from one pole of the construct to the other without developing new constructs. If the slot movement occurs the person is vulnerable to mood shifts . . . .
>
> In common sense terms, depression proneness . . . is not the viewing of oneself (consistently) negatively but instead the viewing of oneself inconsistently, both negatively and positively, along specific interrelated dimensions. (p. 157)

Working within a very different research paradigm, Davis (67) also has reported results that clarify the relationship between negative self-construing and depression. Davis was particularly interested in investigating the "self-schema" of depressives, that is, the relatively stable cognitive patterns that enable individuals to interpret situations relevant to the self. Defined in this way, the notion of self-schema bears striking resemblance to Kelly's concept of "core role structure," the constructions that a person uses to interpret and organize information related to his or her identity (33). Noting that some depressed patients tend to talk about themselves in positive as well as negative terms, Davis (67) theorized that

> not all depressives have negative self-schema as a basis for their negative self-references; perhaps only those who have been depressed over a period of time have developed negative self-schema. Others may be responding to their observations of environmental changes. (p. 98)

He sought to test these hypotheses using a "depth of processing" methodology designed to study information processing and memory.

Essentially, the depth of processing model states that accuracy of recall for material (e.g., adjectives) is a function of the encoding strategies employed by the respondent. These strategies range from relatively superficial ones, such as attending to the word's structure (e.g., its length) or phonemic qualities (e.g., its rhythm), to deeper level semantic strategies focusing on the word's meaning. At the deepest level is self-reference encoding, in which the subject assesses the degree to which the material to be recalled relates to himself or herself. The deeper the level of the encoding strategy, the better the subsequent recall for the material.

Davis reasoned that the enhancement of recall under self-reference encoding was "an effect due to word fit with a structure or schema; if the word fits a pre-existing structure in long term store, it gains in probability of recall" (67, p. 100). From this it follows that the presence or absence of such enhancement reflects the presence or absence of a consistent self-schema that can be used to organize the information to be remembered.

Subjects in the Davis study were 29 depressed psychiatric patients and a similar numer of controls drawn from a college population and a clerical pool. Each subject rated a list of 48 adjectives on one of four orienting tasks corresponding to one of the four depths of processing (e.g., phonemic: "Rate whether you feel the word had a rhythmic sound"; self-reference: "Rate whether you feel the word describes you"), and each then was asked to recall as many of the adjectives as possible in a three-minute period. Both hypotheses were supported. Relative to normals, depressives failed to show enhancement of recall under the self-reference condition, although they did not differ significantly from controls when using more superficial encoding strategies. Furthermore, the duration of the depression was predictive of the amount of material recalled under the self-reference orienting task. Davis (67) interpreted these findings as indicating that depressives generally lack the coherent self-schemata of normals, but that consistently negative self-schemata develop over time as the depression continues.

Kuiper and Derry (68) have questioned this interpretation. They noted that the adjective list used by Davis in his recall task had been compiled by an earlier investigator specifically to represent nonpathological self-descriptions. This left open the important possibility that "depressives have an integrated self-prototype but that it is organized for the processing of different personal information than nondepressives" (62, p. 225). As an alternative, Kuiper and Derry forwarded a content-specificity hypothesis: if depressives had integrated, but negative self-prototypes (self-schemata), then self-referent enhancement would obtain only for adjectives having depressive content. Normals, on the other hand, should show recall superiority for self-reference encoding only when positively valenced material was being recalled.

The results of two studies were congruent with this model. Nondepressed subjects displayed self-reference enhancement only for material of nondepressive content. Mild depressives did not benefit from self-reference orientation under either content condition. Moderate depressives, however, showed self-referent effects for both positive and negative adjectives. Finally, severe depressives displayed superior self-referent recall only for negatively valenced material. These findings clearly implied that "the degree of cohesiveness or organization of the self-schema may change with differing degrees of psychopathology" (68, p. 227).

The most general conclusion to be drawn from the studies reviewed in this section is that negative self-construing increases gradually with severity of depression (37, 52), such that very mildly depressed persons cannot reliably be distinguished from normals (62). Case studies of depressives (63) reinforce this conclusion and implicate increasingly negative self-construing in suicidal behavior as well (64, 65).

But other research suggests that negative self-construing, although more prevalent among depressives than normals, is not necessarily pervasive or consistent for depressives as a whole. Instead, most depressives are characterized by inconsistent self-construing, which may render them susceptible to rapid mood shifts in response to relatively minor environmental changes (52). Mixed self-valence in the core role structure of depressives also may lessen their ability to encode and retrieve positive occurrences (67). This provides an explanation for Beck's observation (32) that depressives show a perceptual bias, such that they "selectively attend" to negative events while minimizing the significance of positive ones. From the standpoint of the emerging cognitive model, this bias follows logically from the relatively greater proportion of the depressive's construct system that is tailored to encoding, storing, and recalling negatively valenced information.

Finally, it appears that the symptomatic severity of depression is related to the stability of the self-structure (cf. 69). The nondepressed individual operates with a consistent and predominately positive core role structure. At mild levels of depression, the self-schema begins to lose some of its organization as it begins to assimilate negative as well as positive self-referent information. This process continues until, at moderate levels of depression, inconsistent self-construing dominates the system. Eventually, as depression reaches peak severity, a stable and consistent self-schema again emerges, but one that is organized along negative lines (68).

The model propounded here prompts a reinterpretation of the common clinical observation that severe depressives are most prone to suicide at the point that their mood begins to lift. Traditional explanations account for this phenomenon by suggesting that improved mood provides the depressive the energy to carry out preexisting impulses toward self-injury (e.g., 70). From a personal construct perspective, however, suicide would be most likely during the transitional phase between one consistent self-structure and another, because it is at that point that one's construct system would be most disorganized (44, 68). This and other process-oriented implications of the negative self-construing model need to be corroborated by longitudinal as well as cross-sectional research.

Polarized Construing

One of the distinctive features of personal construct theory is its emphasis on the bipolarity of our cognitive processes. Kelly (33) clearly regarded constructs as essentially dichotomous, so that any particular concept (e.g., success) makes sense only against the background of its implied contrast (e.g., failure). Kelly (33) was equally explicit, however, in pointing out that this need not lead to absolutistic thinking, because an individual can employ the same basic dimension repeatedly to make fine perceptual discriminations within a field of elements (e.g., "Relative to John, I am successful; but relative to my father, I am a failure"). In this way, a basically bipolar construction can be used to "build up" subtle, graded dimensions for interpreting experience. Developmental research within construct theory has demonstrated that children increasingly display more "shades of grey" in their construing as they mature (71).

The tendency (among adults) to construe events in highly dichotomous or "polarized" terms has been theorized to be a function of two factors (72). The first is the individual's degree of pathology: the more maladjusted the person, the more polarized his or her construing will be. The second is the meaningfulness of the elements and constructs themselves: evaluations of highly significant elements on personally relevant construct dimensions will be more polarized than evaluations in which either the elements or the constructs are less meaningful.

Bonarius (73) attempted to test this two-factor theory by having 125 Dutch university students rate five intimate and five superficial acquaintances on four different construct scales, two of which were personally elicited from each respondent and two of which were provided by the experimenter. Subjects also completed a standardized personality questionnaire that yielded a score for "neuroticism." Results of the experiment supported the meaningfulness proposition; ratings were most extreme when intimate acquaintances were rated on personal constructs. But contrary to expectation, more neurotic students did not show more polarized construing than their less neurotic peers, a finding that appeared to cast doubt on the validity of the maladjustment proposition.

Two features of Bonarious's experimental design, however, limit the confidence that can be placed in this second conclusion. First, the subjects in his study were (presumably well-adjusted) college students, making inferences regarding genuinely psychopathological groups questionable. Second, his treatment of neuroticism as a unidimensional variable may have masked important differences in diagnostically distinct subgroups (e.g., one might expect hysterics and obsessives to differ in the degree to which they would utilize many shades of grey in construing other persons). Thus, the possibility remains that in a clinical sample that is diagnostically homogeneous, a positive relationship between polarized construing and degree of psychological disturbance might yet emerge.

In particular, Beck and his colleagues (34) have contended that "dichotomous thinking," the tendency to interpret events in an extreme, "black-or-white" fashion, is one typical cognitive correlate of depression. Neimeyer and his colleagues (37) have reported evidence that supports this contention. Examining the Reptests of 68 unipolar depressives, they found that those who were more symptomatic tended to construe themselves in more extreme terms. Moreover, the relationship between polarized self-construing and depression remained significant even when the effects of negative self-construing were partialed out. That is, irrespective of the valence of their self-descriptions, more depressed respondents tended to construe themselves more dichotomously than their less depressed counterparts.

Neuringer (74, 75) has demonstrated the operation of similar cognitive processes in suicidal individuals. In his first study (74) Neuringer selected nine semantic differential scales (e.g., good versus bad) that loaded highly on the evaluative factor and 18 concepts (e.g., God, democracy, myself) that were likely to elicit strong evaluative reactions. "Dichotomous evaluative thinking" was operationalized as extreme ratings of the concepts on the 7-point semantic differential scales, as well as the perceived value difference between concepts pairs (e.g., God and devil). Three groups of 15 hospitalized patients completed the scales: (a) a suicidal group, composed of persons who had recently made serious suicide attempts, (b) a group of medical patients, without serious psychiatric problems, and (c) a group of patients diagnosed as psychosomatic. All participants were males, none of whom were currently being treated by psychotherapy, electroshock, or ataractic drugs. Analysis of the results, however, disclosed that Neuringer's predictions were only partially supported. Although the suicide group did display more dichotomous judgment than the normal controls, they were not distinguishable in this regard from the psychosomatic group, whose cognitive processes also tended to be polarized.

In his second study, Neuringer (75) substituted "activity" (e.g., changing versus static) and "potency" (e.g., strong versus weak) scales for the evaluative dimensions that he had originally employed. The same patient groups again were asked to rate such concepts as "communism" and "God" on the scales, and an index of dichotomous thinking was computed based on the extremity of their responses. The predicted results were obtained: although absolutistic construing was found to exist in all patient groups to some extent, it was significantly more common among the suicidal individuals.

Finally, Neuringer and Lettieri (76) have investigated the stability of dichotomous thinking in a longitudinal research design. Subjects were women recruited from the clientele of a suicide prevention center, representing high, moderate, low, and zero lethality groups ($n = 10$ per group) as judged by center staff. Following her initial contact with the agency, each woman was asked to rate nine different concepts (e.g., myself, life) on an 18-item semantic differential and to fill out a brief self-report measure of current suicidal feelings. These same forms were completed independently by each subject on a daily basis for the next 21 days.

Results were in line with predictions. The high lethality group consistently showed the greatest amount of dichotomous thinking throughout the 21-day period, and the zero lethality group the least, with the other two groups falling in between. No differences in trend over time were observed, suggesting that what was being assessed was a relatively stable cognitive style. Moreover, the degree of polarization in construing was independent of daily self-ratings of suicidality within all but the high lethality group. These more self-destructive subjects were the only ones who, when they were feeling more depressed than usual, tended to think more dichotomously than when they were less suicidal.

Convergent support for the relation between dichotomous construing and suicidality comes from the work of Osgood and Walker (48). Comparing 33 genuine and 33 simulated suicide notes, these authors discovered that the genuine notes included significantly more "allness terms" (e.g., always, never), a finding that buttresses the conclusion that suicidal individuals think in highly polarized, absolutistic terms.

The above studies are quite cosistent in pointing to the relation between polarized construing and life-threatening behavior. Only in Neuringer's first study (74) did suicidal respondents fail to show more dichotomous thinking than a control group, and this may well be attributable to the particular comparison group (psychosomatic patients) that was studied. As Winokur

(77) notes, "vague somatic complaints" occur with great frequency among depressed patients, leaving open the possibility that Neuringer's (74) psychiatric controls were depressed, even if nonsuicidal. Because dichotomous thinking appears to typify severe depressives generally (37), this could have confounded Neuringer's comparison.

The potential importance of these results is underscored by their generality. Depressed and suicidal groups, relative to controls, display more polarized construing regarding both themselves (37) and other, more external concepts (74, 75, 76). This trend is apparent regardless of whether the constructs are evaluative (37, 74) or nonevaluative (75) and irrespective of whether the polarization is assessed in a rating scale format or through content analysis of spontaneous productions (48).

Perhaps the most provocative of these findings concerns the apparent stability of this cognitive style over time. Self-destructive persons tend toward absolutistic construing both prior to (48, 76) and (if they survive) following their suicide attempts (74, 75). The fact that Neuringer and Lettieri (76) found little day-to-day variation in the extremity of responses made by several subject groups further implies that dichotomous thinking represents a characteristic and resistant-to-change way of construing oneself and the world. For high lethality individuals, this cognitive style becomes even more exaggerated at the point of suicide crisis (76). Whether this style can be modified by psychotherapy remains to be investigated.

Interpersonal Isolation

Psychological theories that place great emphasis on individuality are inherently vulnerable to the charge that they fail to give sufficient attention to interpersonal processes. Certainly, personal construct theory is not immune to this criticism, as Holland (78) has demonstrated. Yet in writing his basic theory, Kelly (33) attempted to provide at least a rudimentary treatment of the social context and its implications for the individual's constructive efforts. His discussions of such concepts as commonality, sociality, and core role structure exemplify this attempt. In recent years a number of construct theorists have applied and elaborated Kelly's original ideas to explore inter-personal dimensions of individual behavior (79). Though still germinal, similar trends can be discerned in the personal construct literature on depression.

Rowe (80) has studied the constructs or propositions employed by depressed psychotherapy clients to govern their relations to others. On the basis of her case studies of nine individuals, she concluded that depression was

> that experience which accompanies the selection from the set possible groups of propositions of a person's language structure of that particular group of propositions whereby the person sees himself as being cut off from and as choosing to be cut off from interactions with others, both people in his external reality (e.g., wife, friends) and figures in his internal reality (e.g., his God, happy memories of his dead mother ...) ... When we operate with a group of propositions that enclose, we feel that we merely exist, that we are diminished, constricted, isolated, inhibited, helpless, despondent, anguished, barren, desolate, fearful, pessimistic, and bitter. (p. 235)

Examples of isolating propositions include such beliefs as "I am different from everyone else," "If I depend on anyone that person will reject me," and "My relatives do not allow me to be myself." Rowe observes that living one's life on the basis of such principles (e.g., by avoiding self-disclosure or dependency) may provide some short-term protection from being hurt by others but only at the cost of increasing one's sense of desolation in the long run.

Interestingly, Space and Cromwell (52) arrived at a similar formulation on the basis of repertory grid analysis. They had equal numbers of depressive patients, general psychiatric patients, and normal controls (total $n = 57$) complete a standard Reptest and then rate 22 role figures (e.g., self, mother, friend) on 6-point scales flanked by each of their personal construct dimensions. These ratings were used to complete various "identification" indices reflecting the closeness of the respondent's self-descriptions to descriptions of other roles or groups of roles (e.g., parents, same-sex figures). Comparisons of the three groups showed the depressed patients to have the lowest mean identification score on every index. Moreover, when BDI scores for the entire sample were correlated with the identification indices, a significant negative linear trend was found in each instance. These between-group differences were all the more noteworthy because they remained significant even when the tendency of depressives to construe themselves more negatively than others was statistically controlled.

Both of the above studies (52, 80) lead to the general conclusion that depressives perceive themselves as distant from other persons. Ample evidence exists that this sensed interpersonal isolation is not merely phenomenological; it is associated with actual limitations in the quality and quantity of close relationships available to the depressed individual (81–83). The repercussions of this lack of identification with others might be expected to be felt throughout much of the person's construct system.

One domain of construction that would be particularly affected by social isolation would be one's core role structure, that part of the system by which the individual posits an identity and attributes stable meaning to his or her behavior. As Stefan (84) notes, "core constructs are more difficult to validate or invalidate than are first order constructs, because they operate at a less direct level of experience" (p. 283). Thus, although the accuracy of first-order self-constructs (e.g., "I enjoy painting and visiting art exhibits") can be assessed rather directly (e.g., by my being aware of my preferences and how I spend my free time), core role constructs (e.g., "I am creative and artistic") are seldom amenable to such direct confirmation. Instead, these deeper level constructions rely on consensual validation (cf. 85, 86). That is, we confirm or disconfirm them by comparing our self-evaluations with the way that significant others evaluate us. If the depressed individual holds others at a distance or simply lacks suitably initimate relationships to support this process of social comparison, his or her most basic self-understanding may be eroded, leading to the instability in the depressive self-schema noted by several investigators (52, 67, 68).

Unfortunately, construct theorists have given less attention to studying the possible role played by interpersonal isolation in suicide, although other cognitively oriented research suggests a clear link between the two. Jacobs (87), for example, has constructed a theory of self-injury based on interviews with 50 adolescent suicide attempters and their parents. His data led him to conclude that the perception of "increasing social isolation" represents one crucial link in the cognitive chain that eventuates in the suicidal act. Whether suicidal persons can be differentiated from depressives in general on the basis of their interpersonal construing remains to be investigated.

Idiographic Study

Thus far, the bulk of this paper has been devoted to a survey of studies that bear on a nomothetic analysis of depression and suicide from a personal construct perspective. That is to say, the research projects reviewed above were included precisely because they highlighted certain features (e.g., constriction, polarized construing) that characterize the construing of depressed or self-destructive individuals in general. In combination, these features may provide an abstract model or prototype of cognitive processes involved in the two disorders.

But such abstract models, while important in advancing our scientific understanding of clinical phenomena, necessarily lack the richness and depth of more idiographic studies. Given Kelly's (33) great emphasis on individuality, it seems fitting to touch on the value of personal construct theory in illuminating the single case before concluding the paper with a summary of the nomothetic model.

As a straightforward example, consider the case of a university professor who experiences a chronic sense of depression in the face of an impending departmental decision regarding his tenure. At the risk of oversimplification, his mood could be explained by a number of cognitive theories: he may perceive the valued outcome of being granted tenure to be beyond his control (Seligman's "learned helplessness"; 27), or he may despair of being given serious consideration by the committee (Beck's "hopelessness," 32, 60). But these partial explanations do not address the important question of why, psychologically, tenure is so important to him and by implication why its denial appears so devastating. To answer these questions requires a closer examination of his core role structure, that aspect of his construct system that encompasses his sense of who he is, who he would like to be, and who he feels he is becoming.

Let us suppose that one core role that our hypothetical professor applies to himself is that of being an academician. For him, enacting the role of academician carries pervasive implications for his construal of himself (e.g., that he is intelligent, respectable, cultured) and his interpersonal relationships (e.g., he behaves one way in relation to students, another in relation to other faculty, administrators, and so on). In Kelly's (33, p. 21) terms, this exemplifies the control that a superordinate construction (e.g., "I am an academician") has over its subordinate elements (e.g., other self-perceptions and behaviors). If the professor has identified too exclusively with his academic role and lacks alternative core structures, the prospect of denial of tenure may appear to invalidate a cherished construction as well as a major portion of his construct system that is implicatively tied to it (84). The awareness of this invalidation produces sadness (88), an affective state that would continue until a viable core structure could be reconstituted along other lines.

The above example illustrates the depression that can accompany superordinate commitment to a vulnerable core role structure. Such depression can be overcome only in the context of diminished commitment to the endangered core role and a reinvestment in an alternative superordinate identity. Depression also can be associated with the invalidation of interpersonal constructions, as Ryle (89) has demonstrated in his case study of a suicidal young woman.

Susan was a 19-year-old university student who consulted Ryle at the insistence of a friend the day after making two suicide gestures (swallowing up to 20 aspirin). These gestures apparently were precipitated by the decision of her boyfriend Brian to terminate their relationship, which had been deteriorating for several months. This decision was at variance with Susan's general impression of Brian as someone who was weak and easily influenced and who had little idea of what he wanted beyond the wish to please everyone all the time.

Susan was seen twice for therapy over the next two weeks,

during which time she continued to have sporadic contact with Brian. Shortly after her second session, Brian consulted Ryle, bringing with him a note from Susan that challenged him "to prove he was not scared of her or impotent." This drew Brian back to her for a short time, but he soon broke off the relationship again. Following this, Susan made a near lethal attempt on her life, taking 50 aspirin along with a quantity of alcohol, turning on the gas in her room, and writing a suicide note to her family. She was found by friends and hospitalized before losing consciousness.

After discharge from the hospital, Susan was seen alone or conjointly with Brian several times a week for the remaining five weeks of the term. During this period she held to the conviction that their relationship would recommence, despite Brian's decision to begin dating another woman. When Susan consulted Ryle at the beginning of the second term, her depression had abated, and she reported that Brian had given up the other woman and had returned to her. Two weeks later Brian consulted, complaining that he again felt trapped and suffocated by the relationship. Susan continued in therapy throughout the semester at increasing intervals, with some reported gains in the maturity of her involvement with Brian.

Twice over the course of his contact with the two students— shortly after Susan's serious suicide bid and again near the end of therapy—Ryle administered Reptests to both partners. By requiring them to rate themselves and a number of significant others on personal construct scales, Ryle sought to elicit the cognitive framework each used to construe interpersonal relationships. Examining the structure of their individual grids across time, he attempted to answer the following questions: (a) What is the explanation for Susan's and Brian's mutual attraction, in light of their uncomplimentary views of one another? (b) What led Susan to attempt suicide? (c) To what extent was the relationship modified over the course of therapy?

Subjecting Susan's first Repgrid to principal components analysis, Ryle discovered that she dimensionalized persons primarily in terms of two constructs: effective versus ineffective and submissive versus domineering. Furthermore, in every male-female pair in Susan's family constellation (e.g., father/mother, grandfather/grandmother) she construed the female as more effective and more domineering than the male. This was particularly pronounced in her interpretation of her own position relative to Brian; that is, their relationship seemed to repeat, in exaggerated form, the pattern she took to be characteristic of all male-female relationships within her family. Similarly, analysis of Brian's Repgrid disclosed that he construed persons principally along the constructs strong versus weak and trusted versus distrusted. Although Brian appeared to agree with Susan in his placement of them on the first axis (by construing himself as very weak and her as very strong), he also perceived her as distrusted and himself as trustworthy. This pattern was found to be a repetition, again in exaggerated form, of his father's relation to his mother.

Ryle (89) interpreted these results as indicating that for Susan, relative ineffectiveness was an expected and appropriate male trait, and for Brian, relative strength was an expected female one. Each apparently found in the other qualities that were characteristic of opposite-sex figures in their own families, and each appeared to value their mutual relationship more than other relationships on the grid (with previous lovers) that did not fit this pattern. Brian's ambivalent decision to escape Susan's domination, however, enabled him

> to challenge Susan's construct of him as weak, and in so doing he successfully challenged her construct of herself as strong. One could argue that Susan's self-destructive act was carried out because to die seemed less painful than to face so radical a revision of her construct system. (89, p. 1396)

Retesting of both partners suggested that a moderate degree of reconstruction of their relationship took place over the course of therapy. At the second testing, Susan's self-element had lower loadings for strength, and her placement of Brian had higher loadings on the same dimension. Her second component seemed to take on a different character, referring more to rational versus expressive behavior than to effectiveness versus ineffectiveness. The distance between herself and Brian collapsed somewhat on this dimension as well, relative to the first testing. For Brian, reconstruction mainly took the form of moving his self-element closer to the "strong" end of his first component, with a concomitant reduction in Susan's extreme loading for strength. In sum, Ryle's Reptesting of the two students helped him to understand the basis for their ambivalent attraction to one another, to trace changes in their role relationship over the course of therapy, and to pinpoint a possible psychological precipitant for Susan's attempt on her life.

Summary and Conclusions

The prevalence of depression has given rise to numerous theories—ranging from the psychodynamic to the biochemical—that attempt to account for its etiology and offer guidelines for treatment. One of the more striking recent trends in this literature has been the shift toward cognitive and attributional conceptualizations to the disorder (90). Given its position at the interface of clinical psychology and research in social cognition, personal construct theory would seem to be well situated to contribute to this effort.

The Personal Construct Model

The foregoing review suggests that the personal construct systems of depressed and suicidal individuals are characterized by at least six general features, three of which were implicit in Kelly's original discussions of these disorders (33, 41) and three of which derive from more recent research by construct theorists and other cognitively oriented investigators. These features include the following:

1. *constriction* in the content and application of constructs,
2. *disorganization* of the construct system,
3. *anticipatory failure,* the minimally elaborated perception of a future devoid of possibility,
4. *negative self-construing,* the tendency to construe the self in mixed or predominantly negative terms,
5. *polarized construing,* the tendency to interpret events in extreme, dichotomous fashion, and

6. *interpersonal isolation,* the tendency to construe the self as distant from other people.

Three of these processes, anticipatory failure, negative self-construing, and polarized construing, appear to be implicated in both depression and suicide:

> Depressives, relative to normals, are less oriented to the future and conceptualize it in less extended, less elaborated, and more negative terms. Suicidal individuals show these same tendencies but to an even more exaggerated degree.
>
> As depression deepens, the core role structure gradually loses its coherence and positivity, until at moderate levels, an unstable mixed self-valence dominates the system. Finally, at the deepest levels of depression, a consistent self-structure again emerges, but one that is organized along negative lines. Suicidal behavior appears most likely at the point of transition from one stable core structure to another.
>
> Severe depressives construe events in highly polarized or dichotomous terms. This tendency becomes more pronounced with increasing suicidality.

Two additional processes, constriction and system disorganization, have been linked only with suicidal behavior:

> The constructs of self-destructive individuals tend to be concrete in content and may be inapplicable to many of the realities with which they are confronted. The possible role played by this constriction in depression per se has not been investigated.
>
> Some evidence suggests that seriously suicidal individuals have excessively differentiated, loosely organized interpersonal construct systems. Because this is not true of depressives in general, it is possible that system disorganization provides a unique instigating context for self-destructive behavior.

Finally, interpersonal isolation has been demonstrated most clearly in relation to depression:

> Depressed individuals construe themselves as unidentified with and distant from other persons. Although there is some suggestion of a similar connection between perceived interpersonal isolation and self-injury, the relationship between these two processes has been less adequately examined.

Directions for Future Research

In addition to the specific implications for further studies detailed in the preceding sections, a few more general research recommendations should be made. One of these concerns the fundamental issue of whether the cognitive processes discussed above should be considered symptom-linked or vulnerability-linked variables. Essentially, the former covary with symptomatic distress: they are detectable only when the person is actively displaying the clinical syndrome and not when he or she is in remission. Vulnerability-linked variables, on the other hand, are more or less stable constants that predispose the person to become symptomatic in the face of relevant environmental stress. As such, these latter variables could be evident even in persons who have not (yet) experienced the clinical syndrome because their vulnerabilities have not been triggered by unfavorable life events. For example, a man who is markedly constricted might function quite adequately until he encounters pressing interpersonal events that cannot be meaningfully construed within his existing construct system. It would be only at that point that his predisposition to self-destructive behavior might become apparent. Present evidence suggests that some of the cognitive factors outlined here may qualify as vulnerability linked, others as symptom linked. Degree of negative self-construing, for instance, seems to covary longitudinally with symptom intensity, while polarized construing appears to be very stable across time. If several of the above variables are of the latter type, they might lay the groundwork for a cognitive conceptualization of the depressive or suicidal "personality."

A second issue concerns the need for diagnostic differentiation in further cognitive research in this area. A growing literature (77, 91) indicates that "depression" cannot be regarded as a homogeneous diagnostic entity, but instead includes a variety of disorders that are heterogeneous in terms of both etiology and treatment response. Although it is unclear what implications traditional diagnostic distinctions might have for the development of a cognitive model, it is likely that taking into account such basic discriminations as unipolar versus bipolar disorder and psychotic versus nonpsychotic depression would clarify the cognitive processes associated with each. Likewise, "suicide" cannot be adequately regarded as a unidimensional concept. Kelly (41), for example, differentiated between the anxious and the depressive suicide, a potentially important distinction that has not been pursued in the subsequent research literature.

A third point that deserves emphasis has to do with the value of methodological diversity in investigating cognitive processes such as those dealt with above. Modifications of the Reptest or Repgrid (45, 46) seem especially promising in this regard. As the above studies demonstrate, they can be adapted to assess constructions of significant others or to tap the individual's self-schema or core role structure. Moreover, they yield data concerning the content, application, and organization of the construct system, and they are equally appropriate for nomothetic and idiographic studies. The great value of such instruments is that they appear to elucidate what Arnkoff (92) has referred to as the "deep structure" of our interpretative frameworks, the conceptual scaffolding that undergirds our more surface-structural thoughts, self-statements, and so on. Several alternative methodologies also can contribute a great deal to this line of research, including the depth-of-processing paradigm, standard questionnaires and interviews, content analyses of spontaneous productions, and qualitative/phenomenological research strategies.

Lastly, it is clear that the therapeutic implications of the personal construct model need to be elaborated and tested. Some of this work has already been done. Kelly (33), for example, discussed a number of strategies for dilating the constricted focus of a psychotherapy client and for tightening loosely organized constructs into an integral system. In addition, Beck and his colleagues (34) have developed a cognitive therapeutic approach designed to help the client test out and revise unrealistically negative self-evaluations, to identify and correct dichotomous thinking, and to undercut the sense of hopelessness that characterizes the depressive's orientation toward the future. Finally, Klerman and Weissman's Interpersonal Psychotherapy (93) would seem particularly valuable in breaking down the depressed person's sense of distance from others, as would the group therapy approaches advocated by Space and Cromwell (52) and Hollon and Shaw (94). Future work could extend and refine these existing intervention strategies and perhaps integrate them into a single coherent treatment program.

In conclusion, it appears that personal construct psychology can make substantive, methodological, and therapeutic contributions to the emerging cognitive conceptualization of depression and suicide. This illustrates the continuing richness of Kelly's theory (33), a theory whose clinical possibilities are only beginning to be explored.

References

1. American Psychiatric Association. *Diagnostic and statistical manual of mental disorders* (3rd ed.). Washington, D.C.: Author, 1980.
2. Secunda, S. K., Katz, M. N., Friedman, R. J., & Schuyler, D. *Special report: 1973—The depressive disorders.* Washington, D.C.: U.S. Government Printing Office, 1973.
3. Shneidman, E. S. *Deaths of man.* New York: Quadrangle, 1973.
4. Levitt, E. E., & Lubin, B. *Depression: Concepts, controversies, and some new facts.* New York: Springer, 1975.
5. Menninger, K. *Man against himself.* New York: Harcourt, Brace, 1938.
6. Shneidman, E. S. The suicidal person: An overview. In L. Hankoff and B. Einsidler (Eds.), *Suicide: Theory and clinical aspects.* Littleton, Mass.: PSG Publishing, 1979.
7. Vandivort, D. S., & Locke, B. Z. Suicidal ideation: Its relation to depression, suicide and suicide attempt. *Suicide and Life-Threatening Behavior,* 1979, *9*(4), 205–218.
8. Beck, A. T. *The diagnosis and management of depression.* Philadelphia: University of Pennsylvania Press, 1973.

9. Fredrick, C. J. Current trends in suicidal behavior in the United States. *American Journal of Psychotherapy*, 1978, *32*, 172-200.

10. Hollister, L. E. The amine hypothesis revisited: A clinician's view. In J. Cole, A. Schatzberg, & S. Frazier (Eds.), *Depression: Biology, psychodynamics and treatment.* New York: Plenum, 1978.

11. Coppen, A. The biochemistry of affective disorders. *British Journal of Psychiatry*, 1967, *113*, 1237.

12. Glassman, A. Indoleamines and affective disorders. *Psychosomatic Medicine*, 1969, *31*, 197-120.

13. Schildkraut, J. J., et al. Norepinephrine metabolism in depressive disorders. In J. Cole, A. Schatzberg, & S. Frazier (Eds.), *Depression: Biology, psychodynamics, and treatment.* New York: Plenum, 1978.

14. Goodwin, F. K., & Potter, W. Z. The biology of affective illness: Amine neuro-transmitters and drug response. In J. Cole, A. Schatzberg, & S. Frazier (Eds.), *Depression: Biology, psychodynamics, and treatment.* New York: Plenum, 1978.

15. Mendels, J., & Frazier, A. Brain biogenic amine depletion and mood. *Archives of General Psychiatry*, 1974, *30*, 447-451.

16. Hollon, S. D., & Beck, A. T. Cognitive therapy of depression. In P. Kendall & S. Hollon (Eds.), *Cognitive-behavioral interventions.* New York: Academic, 1979.

17. Freud, S. Mourning and melancholia. *Standard edition* (vol. 18), London: Hogarth, 1955.

18. Litman, R. Sigmund Freud on suicide. In E. Shneidman (Ed.), *Essays in self-destruction.* New York: Science House, 1967.

19. Bibring, E. The mechanism of depression. In P. Greenacre (Ed.), *Affective disorders.* New York: International Universities Press, 1953.

20. Klein, M. Mourning and manic depressive states. *International Journal of Psychoanalysis*, 1949, *21*, 125-153.

21. Rado, S. Psychodynamics of depression from the etiologic point of view. *Psychosomatic Medicine*, 1951, *13*, 51-55.

22. Shneidman, E. 58 years. In E. Shneidman (Ed.), *On the nature of suicide.* San Francisco, Jossey-Bass, 1969.

23. Isenberg, P. L., & Schatzberg, A. F. Psychoanalytic contributions to a theory of depression. In J. Cole, A. Schatzberg, & S. Frazier (Eds.), *Depression: Biology, psychodynamics and treatment.* New York: Plenum, 1978.

24. Friedman, A. S. Hostility factors and clinical improvement in depressed patients. *Archives of General Psychology*, 1970, *23*, 524-537.

25. Hauri, P. Dreams in patients remitted from reactive depression. *Journal of Abnormal Psychology*, 1976, *85*, 1-10.

26. Paykel, E. S., Weissman, M. M., Pinsoff, B. A., & Tonks, C. M. Dimensions of social adjustment in depressed women. *Journal of Nervous and Mental Disease*, 1971, *152*, 158-172.

27. Seligman, M. E. P. *Helplessness: On Depression, development, and death.* San Francisco: Freeman, 1975.

28. Abramson, L. Y., Seligman, M. E. P., & Teasdale, J. D. Learned helplessness in humans: Critique and reformulation. *Journal of Abnormal Psychology*, 1978, *87*(1), 49–74.

29. Seligman, M. E. P., Abramson, L. Y., Semmel, A., & Van Baeyer, C. Depressive attributional style. *Journal of Abnormal Psychology*, 1979, *88*, 242–247.

30. Beach, S. R., Abramson, L. Y., & Levine, F. M. Attributional reformulation of learned helplessness: Therapeutic implications. In J. Clarkin and H. Glazer (Eds.), *Depression: Behavioral and directive intervention strategies.* New York: Garland, 1981.

31. Beck, A. T. *Depression: Clinical, experimental, and theoretical aspects.* New York: Harper & Row, 1967.

32. Beck, A. T. *Cognitive therapy and the emotional disorders.* New York: International Universities Press, 1976.

33. Kelly, G. A. *The psychology of personal constructs.* New York: Norton, 1955.

34. Beck, A. T., Rush, A. J., Shaw, B. F., & Emergy, G. *Cognitive therapy of depression.* New York: Guilford, 1979.

35. Bedrosian, R. C., & Beck, A. T. Principles of cognitive therapy. In M. Mahoney (Ed.), *Psychotherapy process.* New York: Plenum, 1980.

36. Lefebvre, M. F. Cognitive distortion and cognitive errors in depressed psychiatric and low back pain patients. *Journal of Consulting and Clinical Psychology*, 1981, *49*, 517–525.

37. Neimeyer, R. A., Klein, M. H., Gurman, A. S., & Griest, J. H. Cognitive structure and depressive symptomatology. *British Journal of Cognitive Psychotherapy*, 1983, *1*, 65–73.

38. Rush, A. J., Beck, A. T., Kovacs, M., & Hollon, S. Comparative efficacy of cognitive therapy and imipramine in the treatment of depressed outpatients. *Cognitive Therapy and Research*, 1977, *1*, 17–37.

39. Coleman, R. E., & Beck, A. T. Cognitive therapy for depression. In J. Clarkin and H. Glazer (Eds.), *Depression: Behavioral and directive intervention strategies.* New York: Garland, 1981.

40. Neimeyer, R. A. George Kelly as therapist: A review of his tapes. In A. W. Landfield and L. Leitner (Eds.), *Personal construct psychology: Psychotherapy and personality.* New York: Wiley-Interscience, 1980.

41. Kelly, G. A. Suicide: The personal construct point of view. In N. Farberow and E. Shneidman (Eds.), *The cry for help.* New York: McGraw-Hill, 1961.

42. Ringel, E. The presuicidal syndrome. *Suicide and Life-Threatening Behavior*, 1976, *6*, 131–149.

43. Shneidman, E. S. A psychological theory of suicide. *Psychiatric Annals*, 1976, *6*, 51–66.

44. Landfield, A. A personal construct approach to suicidal behavior. In P. Slater (Ed.), *Explorations of Intrapersonal Space.* New York: Wiley, 1976.

45. Fransella, F., & Bannister, D. *A manual for repertory grid technique.* London: Academic, 1977.
46. Neimeyer, G. J., & Neimeyer, R. A. Personal construct perspectives on cognitive assessment. In T. Merluzzi, C. Glass, & M. Genest (Eds.), *Cognitive Assessment.* New York: Guilford, 1981.
47. Shneidman, E., & Farberow, N. The logic of suicide. In E. Shneidman and N. Farberow, *Clues to suicide.* New York: McGraw-Hill, 1957.
48. Osgood, C. E., & Walker, E. G. Motivation and language behavior: A content analysis of suicide notes. *Journal of Abnormal and Social Psychology,* 1959, *59,* 58-67.
49. Landfield, A. W. *Personal construct systems in psychotherapy.* Chicago: Rand McNally, 1971.
50. Adams-Webber, J. R. *Personal construct theory: Concepts and application.* New York: Wiley, 1979.
51. Lester, D. Cognitive complexity of the suicidal individual. *Psychological Reports,* 1971, *28,* 158.
52. Space, L. G., & Cromwell, R. L. Personal constructs among depressed patients. *Journal of Nervous and Mental Disease,* 1980, *168*(3), 150-158.
53. Feighner, J., Robins, E., Guze, S., et al. Diagnostic criteria for use in psychiatric research. *Archives of General Psychiatry,* 1972, *26,* 57-63.
54. Derogatis, L. R. SCL-90-R: Manual I. Baltimore: Johns Hopkins University School of Medicine, 1977.
55. Kelly, G. A. A brief introduction to personal construct theory. In D. Bannister (Ed.), *Perspectives in personal construct theory.* London: Academic, 1970.
56. Bakan, D. Suicide and the method of introspection. In D. Bakan, *On method.* San Francisco: Jossey-Bass, 1969.
57. Dilling, C. A., & Rabin, A. I. Temporal experience in depressive states and schizophrenia. *Journal of Consulting Psychology,* 1967, *31*(6), 604-608.
58. Yufit, R. I., Benzies, B., Fonte, M. E., & Fawcett, J. A. Suicide potential and time perspective. *Archives of General Psychiatry,* 1970, *23,* 158-163.
59. Wyrick, R. A., & Wyrick, L. C. Time experience during depression. *Archives of General Psychiatry,* 1977, *34,* 1441-1443.
60. Kovacs, M., Beck, A. T., & Weissman, A. Hopelessness: An indicator of suicidal risk. *Life-Threatening Behavior,* 1975, *5*(2), 98-103.
61. Cook, T. D., & Campbell, D. T. *Quasi-experimentation.* Chicago: Rand McNally, 1979.
62. Ross, M. Depression, self-concept, and personal constructs. Unpublished manuscript, University of Nebraska, 1980.
63. Rowe, D. Grid technique in the conversation between patient and therapist. In P. Slater (Ed.), *Explorations of intrapersonal space* (vol. 1). London: Wiley, 1976.
64. Norris, H., & Makhlouf-Norris, F. The measurement of self-identity. In

P. Slater (Ed.), *Explorations of intrapersonal space* (vol. 1). London: Wiley, 1976.

65. Rigdon, M. Personal communication, April 1982.
66. Rigdon, M. A., Epting, F. R., Neimeyer, R. A., & Krieger, S. R. The Threat Index: A research report. *Death Education*, 1979, *3*, 245-270.
67. Davis, H. Self-reference and the encoding of personal information in depression. *Cognitive Therapy and Research*, 1979, *3*, 97-110.
68. Kuiper, N. A., & Derry, P. A. The self as a cognitive prototype: An application to person perception and depression. In N. Cantor & J. F. Kihlstrom (Eds.), *Personality, cognition, and social interaction*. Hillsdale, N.J.: Erlbaum, 1981.
69. Merluzzi, T. V., Rudy, T. E., & Gloss, C. R. The information processing paradigm: Implications for clinical science. In T. Merluzzi, C. Glass, & Myles Genest (Eds.), *Cognitive assessment*. New York: Guilford, 1981.
70. Hatton, C., Valente, S., & Rink, A. *Suicide: Assessment and intervention*. New York: Appleton, 1977.
71. Applebee, A. N. The development of children's response to repertory grids. *British Journal of Social and Clinical Psychology*, 1976, *15*, 101-102.
72. O'Donovan, D. Rating extremity: Pathology or meaningfulness. *Psychological Review*, 1965, *72*(5), 358-372.
73. Bonarius, H. The interaction model of communication: Through experimental research towards existential relevance. In A. Landfield (Ed.), *The Nebraska symposium on motivation: 1976*. Lincoln: Nebraska Press, 1977.
74. Neuringer, C. Dichotomous evaluation in suicidal individuals. *Journal of Consulting Psychology*, 1961, *25*(5), 445-449.
75. Neuringer, C. The cognitive organization of meaning in suicidal individuals. *Journal of General Psychology*, 1967, *76*, 91-100.
76. Neuringer, C., & Lettieri, D. Cognition, attitude and affect in suicidal individuals. *Life-Threatening Behavior*, 1971, *1*(2), 106-124.
77. Winokur, G. *Depression: The facts*. New York: Oxford, 1981.
78. Holland, R. *Self and social context*. New York: St. Martins, 1977.
79. Stringer, P., & Bannister, D. *Constructs of sociality and individuality*. London: Academic, 1979.
80. Rowe, D. *The experience of depression*. New York: Wiley, 1978.
81. Brown, G. W., Harris, T., & Copeland, J. R. Depression and loss. *British Journal of Psychiatry*, 1977, *130*, 1-18.
82. Henderson, S., Duncan-Jones, P., McAuley, H., & Richie, K. The patient's primary group. *British Journal of Psychiatry*, 1978, *132*, 74-86.
83. Paykel, E. S., Myers, J. K., Dienelt, M. N., Klerman, G. L., Lindenthal, J. J., & Pepper, M. P. Life events and depression: A controlled study. *Archives of General Psychiatry*, 1969, *21*, 753-760.
84. Stefan, C. Core structure theory and implication. In D. Bannister (Ed.),

New perspectives in personal construct theory. London: Academic, 1977.

85. Duck, S. W. Inquiry, hypothesis, and the quest for validation. In S. W. Duck (Ed.), *Theory and practice in interpersonal attraction*. New York: Academic, 1977.

86. Neimeyer, G. J., & Neimeyer, R. A. Functional similarity and interpersonal attraction. *Journal of Research in Personality*, 1981, *15*, 427–435.

87. Jacobs, J. *Adolescent suicide*. New York: Wiley, 1971b.

88. McCoy, M. M. A reconstruction of emotion. In D. Bannister (Ed.), *New perspectives in personal construct theory*. London: Academic, 1977.

89. Ryle, A. A repertory grid study of the meaning and consequences of a suicidal act. *British Journal of Psychiatry*, 1967, *113*, 1393–1403.

90. Shaw, B. F., & Dobson, K. S. Cognitive assessment of depression. In T. Merluzzi, C. Glass, & M. Genest (Eds.), *Cognitive assessment*. New York: Guilford, 1981.

91. Rush, A. J. Diagnosing depressions. In A. J. Rush (Ed.), *Short-term psychotherapies for depression*. New York: Guilford, 1982.

92. Arnkoff, D. Psychotherapy from the perspective of cognitive theory. In M. Mahoney (Ed.), *Psychotherapy process*. New York: Plenum, 1980.

93. Klerman, G. L., & Weissman, M. M. Interpersonal psychotherapy: Theory and research. In A. J. Rush (Ed.), *Short-term psychotherapies for depression*. New York, Guilford, 1982.

94. Hollon, S. D., & Shaw, B. F. Group cognitive therapy for depressed patients. In A. Beck, A. J. Rush, B. Shaw, & G. Emery (Eds.), *Cognitive therapy of depression*. New York: Guilford, 1979.

∞∞∞

BEREAVEMENT AND PERSONAL CONSTRUCTS: OLD THEORIES AND NEW CONCEPTS

∞∞∞

ALICE C. HOAGLAND

University of Rochester

This paper reviews several traditional and current theories regarding the nature of bereavement and argues that conceptualizing grieving in personal construct terms can clarify and extend existing work in this area. In particular, it is contended that a personal construct view of the importance of "core role" (self) structure helps explain Bowlby's theory of "defensive exclusion" of the reality of the death: because an individual's perceived relationship with a significant other helps define his or her core role, loss of the relationship through death directly challenges the most central dimensions of the bereaved person's construct system. Implications of this cognitive theory of bereavement are detailed, and several testable hypotheses are put forward.

Pathological or morbid responses to loss have been strongly implicated in the disruption of personal relationships and deterioration of physical and mental health (1-4). In spite of the mounting evidence that bereavement is a significant contributor to psychological sequelae, a clear delineation of what constitutes an abnormal grief response has not been well formulated. This may be due in part to the lack of agreement on what is involved in a "normal" grief response. Diagnosing pathological grief is clearly different from diagnosing other mental illnesses, because there are sets of grief responses that are by and large considered normal. In contrast there is no such entity as normal schizophrenic symptomatology.

Current psychiatric nomenclature recognizes the normality of grief. The recent DSM-III manual (5) classifies Uncomplicated Bereavement as a "V" code, a condition that is not attributed to a mental disorder.

V62.82 Uncomplicated Bereavement: This category can be used when a focus of attention or treatment is a normal reaction to the death of a loved one (bereavement).

A full depressive syndrome frequently is a normal reaction to such a loss, with feelings of depression and such associated symptoms as poor appetite, weight loss, and insomnia. However, morbid preoccupation with worthlessness, prolonged and marked functional impairment, and marked psychomotor retardation are uncommon and suggest that the bereavement is complicated by the development of a Major Depression

In Uncomplicated Bereavement, guilt, if present, is chiefly about things done or not done at the time of the death by the survivor; thoughts of death are usually limited to the individual's thinking that he or she would be better off dead or that he or she should have died with the person who died. The individual with Uncomplicated Bereavement generally regards the feeling of the depressed mood as "normal," although he or she may seek professional help for relief of such associated symptoms as insomnia and anorexia.

The DSM-III system clearly suggests that "complicated" bereavement does not exist and is in fact something else, such as "Major Depression" or a "Somatiform Disorder." The clinician as well as the researcher, when faced with what appear to be symptoms of morbid grieving, is asked to provide an alternate diagnosis. Diagnosing a complicated grief response as a depressive episode or as anorexia may lead to inappropriate and perhaps only symptomatic treatment of the grief problem.

The problem lies not just with the authors of DSM-III; rather, it lies initially with the lack of agreement in the field on the symptoms or chronology of normal bereavement. Part of the problem lies also within the nature of grief itself. As an emotional process, it elicits such a wide range of behaviors that it is difficult to generate a single unified description. Also, grieving can occur as a response to the loss of a variety of objects, both imagined and real, raising problems in pinpointing a specific stimulus for the grief response. Finally, bereavement behavior has clear social normas that vary considerably according to culture, religion, and custom. What is considered normal grieving in one society is considered bizarre or pathological in another. For example, Matchett (6) has documented the existence of repeated hallucinatory experiences in Hopi Indian women after the death of the spouse.

This paper examines the prevalent approaches toward describing and understanding bereavement. An alternative theoretical approach is proposed as an attempt to provide a clearer understanding of the grief response.

Normal Bereavement

The Focus on Symptoms

Historically, bereavement has been most eloquently described in literature.

ON MY FIRST SON

Farewell, thou child of my right hand, and joy;
My sin was too much hope of thee, loved boy:
Seven years thou 'wert lent to me, and I thee pay,
Exacted by thy fate, on the just day.
O could I lose all father now! for why
Will man lament the state he would envy,
To have so soon 'scaped world's and flesh's rage,
And, if no other misery, yet age?
Resit in soft peace and asked, say, "here doth lie
Ben Jonson his best piece of poetry."
For whose sake henceforth all his vows be such
As what he loves may never like too much.

Ben Jonson, 1616

As the loss of an important person universally elicits intense emotional responses, it almost seems that the job of describing the feelings associated with grief has been best left to poets and the literate. It is they who can, by virtue of their expertise, elicit an empathic response from their audience when they describe mourning and sadness. The understanding of grief has been in these instances an emotional rather than intellectual experience. Any systematic description from an objective or scientific point of view has appeared impoverished and somehow inaccurate. Indeed, one of the first attempts at an objective delineation of the laws and regularities of grief relied heavily on examples from literature to support hypotheses (7).

For centuries, the most salient characteristics of bereavement were the intense emotional reactions as described by literature. It is therefore not surprising that some of the first attempts at scientific analyses of the process of bereavement involved descriptions of affect and associated physiological symptoms. Lindeman's (8) careful observations of survivors of the Coconut Grove Fire and of relatives of those who died in the disaster remain the definitive work on grief symptomatology. He noticed that five characteristics were universal to all who grieved. These were (*a*) somatic distress (e.g., tightening of throat, abdominal pain, weakness), (*b*) preoccupation with the image of the deceased, (*c*) guilt, (*d*) hostile reactions, and (*e*) loss of normal pattern of conduct. Lindeman believed that these symptoms were essential to normal grief. In fact, he stressed that delays or distortions in these symptoms were prognostic of abnormal grief. Suffice it to say that Lindeman's conclusions were based on observations of survivors of a large natural diaster and are probably not totally representative of normal grieving patterns in the general population. In particular, feelings of guilt have not been uniformly found in widowhood, even when grief was considered pathological (9). In contrast, some researchers have expressed the opinion that self-blame is found more frequently in "morbid" or abnormal grievers than in the "normally" bereaved (10, 11). Finally, Clayton and her co-workers (12) reported that 87 percent of the bereaved whom they studied denied self-condemnation and 82 percent denied experiencing the somatic symptoms described by Lindeman.

The confusion over what constitutes a "typical" grief response has been exacerbated by the continually growing list of potential symptoms. Clayton and her colleagues (12) found that only three symptoms (depressed mood, sleep disturbance, and crying) were acknowledged within a month after a loss by more than one-half of their subjects. Difficulty in concentrating, loss of interest in TV or news, anxiety attacks, irritability, and anorexia were symptomatically reported in more than one-third of their subjects. A variety of other symptoms, including suicidal ideation, depersonalization, and increases in alcohol and drug consumption, were reported in less than one-third of the subjects. Subsequent interviews revealed that the three primary symptoms quickly dissipated.

Another major problem with some symptomatic descriptions of normal grief has been that the observed symptoms are very similar to those experienced in depression. The list of symptoms for a major depressive episode provided by DSM-III is nearly identical to the one generated by Clayton and her colleagues (12) in their study of normal bereavement (see Table 1). As can be seen, a differential diagnosis between a major depressive episode and normal bereavement based on symptoms alone is nearly impossible. Clayton (Note 1) has indicated that psychomotor retardation is the only symptom of depression that appears absent in bereavement. Yet psychomotor retardation is present in only a small percentage of cases of depression. Thus prediction of the natural direction of bereavement cannot be accomplished from an examination of symptoms that mimic

TABLE 1 Symptomatic Comparisons of Depression and Bereavement

Symptoms of major depressive episode (DSM III)	Symptoms of bereavement (Clayton, Desmarais, and Winokur)
Dysphoric mood	Depressed mood (89%)
Four of the following:	
Poor appetite or significant weight loss	Anorexia or weight loss (85%)
Insomnia or hypersomnia	Sleep disturbance (36%)
Psychomotor agitation	Anxiety attacks (36%)
Loss of interest or pleasure in usual activities	Loss of interest in TV or news (42%)
Loss of energy	Tired (29%)
Feelings of worthlessness, self-reproach, or excessive or inappropriate guilt	Self-condemnation (13%)
Complaints or evidence of diminished ability to think or concentrate	Difficult concentrating (47%)
Recurrent thoughts of death, suicidal ideation, wishes to be dead, or suicide attempt	Suicidal thoughts (13%)

Sources: 5, 12.

depression. Clearly then, alternative approaches to the description of bereavement symptomatology are needed, not only to distinguish it from depression but also to provide a basis for understanding the normal course of bereavement behavior.

Time as a Predictor

One of the most important discoveries about bereavement is that, unlike the case for depression, the symptoms tend to follow a predictable course over time. The symptoms enumerated by Clayton and co-workers (12) were found to dissipate very rapidly. Within 6–10 weeks following the death, 81 percent of their subjects reported symptomatic improvement.

In a correlational study of variables that predicted outcome for American widows and widowers, Parkes (13) concluded that intense grief, anger, and self-reproach after six weeks were associated with diminished psychological, social, and physical adjustment one year later. The researchers presumed that prior to the six-week deadline those symptoms were considered normal. Similarly, widows from Great Britain also reported gradual improvement in anxiety and depression during the first three months of bereavement (14).

Although research indicates that the most intense emotional responses dissipate within 6–10 weeks, the duration of the more subtle symptoms of normal grief has not been adequately established. Bornstein and his co-workers (9) divided a group of 106 widows and widowers into "depressed" or "not depressed" groups; 35 percent of their subjects qualified for a diagnosis of depression on the basis of criteria similar to those for Major Depression in DSM-III. All were reassessed for signs of depression at 13 months. At that time, 75 percent of those who were diagnosed as depressed at 13 months had been in the 1-month depression group. The investigators concluded after examining genetic, familial, and social variables that the presence of depression at one month was the greatest single predictor for depression a year later. It is important to note, however, that two-thirds of the one-month depression group was not considered depressed on year later.

Bornstein's study highlights the continuing difficulty in distinguishing between symptoms of depression and bereavement, even when chronology is considered. Obviously, some investigators and clinicians would not see the symptoms of depression at one month as pathological. It is certainly feasible that this group was actually displaying normal symptoms of bereavement rather than depression.

One of the more interesting hypotheses regarding the chronology of grief is that the symptoms of bereavement follow a course similar to that of an injury or disease (15, 16). Physical injury results in an immediate increase in body cortisols, which in turn suppresses natural immune mechanisms. Over time, cortisol levels diminish as the system begins to heal. Hofer and his co-workers (17) found that "over-secretion" of corticosteroids occurred during bereavement and persisted until normal levels were achieved after 18 months. Although this disease model is intriguing, it is limited in its ability to distinguish between the stress of bereavement and any other stressor. This model also fails to account for the wide variation in grief symptomatology.

Very few researchers or clinicians would aruge that in normal bereavement the depressive symptoms previously described would not diminish over time. Time, however, is at best a gross predictor for symptom reduction. Many other variables (e.g., extent of social supports, previous coping styles with other deaths, significance of relationship with the deceased) interact with time and each other to vary the course and extent of symptom reduction (18). Thus, predicting the process of normal bereavement on the basis of time alone is insufficient. This is apparently due to two factors, lack of agreement on a time frame for reduction of symptoms and insufficient knowledge about the psychosocial factors that may influence symptomatology.

Cognitions as Predictors

Alternative approaches to the study of bereavement have been proposed primarily by those who take a psychodynamic approach. These theoreticians recognized the general pattern of symptom reduction over time as a very good indicator for grief resolution. They proposed, however, that the most significant predictions of symptoms reduction and consequently grief resolution were the patterns of thoughts about the deceased that changed over time. As these cognitions changed, distressing symptomatology decreased. Freud (19) was one of the first to propose that mourning was actually a cognitive process that involves an identification with the lost object. According to him, the cognitive task in mourning involved a gradual detachment (libidinal decathexis) from the object. The symptoms of grief then are seen as a result of the conflict between desire to maintain libidinal involvement with the deceased and the demands of reality. Freud distinguished grief and depression by elucidating different cognitive processes rather than different symptomatic responses. Initially Freud believed that identification with the deceased was present only in melancholia or depression. He later abandoned this theoretical stance and essentially described the difference between normal grief and depression as a disruption of self-regard (20). Freud believed that at the core of depression was a distinct hatred for the lost object, which was either openly expressed or more frequently displaced onto the self. Today there is sufficient evidence to indicate that anger expressed openly or in the form of self-reproach is also characteristic of normal grieving. The literature already reviewed on symptoms of grief indicates that even healthy mourners engage in anger or self-condemnation. Furthermore, outward expressions of hostility toward the deceased have been found common to different cultures (21, 22).

Lest Freud's contribution to the understanding of grief be abandoned altogether, it should be stressed that Freud's notion, regardless of libidinal direction, was that bereavement is a cognitive process involving a gradual change in a person's view of the world. His was an attempt to explain how an external event that is not desired becomes part of an individual's psychological makeup. Symptoms and their subsequent diminution are then reflective of the different attempts to cope with a dramatic change in reality. This was seen as an important step in the understanding of grief; and Freud's emphasis on the cognitive task, rather than a symptomatic display, laid the groundwork for future theorists.

Perhaps the most eminent theoretician and researcher in the field of bereavement today is John Bowlby (23, 24). His approach to the understanding of grief is based on a view of processing information that has become known as the "New Look" (25). New Look theoreticians suggest that perception and processing of external stimuli are selectively biased by internal events such as needs, defenses, and values. Examples of these perceptual distortions are found in the growing body of literature on selective attention (26–28), and their impact has in some circles become known as the "perceptual defensive-vigilance effect." The basic premise advanced in this view is that there is continuous selective contact of all processing systems with long-term memory, which enables certain material to be retrieved (perceptual vigilance) and other material to be simultaneously excluded (perceptual defense).

In espousing the New Look theory of information processing, Bowlby believes that perceptions of external events are first appraised before the event has any effect on behavior. Ultimately, it is this appraisal of reality that influences mood and action. Appraisals are based on the representational models or templates a person creates of his world, so that events can fit more easily into a pre-existing structure. In order to understand the appraisals of those who are grieving, it is important to understand those models that an individual builds around the lost object. Bowlby suggests that with the loss of a significant person the models are based on the extent and nature of attachment to the deceased. Information is exluded from processing when an individual can no longer use the model previously formulated of the deceased. Bowlby calls this exclusionary process in bereavement "defensive exclusion." The difference between defensive exclusion and exclusion of any stimuli from the system lies in the nature of the stimuli itself. Bowlby suggests that information most likely to be excluded from processing is that leading a person to encounter psychological distress or suffering and that in dramatic conflict with previously formed models of the situation. The individual defensively excludes information of this sort until the circumstances of reality require that new representations be generated. The death of a significant individual is the kind of information that if taken in toto would immediately challenge pre-existing psychological models of the individual's relationship with the deceased. The easiest course of action then is slowly to modify or replace old representations with new ones.

Thus, according to Bowlby, the process of normal bereavement is a gradual inclusion of the information that was defensively excluded so that over time the full force of reality is understood. He suggests that this process occurs in four successive stages:

1. *Phase of numbing.* This stage is characterized by a sense of disbelief. Bowlby suggests that cognitively this is the stage in which defensive exclusion is used to its greatest degree. The loss of a significant individual violates the previously formed models of this relationship so extensively that the initial response is almost total denial of the reality of this death. Symptomatically, the bereaved may appear to act as if nothing significant had happened. Normal activities, including hosting elaborate wakes or funerals, are frequently carried on without difficulty. During this stage, occasional displays of intense emotional response (e.g., crying, outbursts of anger, panic attacks) occur as the bereaved begins to register the reality of the loss. This phase may last from a few hours to approximately a week.

2. *Phase of yearning and searching for the lost figure.* The cognitive and subsequent symptomatic responses seen in the bereaved during this phase have their roots, according to Bowlby, in the developmental history of any human being. In his earlier works, Bowlby held that the crying and intense distress of a baby during separation from its mother was an attempt to recover the missing parent (23). In most children, more often than not, these emotional outbursts are effective in facilitating a reunion. As the child develops, anger is also employed as an attempt to recover the lost object. Bowlby notes that anger is indeed useful when a loss or separation is perceived as temporary, as it mobilized other individuals to help and, subsequent to the reunion, makes separation less likely to occur. Anger, however,

has a useful function only in temporary separations and is out of place in permanent losses. Bowlby contends that there is a biological basis for this type of response to loss:

> There are therefore good biological reasons for every separation to be responded to in an automatic instinctive way with aggressive behavior; irretrievable loss is statistically so unusual that it is not taken into account. In the course of our evolution, it appears our instinctual equipment has become to be so fashioned that all losses are assumed to be retrievable and are responded to accordingly. (23)

Thus, Bowlby sees the bereaved acting in accordance with this biologically ordained response to loss. In this respect his theory of defensive exclusion is applied to grief. The first and immediate response to a loss is disbelief, as seen in the stage of numbing. As the reality of the event is registering the first attempt is to maintain the original representational models of the deceased. This can be accomplished only by fully regaining the relationship. The task then is to regain reality as was previously construed and thereby treat the loss as temporary. The bereaved attempts to search for the deceased to validate old constructs. Symptomatically, preoccupation with the deceased and behavior "as if" the individual were still alive is frequently reported. Anger is also highly characteristic during this stage— toward the deceased as well as toward anyone who is perceived as interfering with the desired reunion. Also characteristic of this phase are the sporadic attempts at ridding all reminders of the deceased from one's life, because such reminders highlight the repeated failure to reunite with the deceased. Other symptoms of agitation and preoccupation are also salient during this early stage of grief resolution.

3. Phase of disorganization and despair. This stage begins at the moment in the griever's life when the finality of the loss is realized. Defensive exclusion operates in a much lessened extent as a protective process. Symptoms during this phase involve a variety of behaviors that appear disorganized and listless. Bowlby believes that this disorganization is in part the result of the loss of the task of regaining the deceased. The bereaved attempts to initiate new goals but has considerable difficulty finding new activities that are as meaningful or organized as that of searching for the deceased. Also, symptoms of despair and depression are reported as the individual slowly accepts the destruction of a part of the personality that was exclusively directed toward the relationship.

> Subjectively, because certain key aspects of his total functioning interactions between himself and his world has ceased, not only does he see the world as poor and empty, but he feels himself to be the same. (23)

Bowlby states that despair is universally the result of the loss of activities and goals without adequate replacement. In this regard the bereaved are faced with a dual loss. Not only is there a loss of typical behavior patterns previously associated with the deceased, but the individual also loses the goals and activities associated with the previous stage of mourning.

4. Phase of reorganization. Because realization of the permanence of death necessarily involves attempts at new patterns of conduct and new constructs of reality, the bereaved strive to redefine themselves in relation to new people and new roles. During this stage of recovery, social life has somewhat resumed and the relationship with the deceased is no longer seen as crucial to survival. Behaviorally, the bereaved begins to learn new skills and roles as the self is redefined without the old relationship. This phase is not always marked with a sense of well-being. Loneliness is frequently reported as are periods of depression. By this time, however, the protective process of defensive exclusions is no longer necessary as new constructs of reality have been formed with which inclusion of the deceased is no longer relevant.

Bowlby's conceptualization of the process of grief has been applauded as a significant contribution to the understanding and prediction of bereavement outcome (11, 29–30). Most investigators concur that the reduction in overt symptoms observed in the bereaved follows logically from his hypothesis about the processing of information. Mendelson (31), however, has criticized Bowlby for not providing an even closer match between observations of the bereaved and the proposed stages of grief. He suggests that not all adults experience the phases of mourning and that Bowlby oversimplifies the biological basis for attachment behavior. Bugen (32) also finds fault with a "stage" approach to the process of grieving. He notes that stages are rarely the separate entities proposed; rather, he proposes that they subsume one another. Further, mourners have been observed to experience stages out of the prescribed order. Finally, the intensity and duration of any one stage may vary idiosyncratically among those who grieve.

Interestingly, such criticisms of Bowlby's conceptualization rarely indict his theoretical stance on the cognitive processes involved in bereavement. Most fault is found with the apparent inability of the cognitive changes proposed by Bowlby to account for the reduction of symptoms. Basically, Bowlby proposed that as the griever's concept of the deceased changed from searching and pining to recognition of the permanency of the loss, symptoms (both emotional and behavioral) changed from very intense with overt expression to less intense, with fewer observable displays.

Bowlby also acknowledges the influence of psychosocial variables on the course of mourning. He would argue, however, that regardless of the presence of psychological or sociological stressors, the cognitive changes in bereavement are universal, based on an innate biological mechanism. Thus, such stressors can retard or even permanently disrupt the course of grief by their effects on the eventual acceptance of the finality of the loss. For example, an individual who finds that she has no money and no skills with which to earn a living may not be able to grasp cognitively the permanence of her husband's death. She would therefore continue to search for him, and symptomatically we would observe intense and overt expressions of grief. Should the same individual subsequently acquire a vocation or other financial resources, the process of accepting death's permanence would continue with a concomitant reduction of symptoms. This is certainly a gross oversimplification of the effects of psychosocial stressors on cognitive changes during bereavement, which does not do justice to the complexities of the process. The example does, however, highlight Bowlby's reliance on cognitions as predictions of grief solution. Reduction in symptoms then is seen as a readily observable by-product of cognitive changes. Therefore, validation of Bowlby's theory of cognitive change during bereavement can best be achieved by comparing the actual cognitive structures of the bereaved as proposed by Bowlby with symptoms characteristic of grief. Indeed, it is possible that his conceptualization of the cognitive changes in bereavement have not been supported for lack of appropriate empirical evidence, rather than an inherent weakness in the theoretical position. The apparent gap between theory and observable data is not insurmountable. Closer scrutiny of the cognitive structures of the bereaved should provide a more adequate basis for a critique of Bowlby's theories. Changes in cognitive structures have been studied by researchers of personal construct theory, originally developed by George A. Kelly (33-36).

The Evaluation of Personal Constructs

Basic Theory

It is not within the scope of this paper to provide an extensive discourse on Kelly's theory of personal contructs. For our purposes, a truncated version of its principles provides a framework for examining issues of bereavement. Kelly proposed that all individuals are psychologists, that is, they are continually attempting to predict and ultimately to control behavior. As scientists and as students of behavior, human beings continuously generate hypotheses about the future in order to behave accordingly. This is the cornerstone for Kelly's fundamental postulate: "A person's processes are psychologically channelized by the ways in which he anticipates events" (33).

From this basic axiom, Kelly generated several logical corollaries regarding the nature of human cognitive processes. Several of these are of particular interest to us, for example, the so-called construction corollary: "A person anticipates events by construing their replications." Kelly asserted that "construing" was a process of placing an interpretation or appraisal about the nature of the event so perceived. In creating such a structure or cognitive map, the person notes similarities and differences in the features or elements of the perceived event and erects constructs in this dichotomous fashion. The following diagram should illustrate a rudimentary development of a person's construct.

Event

Elements

a   b   c   d
(+) (+)   (+) (−)
Construct A   Construct B

Thus, elements a, b, and c, are combined to create a new construct (or extend an old construct), which does not contain element d. Features in future events will be evaluated to determine if they fall within the range of convenience of either Construct A or Construct B. Inherent in this notion is the dichotomous nature or shape of a person's constructs: This is expressed in terms of a dichotomy corollary: "A person's construction system is composed of a finite number of dichotomous constructs" (33).

Kelly enumerated several other corollaries to explain the development, range, and change in personal constructs. For the understanding of the cognitive structures during the process of bereavement, we return to Bowlby's basic hypothesis regarding the processing of information. It should be recalled that Bowlby also suggested that events are perceived and encoded according to their relative fit into already existing representations of the world. As has been shown, this view is in accord with Kelly's notions of personal constructs. The key to understanding information processing during bereavement is, according to Bowlby, understanding these previously formed models of the world, because they are directly responsible for what and how materials is "defensively excluded" from processing. Bowlby suggests that representations of the deceased may be a critical key to the understanding of the process by which each individual mourns. This notion is in accordance with recent personal construct theories about the nature of bereavement. Woodfield and Viney

(37) hypothesize that bereavement is a process by which individuals attempt to alter certain core constructs (e.g., those that are identity syntonic). Such core constructs for the bereaved then might very well involve a perception of their personal relationship with the deceased. As bereavement progresses, major revisions in the constructs relating to the deceased vis-à-vis the griever are required in order for the bereaved to better anticipate future events.

As was noted earlier, Bowlby's notion of defensive exclusion suggests that the external reality of death is excluded from processing as it is in conflict with previously formed models of the world. A personal construct theorist would propose that such core constructs are only slowly altered as other constructs take shape and form. Thus the primary difference between the two theoretical positions lies in the proposed reasons for the necessity of time for bereavement. Bowlby states that individuals need time to grieve because of individuals psychological distress and pain. Personal construct theory would propose that time is needed to replace or alter core constructs with new representations. Such positions need not be mutually exclusive, however. Kelly (33) noted that when new constructs are replacing old, symptomatic distress is often observed. Thus psychological pain is indeed an excellent indicator of changing constructs during bereavement, but it does not necessarily play a causal role in the process.

The question remains: What common constructs can we observe that indicate that bereavement is manifest, and how will they change as grief is resolved? Certainly humans' constructual interpretations of themselves and their separate worlds are highly individualistic. Bowlby (24), however, has suggested that commonalities can be found. For example, when symptoms are most salient and distressing, the bereaved are demonstrating a pronounced preoccupation with the deceased. Such preoccupation is a way that grievers "keep alive" (recall the second phase) the lost figure. Thus the personal construct view of this symptom and cognition suggest that grievers would perceive many life events as impoverished without the deceased. Indeed, this attempt to maintain a living relationship makes contemplating events not directly related to the deceased very difficult, as if such events would thwart this desired reunion. Such a world view reflects constructs that are rather impermeable and are in need of change for the bereaved to recover from the loss.

Another characteristic of the griever's inability to accept the finality of the loss deals specifically with how the deceased is cognitively kept alive. We would suggest that when a continuing relationship with the deceased is so intensely desired, then qualities that describe the deceased should be predominantly positive. This would occur regardless of the "real" relationship with the deceased. Thus many personal constructs of the deceased should describe an individual who is rather deified. This perception changes to reflect a more fallible human as bereavement progresses.

In conclusion, this paper has argued that a personal construct conceptualization of the bereavement process is compatible with recent cognitive theories of grieving, particularly that arising from Bowlby's (24) work. It contributes to such theories a number of hypotheses regarding the psychological sequelae of loss, as well as the methodology (38) for testing them. In addition, construct theory may strengthen a New Look model of bereavement by circumventing some of the weaknesses for which Bowlby's work has been criticized (e.g., its emphasis on stages of grieving; its preference for biological, rather than psychological, explanation). It is hoped that the interpenetration of these two approaches will produce a theory of grieving that is more conceptually and clinically useful than either approach taken alone.

Reference Note

1. Clayton, P. Personal communication, March 1981.

References

1. Winokur, G., & Pitts, F. N., Jr. Affective disorder: V. The diagnostic validity of depressive reactions. *Psychiatric Quarterly* 1965, *29*, 727–728.
2. Deutsch, H. Absence of grief. *Psychomatic Quarterly*, 1937, *6*, 12-22.

3. Fleming, J. The problem of diagnosis in parent loss cases. *Contemporary Psychoanalysis*, 1974, *10*, 439-451.
4. Lieberman, S. Nineteen cases of morbid grief. *British Journal of Psychiatry*, 1978, *132*, 159-163.
5. American Psychiatric Association. *Diagnostic and statistical manual of mental disorders* (3rd ed.). Washington, D.C.: Author, 1980.
6. Matchett, W. F. Repeated hallucinatory experiences as a part of the mourning process among Hopi Indian women. *Psychiatry*, 1972, *35*, 185-194.
7. Shand, A. E. *The foundations of character*. London: MacMillan, 1920.
8. Lindemann, E. Symptomatology and management of acute grief. *American Journal of Psychiatry*, 1944, *101*, 141-148.
9. Bornstein, P. E., Clayton, P. J., Halikas, J. A., Maurice W. L., & Robins, E. The depression of widowhood after thirteen months. *British Journal of Psychiatry*, 1973, *122*, 561-566.
10. Parkes, C. M. Bereavement and mental illness. *British Journal of Medical Psychology*, 1965, *38*, 1-26.
11. Raphael, B. The management of pathological grief. *Australia and New Zealand Journal of Psychiatry*, 1975, *9*, 173-180.
12. Clayton, P., Desmarais, L., & Winokur, G. A study of normal bereavement. *American Journal of Psychiatry*, 1968, *125*, 64-74.
13. Parkes, C. M. *Bereavement: Studies of grief in adult life.* New York: International Universities Press, 1972.
14. Parkes, C. M. Psycho-social transitions: A field of study. *Social Science and Medicine*, 1971, *5*, 101-115.
15. Engel, G. Is grief a disease? *Psychosomatic Medicine*, 1961, *23*, 18-22.
16. Frederick, J. F. Grief as a disease process. *Omega*, 1976-1977, 7, 297-305.
17. Hofer, M. A., Wolff, C. T., Friedman, S. B., & Mason, J. W. A psychoendocrine study of bereavement. *Psychosomatic Medicine*, 1972, *34*, 481-504.
18. Schmale, A. H. Reactions to illness: Convalescence and grieving. *Psychiatric Clinics of North America*, 1979, *2*, 321-329.
19. Freud, A. Mourning and melancholia. In *Standard Edition* (Vol. 14). London: Hogarth Press, 1957. (Originally published, 1917.)
20. Freud, S. The ego and the id. *Standard Edition* (Vol. 19). London: Hogarth Press, 1961. (Originally published, 1923.)
21. Hobson, C. J. Widows of Blackton. *New Society*, 1964, *24*,.
22. Marris, P. *Widows and their families.* London: Routledge & Kegan Paul, 1958.
23. Bowlby, J. Process of mourning. *International Journal of Psychoanalysis*, 1961, *42*, 317-340.
24. Bowlby, J. Loss, sadness and depression. *Attachment and Loss* (Vol. 3). New York: Basic Books, 1980.
25. Erdelyi, M. H. A new look at the New Look: Perceptual defense and vigilance. *Psychological Review*, 1974, *81*, 1-25.

26. Neisser, U. *Cognitive psychology.* New York: Appleton-Century-Crofts, 1967.

27. Norman, D. A. Memory while shadowing. *Quarterly Journal of Experimental Psychology*, 1969, *21*, 85-94.

28. Treisman, A. M. Strategies and models of selective attention: *Psychological Review*, 1969, *76*, 282-299.

29. Parkes, C. M. "Seeking and finding" a lost object: Evidence from recent studies of the reaction to bereavement. *Social Science and Medicine*, 1970, *4*, 187-201.

30. Blanco, I. M. Review of attachment and loss: I. Attachment. *International Journal of Psychoanalysis*, 1971, *52*, 197-199.

31. Mendelson, M. *Psychoanalytic concepts of depression* (2nd ed.). New York: Halsted Press, 1974.

32. Bugen, L. A. Human grief: A model for prediction and intervention. *American Journal of Orthopsychiatry*, 1977, *47*, 196-206.

33. Kelly, G. A. *A theory of personality: The psychology of personal constructs.* New York: Norton, 1955.

34. Adams-Webber, J. *Personal construct theory: Concepts and applications.* London: Wiley, 1979.

35. Bannister, D., & Mair, J. M. M. *The evaluation of personal constructs.* London: Academic, 1968.

36. Landfield, A. W. *Personal construct systems in psychotherapy.* Chicago: Rand McNally, 1971.

37. Woodfield, R. L., & Viney, L. L. A personal construct approach toward bereavement. *Omega*, in press.

38. Fransella, F., & Bannister, D. *A manual for repertory grid technique.* London: Academic, 1977.

DEATH THREAT BEFORE AND AFTER ATTEMPTED SUICIDE: A CLINICAL INVESTIGATION

MICHAEL A. RIGDON

University of Utah

While participating in a study of death attitudes, "Cary" (a pseudonym) completed two death orientation measures before and after his attempt to kill himself. Changes in his view of himself and death are examined as they reflect on a hypothesis regarding the impending collapse of a suicidal person's construct system and as they portray the meaning of Cary's self-destructive act. Implications are drawn with respect to a personal construct assessment of suicidal individuals and with respect to future research on suicidal behavior.

Kelly (1) believed the most effective way to understand any aspect of human behavior is to find out what it means to the behaving person. He developed a psychology of personal constructs that he anticipated would enable investigators and clinicians to appreciate the system of meaning that each person constructs to organize personal experience. In line with this approach, Kelly (2) suggested that, as a suicidal person, one might attempt suicide when faced with the impending collapse of the personal construct system that represents the meaning of his or her life. In other words, suicide would be that person's way of preventing total confusion and preserving the last meaningful remnants, at least, of a personal world.

In an initial test of Kelly's hypothesis (3), there was no evidence that suicidal individuals were more disorganized and confused in their interpersonal meaning systems than were nonsuicidal individuals. Landfield (4), however, reported more supportive results. Compared with control group subjects, individuals who had made serious attempts at self-destruction had interpersonal meaning systems that were more disorganized and seemed restricted to more easily organized concrete events. Their chaotic systems simply had failed to organize in a meaningful way a wide variety of complex interpersonal events. Landfield found the characteristics of disorganized and restricted meaning especially in Helen, one of his subjects who tried to kill herself the day after she was tested. Without being directly related to Kelly's hypothesis about the experience of suicide, two other studies (5, 6) focused on the content and features of the personal constructs of a young woman and a young man after their unsuccessful suicide attempts. These two studies explored the personal meaning of suicidal behavior in two individuals after the fact, whereas Landfield examined Helen's personal construct system for indications of the imminence of self-destructive behavior before it occurred. The present paper explores the meaning of suicide for an individual before and after his attempt to kill himself.

During a recent study of death attitudes (7), an unexpected occurrence provided an opportunity to examine the death-related personal constructs of "Cary" (pseudonym for one of the 96 college student participants) for changes resulting from his attempted suicide. Following his completion of the posttest questionnaires seven weeks after the pretest, Cary casually remarked that he had swallowed 33 Quaaludes three days earlier and had begun psychotherapy.[1] Unlike the individuals in the three studies described above, Cary completed the questionnaires before and after his self-destructive behavior. Furthermore, the focus in the previous studies was on constructs that the individuals used to organize their interpersonal experience and their understanding of other people, whereas the focus for Cary is on his death-specific constructs that would be especially critical for an accurate understanding of the meaning of his attempt to cause his own death. The rest of this paper reports the changes

---

[1] At the pretest session, Cary was randomly assigned with 30 other participants to one of the two death-related experiences intended to reduce death threat. His participation in this experience was not thought to have produced his suicidal behavior or the death orientation changes discussed here, in that neither experience had a significant impact on the death attitude scores of the participants.

in Cary's attitudes toward himself and death, particularly as these changes reflect on Kelly's hypothesis about suicidal disorganization and on the meaning of Cary's behavior. Conclusions are drawn regarding the use of a personal construct assessment for psychotherapy with suicidal individuals, and some directions are indicated for future investigations of suicidal behavior.

Impending Construct System Collapse?

Cary, a freshman, did not identify himself as the member of a church, nor did he have any opinion regarding life after death. Religion appeared to be an unimportant factor in his life. He was, on the other hand, one of 22 participants who reported a "close brush with death" in a accident two years previously. Cary's only previous experience of the death of a close relative or friend was the death of a sibling about a year earlier as a result of cancer. There was nothing in Cary's religious behavior and beliefs or in his previous experience with death and dying that was unusual or seemed to place him especially at risk for suicide.

An initial question was whether Cary would have a construct system as disorganized and restricted in meaning as Landfield reported for Helen the day before her self-destructive act. Landfield used his Functionally Independent Construction (FIC) index of construct organization and two indices of meaning restriction. First of all, restriction in applicability was measured by the number of times Helen indicated that neither construct pole applied to the various people. Her boyfriend, for instance, was neither "weak-willed" nor "driven." The second measure was the number of Helen's constructs that appeared to reflect restriction to concrete content (e.g., "likes long-hair music"). A similar methodology was used with Cary, who completed a revised form of the Death Threat Index (8) at pretest and posttest. Cary completed the Threat Index (TI) by rating himself, his own death, and the 10 death-related elements in Table 1 on the 30 death-related dimensions in Table 2. Cary's FIC score was calculated from these ratings, as well as his score on two other indices of construct organization: the ordination

TABLE 1 Ten Death-related Elements Rated on Threat Index Dimensions

1. Three children die when a tornado hits their elementary school.
2. You run over and kill a young child.
3. Your closest friend is killed in a plane crash.
4. Your father dies while trying to save another person from drowning.
5. A terminal patient dies after months of unrelievable pain.
6. President Reagan is assassinated.
7. Your grandmother dies in her sleep.
8. A convicted murderer is executed in the electric chair.
9. A member of the Polish Solidarity union is shot for refusing to obey martial law.
10. A divorced mother of two dies from a drug overdose.

Note. These death-related elements were adapted from previous research on the TI (8). "Myself" and "my own death" were elements 11 and 12, respectively.

and chi-square measures (9, 10). The number of times Cary used the neutral, zero rating provided an index of how restricted in applicability these constructs were. Concreteness of content could not be assessed, however, because the same list of 30 constructs was supplied for all 96 participants.

The results of this methodology indicated that Cary's death-related construct system was normally organized. When the FIC

TABLE 2 Thirty Provided Constructs for Threat Index

caring–not caring	restriction–freedom
purposeful–not purposeful	useful–useless
sick–healthy	unnatural–natural
static–changing	hard–easy
random–predictable	secure–insecure
bad–good	sad–happy
feels good–feels bad	not responsible–responsible
stagnation–growth	weak–strong
peaceful–violent	not learning–learning
not understanding–understanding	helping others–being selfish
calm–anxious	existence–nonexistence
kind–cruel	animate–inanimate
meaningful–empty	satisfied–dissatisfied
open–closed	pleasure–pain
hope–no hope	lack of control–control

Note. Participants rated the death-related elements on 13-point scales.

index of construct organization was applied to Cary's ratings of the death-related elements, his constructs were not abnormally disorganized, with FIC scores before and after his self-destructive act almost identical to the average FIC score (see Table 3). The other two construct organization measures also indicated that Cary's construct system was sufficiently well integrated, with ordination and chi-square scores at pretest and posttest very close to the mean. The chi-square scores, in fact, suggested a slightly tighter than average organization for Cary's death-related constructs. Furthermore, Cary's death-related constructs were certainly useful to him, in that he applied the neutral rating slightly less often than the average participant in the study. In general, Cary's death-related construct system seemed quite normal before and after his attempt to kill himself. There is no suggestion of any lack of organization, no hint of any restricted usefulness, and no indication of an imminent collapse. Kelly's hypothesis is not very useful for understanding Cary's suicidal behavior. Perhaps the interpersonal aspect of his construct system was indeed in a state of chaos, while his sytem remained relatively healthy and stable in the realm of death and dying. In any case, the meaning of Cary's suicidal attempt must be found by examining more carefully changes in his death attitudes and in his personal system of meaning relative to death and dying.

TABLE 3 Cary's Scores and Mean Scores on Measures of Construct Organization and Restricted Meaning

Testing session	Measures			
	FIC	Ordination	$\chi^{2\,a}$	Number of zeros
Pretest				
Cary	14.0	30.5	35.7	21.0
Mean[b]	14.4 (6.6)	34.9 (9.7)	69.3 (49.4)	53.7 (46.5)
Posttest				
Cary	11.0	34.3	43.4	5.0
Mean[b]	9.1 (5.4)	32.2 (9.9)	57.6 (39.7)	24.4 (36.6)

Note. Standard deviations are in parentheses.
[a]For χ^2, lower score indicates more organization.
[b]$N = 96$ (pretest) and 95 (posttest).

Changes in Cary's Death Threat Score

Like the other participants, Cary completed not only the Threat Index, but also a second death orientation questionnaire: the Collett-Lester Fear of Death Scale (FDS) (11). The FDS is scored for four subscales: the fear of the death and dying of self and the fear of the death and dying of others. One might expect that Cary's FDS scores would change between pretest and posttest or that his scores would be notably different from those of the other participants. In fact, none of Cary's four scores were unusual either before or after his suicide attempt. There were no striking changes in his FDS scores, and, although his scores appeared slightly low, all were within one standard deviation of the mean.

The picture with respect to Cary's death threat was more intriguing. Threat is indexed on the TI by the number of "splits," that is, the number of times the person rates self and death on opposite sides of a construct (for example, self as useful and my death as useless). This score is taken as an estimate of death threat because it represents the amount of comprehensive change that must occur before death will be seen as a personal reality, compatible with the person's view of self.

Cary's initial level of death threat was very high, with a score of 21 splits out of a possible 30. His score was about one standard deviation above the mean (15.6) for the 96 participants. With his suicide attempt, however, Cary's TI score dropped to a low score of 7 splits (one and one-third standard deviations below the posttest mean of 17.5). Only nine participants had TI scores below 7 at posttest. This reduction in death threat score suggests that Cary viewed himself and death as more compatible than he had several weeks earlier. What sort of change produced this increased compatibility? A quick glance at Cary's ratings indicated almost no change in his view of his own death, which received 28 negative ratings at pretest and 25 at posttest. A remarkable change took place, however, in Cary's view of himself. Whereas he initially used only three negatives to describe himself (anxious, closed, and lack of control), he used 27 negatives at posttest. The only three positive self-ratings at posttest were predictable, animate, and helping others. Cary changed from an almost entirely positive view of himself to an almost entirely negative one. Whether a cause or an effect of his self-destructive act, Cary's total loss of self-esteem could easily represent a suicidal frame of mind, especially when this negative self-image was matched by a negative image of death. For Cary, it seems that the choice to die was no worse than the choice to maintain a self-identity that was already as bad as death itself.

Changes in Cary's Death-specific Personal Constructs

In addition to the obvious reduction in Cary's death threat score and the radical change to a negative self-image, other changes can be tracked by a more complex analysis of the ratings that reflect Cary's view of himself and death. A principal components analysis of the ratings, using Slater's (12) INGRID program, permits a twofold examination of Cary's death-related construct system according to (a) the primary dimensions according to which he understands self and the death-related elements and (b) the relative distance of the elements from each other in Cary's meaning realm reflected in his rating pattern. As outlined by Warren (13), the application of the INGRID analysis to a person's TI ratings results in a picture of the way that person uniquely thinks, feels, and behaves relative to death. In order to identify some significant changes in the meaning that Cary attributed to death, let us turn to this twofold examination of his death-related constructs.

Principal Components Analysis

The first interesting results of the INGRID analysis of Cary's pretest ratings are from the principal components analysis that grouped together not only the death-related elements but also the constructs in terms of which the elements are similar to or different from each other. The first three components accounted for 72 percent of the variation in the initial ratings. The resulting picture of the way in which Cary viewed himself and death is striking.

The first two components, for example, reveal that Cary saw fundamental differences between self and a cluster of elements that included his own death (see Figure 1). Although this cluster was described by the negative poles of the constructs with high loadings on component I, Cary's self-image was definitely linked to the positive poles (e.g., understanding, healthy, meaningful, purposeful, hope, and happy). On the other hand, Cary saw personal death and a few other elements that loaded on component II as radically different from the mother's death by drug overdose, which he viewed in negative terms like weak, easy, and not caring. This second component also brings out another difference between personal death and suicide, in that Cary considered his death as an event over which he had control (construct 30) but no responsibility (construct 14), whereas he viewed suicide by drug overdose as being out of control and still responsible. One might wonder whether Cary's pretest rating of himself as out of control (one of only three negative self-ratings) was a prelude to his drug overdose several weeks later. Even

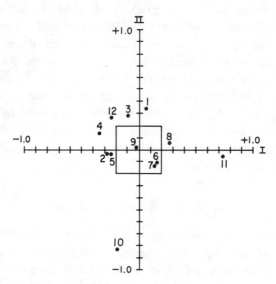

FIGURE 1   Loadings of the 12 elements on principal components I and II at pretest. (See Table 1 for the identification of each element. Constructs with high loadings on these components are indicated in the text.)

though suicide indicated weakness and seemed like the easy way out, it may have been Cary's way of grasping for some sense of responsibility and predictability, at a time when he apparently had little sense of being in control of himself.

Although Figure 1 indicates differences between Cary's perspective on his own death and his perspective on suicide, components I and III indicate some similarities as well, in that he considered both events as somewhat negative on component I constructs (for example, useless, not very purposeful, and somewhat hopeless) and as relatively neutral on component III, in between a calm, peaceful death like grandma dying in her sleep and a more violent, anxiety-producing death like the shooting of a Polish union member.

In general, this initial analysis indicates that Cary viewed self as very different from most aspects of death, particularly his own death and death by drug overdose. The only possible indications of his later suicidal behavior lie in his view of himself as out of control like the suicidal mother and in the similarities between personal death and suicide on components I and III.

For Cary's ratings at posttest, the first three components again accounted for most of the variation (64 percent), and indicated some major shifts in Cary's death-related construct system. First of all, on components I and II, self, personal death, and death by drug overdose (element 10) are close together and relatively neutral on both components. Cary still evaluated death by execution in the positive terms of component I, as a meaningful, useful, healthy event about which he feels happy. And grandma's death during sleep is still viewed as peaceful and natural (component II). Compared to grandma's death, an execution, and the other events, Cary simply did not see himself, his death, or a suicidal overdose as particularly notable in terms of the constructs that loaded on components I and II (see Figure 2).

Self and a suicidal overdose were also neutral on component III, which primarily distinguished between Cary's own death and a father's drowning. The component III constructs highlight some unusual links in Cary's construct system. Contrary to the father's drowning, his own death was described in terms of growth, pleasure, and feeling good or satisfied and, at the same

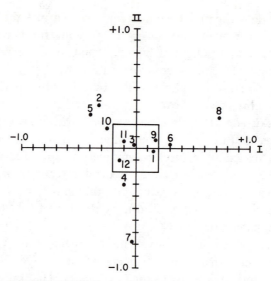

FIGURE 2   Loadings of the 12 elements on principal components I and II at posttest. (See Table 1 for
the identification of each element. Constructs with
high loadings on these components are indicated in
the text.)

time, in terms of being selfish, weak, without hope, and not
learning. These positive aspects of Cary's view of his death may
have produced in part his decision to kill himself. The implication, however, that his death represented not only growth but
also weakness, selfishness, and hopelessness might have resulted
from his suicide attempt as a way to prevent a repetition. On
the other hand, if Cary generally viewed growthful, pleasant
events in his life as also indicative of selfishness and weakness,
this connection may result in his refusal to engage in behaviors
that would lead to growth or in a sense of guilt for engaging in
them.

Cary initially viewed self, personal death, and suicide as very
different from each other. Following his suicidal behavior,
however, he had a similar view of himself and death by suicide.
On the three principal components, these two elements were
together, in that neither stood out notably in comparison with
the other types of death. Cary's suicidal behavior might be
understood in terms of the increased similarity between his

views of self and suicide. Furthermore, Cary's self-image and his perspective on suicide at posttest were similar in many ways to his notions about his own death, except for the unusual representation of personal death as growth and satisfaction, on the one hand, and weakness and selfishness on the other. Let us now turn to the relative distance between the death-related elements as a way of unlocking the changing meaning that Cary attributed to death.

Distances between Elements

As part of the principal components analysis of Cary's ratings, the distances of each element relative to all the others are provided. An examination of the distances of the elements relative to Cary's perception of self and his own death reveals some interesting changes from pretest to posttest (see Table 4). First of all, self, the element he initially viewed as most unlike personal death, became the element most like personal death.

TABLE 4 Distances of Each Death-related Element from Self and Personal Death at Pretest and at Posttest

Element number[a]	Pretest		Posttest	
	Self	My death	Self	My death
1	1.31	.84	.84	.97
2	1.56	.66	.81	1.10
3	1.39	.57	.63	.94
4	1.70	.49	.79	1.14
5	1.58	.69	.79	1.05
6	1.10	.94	.84	1.09
7	1.29	.98	.99	1.11
8	.99	.97	1.20	1.45
9	1.33	.90	.72	1.01
10	1.66	1.03	.66	.99
11	—	1.58	—	.85
12	1.58	—	.85	—

Note. The distance measure has a minimum of 0 (elements are similar), a mean of 1 (elements are indifferent to each other), and seldom exceeds 2 (elements are dissimilar).
[a]For identity of each element, see Table 1.

The various types of death also were generally more like self at posttest. These changes support Cary's reduced death threat, in that self and the general notion of death and dying, as well as self and the specific notion of personal death, were far more compatible following Cary's self-destructive act.

A second interesting change relates to Cary's view of the only death event that describes a suicide: a mother who kills herself with a drug overdose. Cary initially saw this way of dying as most unlike himself. After his own overdose experience, however, he reasonably viewed this manner of dying as most like himself. The opposite sort of change occurred with Cary's perspective on death by execution. Initially most like himself, this way of dying moved to a distance farthest from his later self-image. A likely explanation for this change lies in the fact that Cary viewed execution, according to component I, as an understandable, purposeful, useful event about which he felt happy, hopeful, and secure. Whereas he initially viewed himself in a similar fashion, the difference between self and death by execution at posttest resulted from his later view of himself as unhappy and insecure, with little hope or purpose.

A third notable feature is that Cary's view of his own death changed radically. The initial stimilarities between his personal death and a sudden, accidental type of death (elements 1 to 4) disappeared at posttest, leaving his own death defined primarily as being different from a useful, purposeful death by execution. Unlike the execution of a convicted killer, Cary viewed both self and death as events that were hard for him to understand, events for which he saw no meaning and about which he felt very unhappy. In general, the examination of the element distances, like the principal components analysis, emphasizes the increased similarity in Cary's views of himself, personal death, and suicide. In addition, the increased distance of death by execution from both self and personal death highlights the increased difficulty that Cary had in understanding himself or his death and in attributing some purpose or meaning to these events.

Discussion

An attempt was made to understand Cary's decision to kill himself, with the Threat Index used to assess his death orientation and to track its changes. From his initial death orientation, it would be difficult to predict Cary's decision to take an overdose. There were, it is true, some similarities between his pretest views of personal death and suicide in that both were, first, moderately meaningless and hard to understand and, second, about halfway between a calm, peaceful death and a violent one. There was also the initial description of himself as being out of control—a characteristic feature of his view of the mother who took an overdose. For the most part, however, Cary's initial perspective is characterized by major differences between self and personal death and between self and death by suicide. Death was basically incompatible with his self-image.

Although Cary's suicidal behavior seems difficult to predict, its impact on his death-related constructs is unmistakable. The compatibility between self and death at posttest was evident in the smaller number of TI splits and in the principal components analysis. The increased similarity also appeared in the reduced distances between self, death, and suicide. Cary's image of self and personal death at posttest were both defined as the opposite of a purposeful, meaningful, understandable event like death by execution.

The reduction in Cary's death threat would appear to be a change toward a more "realistic" view of his own mortality. But his risk for suicide appears to remain high, because of the way in which his threat was reduced—by a drastic drop in his self-esteem so that his self-image matched his negative image of death. Cary's psychotherapy would, it is hoped, focus on increasing his self-esteem, perhaps by extending the meaning of one of his few positive self-descriptors: self as helping others. Another issue is the development of a sense of control that Cary indicated is lacking in his life, a lack that matches one of the primary characteristics he attributed to a suicidal death. Effective psychotherapy with Cary might also explore his view of growthful, pleasant experiences as somehow indicative of selfishness and weakness. In general, it would be important for Cary to redevelop the positive self-understanding and sense of purpose he lost sometime after the initial testing.

Contrary to expectation, there was no evidence before or after Cary's suicide attempt that his death-related construct system was in imminent danger of collapse. Plausible reasons for the lack of evidence include that the pretest took place too early, before the construct disintegration had really begun and that the posttest took place too late, allowing several days for reintegration after Cary's overdose. Alternatively, as mentioned earlier, the assessment of Cary's interpersonal constructs might have provided evidence of considerable disorganization, even though his death-related constructs remained intact. For whatever reason, this lack of support for Kelly's (2) hypothetical notions for understanding suicidal behavior emphasizes the importance of examining not only the organizational, structural features of a suicidal person's constructs, but also the actual meaning of death for the person and the relationship between self and death. The failure of the FDS to detect any changes in Cary's attitudes comparable to those found with the TI further indicates the need to assess a suicidal person's death orientation with an assessment methodology that taps the idiosyncratic meaning of death in the manner of the Threat Index. In her clinical work with a variety of people, Rowe (14) discovered that, in order to understand the meaning of a client's life, it was important for her to understand the client's constructions that account for death. This would seem to be especially crucial if one is trying to understand suicidal behavior—that of a psychotherapy client as well as that of subjects in research on suicide.

References

1. Kelly, G. A. *The psychology of personal cosntructs* (2 vols.). New York: Norton, 1955.
2. Kelly, G. A. Suicide: The personal construct point of view. In N. Farberow & E. Shneidman (Eds.), *The cry for help.* New York: McGraw-Hill, 1961.
3. Lester, D. Cognitive complexity of the suicidal individual. *Psychological Reports,* 1971, *28,* 158.
4. Landfield, A. W. A personal construct approach to suicidal behavior. In P. Slater (Ed.), *Explorations of intrapersonal space.* New York: Wiley, 1976.
5. Ryle, A. A repertory grid study of the meaning and consequences of a suicidal act. *British Journal of Psychiatry,* 1967, *13,* 1393–1403.

6. Norris, H., & Makhlouf-Norris, F. The measurement of self-identity: In P. Slater (Ed.), *Explorations of intrapersonal space.* New York: Wiley, 1976.
7. Rigdon, M. A. Reduction in death threat as a basis for optimal functioning: The test of central existential hypothesis. (Doctoral dissertation, University of Florida, 1982). *Dissertation Abstracts International,* 1983, *43*, 3018B. (University Microfilms No. DA8302294)
8. Rigdon, M. A., Epting, F. R., Neimeyer, R. A., & Krieger, S. R. The Threat Index: A research report. *Death Education,* 1979, *3*, 245–270.
9. Landfield, A. W., & Barr, M. A. *Ordination: A new measure of concept organization.* Unpublished manuscript, University of Nebraska, Lincoln, 1976.
10. Landfield, A. W., & Schmittdiel, C. *The chi-square analysis: A continuing search for ordination.* Paper presented at the Fourth International Congress on Personal Construct Psychology, Brock University, St. Catharines, Ontario, Canada, August 1981.
11. Lester, D. *The Collett-Lester Fear of Death Scale: A manual.* Unpublished manuscript, Stockton State College, 1974.
12. Slater, P. *Dimensions of intrapersonal space.* London: Wiley, 1977.
13. Warren, W. G. Personal construction of death and death education. *Death Education,* 1982, *6*, 17–28.
14. Rowe, D. *The constructions of life and death.* New York: Wiley, 1982.

DEATH CONCERNS AND PHYSICAL ILLNESS

∞∞

FEAR OF DEATH AND PHYSICAL ILLNESS:
A PERSONAL CONSTRUCT APPROACH

∞∞

PAUL J. ROBINSON AND KEITH WOOD

Lakehead University

The Threat Index, Templer's Death Anxiety Scale, and the Collett-Lester Fear of Death Scale were administered to 100 respondents in an attempt to assess their personal orientation toward death. Each respondent was a member of one of the following groups: people with no known illness; people attending their family physician for a checkup; rheumatoid arthritics; diabetics; or people recently treated for cancer.

Hierarchical multiple regression analyses indicated that older respondents were significantly less death anxious, less fearful of their own death, and more integrated (that is, showed less self-death discrepancy) than younger respondents. Further analyses revealed no differences between any of the groups on fear of death or death anxiety, indicating that the current state of an individual's health was not related to his or her death orientation. Instead, correlational and regression analyses suggested that anxiety and fear were much more likely to be influenced by a respondent's level of actualization and, to a lesser extent, level of integration. The expected additive effects of actualization and integration did not emerge, a finding that was at variance with previous research.

Research designed to investigate people's attitudes toward death and dying has never been able to describe successfully what factors contribute to the personal meaning of death for any one individual. Part of the problem arises from the fact that the interrelationships between fear of death, death anxiety, personality characteristics, and physical well-being have never been fully delineated. In addition, the majority of the research has focused on healthy populations, and even when the physically unwell

213[127]

have been investigated the assessment techniques often provided insufficient estimates of what death meant to these individuals. In an attempt to deal with these problems, Krieger, Epting, and Leitner (1) constructed the Threat Index (TI), an instrument that has now emerged as one of the most promising measures of individual death orientation available in the literature today (2-6).

Based on Kelly's Personal Construct Theory (7), the current form of the TI requires the respondent to rate "self," "ideal self," and "own death" on each of 40 bipolar constructs. The rating of self and ideal self on the same pole of each of the constructs provides a measure of "actualization" and indicates that the respondent sees no difference between who he or she is and the person he or she would prefer to be. In much the same way, the frequency with which self and own death are given the same ratings on each of the constructs provides a measure of "integration" (the degree to which death is integrated into constructs of self). Recent research (4, 8, 9) has shown that both actualization and integration, as measured by the TI, have an independent as well as additive effect on fear of death and death anxiety as measured by the Collett-Lester Fear of Death Scale (FDS) (10) and Templer's Death Anxiety Scale (DAS) (11). For example, the degree to which an individual has actualized important life goals will influence that individual's fear of death regardless of the degree to which death is integrated into his or her personal construct system. Similarly, an individual's level of integration will significantly influence his or her fear of death regardless of whether the individual is actualized. Moreover, individuals who are highly actualized and highly integrated appear to be significantly less fearful of death and less death anxious than individuals having lower levels of either actualization, integration, or both.

Although the aforementioned findings provide us with a basis for understanding some of the complexities associated with fear of death, death anxiety, actualization, and integration, it does so only for presumably healthy adult populations. It is unknown, at this point, whether these same relationships can be generalized to populations for whom issues of death and dying might be of primary concern.

Much of the research that has investigated the relationship between physical well-being and death attitudes has focused on elderly populations. For example, two studies (12, 13), using self-reports and the Thematic Apperception Test (TAT), each found the elderly physically ill to be more concerned about death and dying as well as more defensive and less emotionally responsive than the elderly healthy. Similarly, elderly respondents who were closer to death than a comparable control group, were found to be more fearful of death as determined by interviews, self-reports, and the TAT (14). Contradictory findings, however, have been reported by several authors (15, 16). For example, one of these studies (15), through the use of a checklist and a forced choice rating scale, indicated that individuals who were in poorer health were less fearful of death. In much the same way (16), it has been found that elderly persons who were active and living in the community were more death anxious, as measured by the DAS and Boyar's Fear of Death Scale (17) than a group of elderly disabled people living in a nursing home. The research is confused even further by several studies that have found no relationship between somatic integrity and attitudes toward death and dying (18, 19). Unfortunately, the research that specifically has examined death orientation in a seriously ill population is no less confusing.

In one series of studies (20–22) no differences in fear of death were found between healthy or ill respondents at either a conscious or fantasy level. Significant differences in fear of death did appear at a nonconscious level when cancer and heart disease patients were compared with a healthy control group. Similarly, in related research, nonfatally ill cancer patients have been found to be less threatened or fearful of death than those with fatal disease (23, 24). In contrast, it was found using interviews and the DAS that there was less death anxiety in a group of cancer patients when compared with a control group of eye clinic patients (25). Finally, several researchers (26–28) have suggested that there is no relationship between physical well-being and orientation toward death, an argument supported by some of the research done with the elderly (18, 19).

In summary, it is clear that very little can be concluded about fear of death in unhealthy populations. Given that the equivocal nature of the findings may be partially attributed to conflicting and inadequate methodologies, the present study was designed to investigate the relationship between death orientation and physical illness through the use of the Threat Index (1). It was hypothesized that those individuals who were highly actualized and highly integrated would demonstrate the least fear of death and death anxiety, regardless of whether they were healthy or ill or of what type of illness they had. In other words, it would not be an individual's medical status that related to fear of death or death anxiety but rather the additive effects of actualization and integration.

Method

Respondents

The respondents were 69 women and 31 men ranging in age from 17 to 79 years, with a mean age of 41.17 years. Recruited from various medical and university facilities in Thunder Bay, Ontario, the respondents were included in one of the following five groups, depending upon their medical status:

Group 1. Healthy people ($n = 20$) who reported no medical problems were recruited from an introductory psychology class at Lakehead University.

Group 2. The Worried well ($n = 20$) were individuals with no major medical difficulties who were attending their family physician at the Port Arthur Clinic in Thunder Bay, Ontario, for a physical checkup.

Group 3. Rheumatoid arthritis patients ($n = 20$) were recruited while receiving treatment at the Rheumatic Disease Unit of St. Joseph's General Hospital in Thunder Bay, Ontario, or while seeing their rheumatologist at the Port Arthur Clinic in Thunder Bay.

Group 4. Diabetes patients ($n = 20$) were respondents suffering from diabetes mellitus. They were recruited from the Diabetes

Education Center at St. Joseph's General Hospital in Thunder Bay or from a diabetes fitness class at Confederation College, also in Thunder Bay.

Group 5. Cancer patients ($n = 20$) were suffering from Hodgkin's Disease, malignant melanoma, or cancer of the lung, breast, or colon and were recruited from the Thunder Bay Cancer Clinic.

It should be noted that, except for age, all the groups were roughly comparable on various demographic variables. A post hoc student Newman-Keuls multiple comparison indicated that the respondents in Group 1 were significantly younger than the respondents in any of the other groups and that the respondents in Group 2 were significantly younger than those in Groups 3, 4, and 5 (who were all of comparable age).

Assessment Materials

Threat Index (TI). The TI provides 40 bipolar dimensions on which the respondent rates "self," "ideal self," and "own death," thinking about the latter as if it were personally imminent. The number of times the individual places self and own death on the same pole of each dimension is counted to yield an overall integration score. A higher integration score is indicative of a greater congruency between constructs of self and the constructs of death. A score for actualization is also derived from this scale by counting the number of congruencies between self and ideal self. The higher the actualization score, the greater the congruency between the constructs of self and preferred self. Scores on either actualization or integration can range from 0 to 40.

Templer Death Anxiety Scale (DAS). The DAS requires the respondent to answer "true" or "false" to 15 statements dealing with emotional reactions to death and dying. The total score (ranging from 0 to 15) represents the number of times the respondent answered in the direction indicative of death anxiety.

Collett-Lester Fear of Death Scale (FDS). This multidimensional scale comprises 36 items about death and dying and is designed to assess an overall fear of death and dying as well as four separate fears: fear of death of self (DS); fear of death of other (DO); fear of dying of self (DYS); and fear of dying of other (DYO). The respondent is required to indicate, using a 6-point Likert-type scale, agreement or disagreement with each of the 36 statements. The four subscales on the FDS are each composed of a different number of items. Therefore, the possible total score for each subscale is different. For this reason each subscale score was transformed such that the scores could range from 0 to 100 to give a sense of the magnitude of death concern associated with each subscale and to make the scales more directly comparable with one another. A higher score is indicative of an endorsement of the fear-indicating items.

Procedure

The TI, the FDS, the DAS, and a demographic questionnaire were administered to respondents in all five groups. Group 1 was the only large group administration, with members of the other groups being seen on an individual or small group basis.

Because it was thought that issues of death and dying might have been more salient and potentially more upsetting for people with cancer, every effort was made to be sure that they experienced no adverse effects from participating in the study. All patients were contacted at the Cancer Clinic, where the study was described to them and their participation requested. Patients who agreed to take part in the study were contacted at a later date for the administration of the questionnaire. This was followed by a further contact sometime later to be sure that any questions or concerns resulting from participation in the study were taken care of.

Except for the cancer patients, all respondents were tested in the setting from which they were recruited, and any issues or concerns that arose during the administration session were dealt with at that time. Every respondent was also urged to contact either author in the future if they had any concerns, comments, or questions associated with the study.

Results and Discussion

As a first step in analyzing the data, scores were calculated for each respondent on each of the eight variables of interest: actualization (ACT), integration (INT), death anxiety (DAS), overall fear of death and dying (FDS), fear of death of self (DS), fear of death of other (DO), fear of dying of self (DYS), and fear of dying of other (DYO). The relationship between these variables and various demographic variables was then investigated using hierarchical multiple regression.

Age

According to the regression analyses, none of the demographic variables, except for age, accounted for a significant proportion of the variance on any of the eight variables of concern. Specifically, it was found that age accounted for 10 percent of the variability on the DAS, $F(1, 74) = 11.16$, $p < .01$, 8 percent of the variability on the DS subscale, $F(1, 74) = 9.04$, $p < .01$, and 16 percent of the variability on INT, $F(1, 74) = 20.17$, $p < .001$. In other words, within the total sample of 100 respondents, people who were older were less anxious about death, were less fearful of their own death, and had integrated death into their personal construct systems more completely than younger respondents.

These findings are interesting in light of the conclusions of previous research (29, 30), which indicated that age influenced attitudes toward death only up to the point of stabilization of cognitive development. Moreover, Lester (29) has argued that subsequent changes in attitudes toward death are more likely to be attributable to life experiences and changes in personality than to aging per se. Such a possibility could account for the relationship between age and reduced anxiety, fear of death, and the higher levels of integration reported in the present study. In any event, the complexity of these relationships makes a definitive explanation of these findings impossible at this time.

Medical Status

Mean scores on each of the death concern measures for each medical subgroup appear in Table 1. With the effects of age controlled for, a hierarchical multiple regression was performed to determine whether fear of death or death anxiety differed among the five groups. No significant differences were found on any of the eight variables. This suggests that attitudes toward death and dying are independent of the respondent's medical status.

Although the results of past research have been equivocal, the lack of a relationship between medical status and death concerns in the present study is in agreement with Templer's (19) conclusion that "death anxiety is usually related more to degree of personality adjustment and subjective state of well-being than to reality-factors" (p. 523). The present findings clearly demonstrate that disease (a reality-based factor) has little to do with a respondent's orientation toward death. It may be that any patient diagnosed as having a life-threatening illness who responds with marked fear and apprehension is doing so because he or she has always been very much afraid of death and not because the illness created the fear.

In a further analysis of the data, healthy respondents (Groups 1 and 2 combined) were contrasted with physically ill respondents (Groups 3, 4, and 5 combined) through the use of contrast coding, a multiple regression procedure essentially equivalent to an a priori comparison (31). It was found that the healthy group scored higher on ACT than the ill group, $F(1, 94) = 4.29$, $p < .05$, indicating that respondents who were healthy saw themselves as being more like their preferred selves than those who were ill. This result was not surprising considering the fact that most people who are ill would see a discrepancy between self (someone who was ill) and preferred self (someone who was healthy). Furthermore, as a logical extension of this argument, it is plausible that the difference between the two groups resulted from a decrease in the patients' level of actualization as a result of becoming ill. Another, perhaps equally viable, explanation for these findings could be that the physically ill group, because of their illness, interpreted some of

TABLE 1 Means and Standard Deviations of All Measures for Each Group and the Entire Sample

	Well (n = 20)		Worried well (n = 20)		Rheumatoid arthritics (n = 20)		Diabetics (n = 20)		Cancer patients (n = 20)		Entire sample (n = 100)	
	M	SD	M	SD	M	SD	M	SD	M	SD	M	SD
ACT	35.05	4.58	36.45	2.70	33.60	4.95	34.50	5.38	35.20	4.76	34.96	4.57
INT	19.25	10.64	20.20	11.71	23.80	9.34	26.75	10.06	26.05	8.87	23.21	10.42
DAS	7.75	2.90	7.45	3.65	6.20	3.00	7.45	2.72	7.05	2.82	7.18	3.02
FDS	53.90	14.95	49.10	14.33	49.15	11.25	50.35	9.59	51.75	13.19	50.85	12.69
DS	54.55	26.01	55.10	24.51	42.95	16.37	49.50	16.07	49.00	19.75	50.22	20.99
DO	61.00	16.84	51.65	20.52	48.00	15.94	52.80	13.81	58.00	16.29	54.29	17.13
DYS	56.30	20.27	58.10	16.27	63.10	14.79	56.90	15.86	60.35	15.84	59.49	16.53
DYO	43.00	17.34	31.50	15.15	42.70	14.33	39.50	17.79	39.45	18.48	39.23	16.88

the construct dimensions on the TI as referring to their physical well-being. By contrast, the healthy respondents may have incorporated the same items differently. Such differences in the interpretation of the TI may account for the variation observed on the actualization measure.

Actualization and Integration

Analyses were performed on the entire sample, by collapsing across groups, in order to investigate the separate and additive effects of actualization and integration. The first analysis assessed the separate effects of ACT and INT by calculating the correlations between ACT and INT and the various measures of death concern for the entire sample. These correlations, presented in Table 2, are consistent with past research and indicate significant relationships for ACT and INT with the DAS, the FDS overall, and with DYS, in addition to a significant ACT-DS correlation coefficient.

In a further test of the separate effects of ACT and INT, multiple regression basically substantiated the results of the correlational analyses (Table 3). Specifically, those people who were highly actualized, regardless of their age, were significantly less death anxious, less fearful of death and dying overall, less fearful of death of self, and less fearful of dying of self and others. Because the only significant unique contribution made by INT was on the DYS subscale, it was concluded that ACT was a much more potent measure with regard to predicting fear of death and death anxiety in the present sample.

The present findings concerning the effects of actualization

TABLE 2   Product-Moment Correlations for Actualization (ACT) and Integration (INT) with Various Measures of Death Anxiety and Fear of Death for the Entire Sample ($n = 100$)

	DAS	FDS	DS	DO	DYS	DYO
ACT	−.31**	−.30**	−.23*	−.17	−.27**	−.20
INT	−.22*	−.22*	−.16	−.16	−.21*	−.10

$*p < .05.$
$**p < .01.$

TABLE 3 Separate Hierarchical Multiple Regression Analyses for Actualization (ACT) and Integration (INT) on Various Measures of Death Anxiety and Fear of Death

Criterion	DAS		FDS		DS		DO		DYS		DYO	
Variable[a]	R^2 Change	p	R^2 Change	p	R^2 Change	p	R^2 Change	p	R^2 Change	p	R^2 Change	p
Age	.08	.01	.02	n.s.	.01	.01	.04	n.s.	.00	n.s.	.01	n.s.
ACT	.09	.01	.09	.01	.05	.05	.03	n.s.	.07	.01	.04	.05
Age	.08	.01	.02	n.s.	.10	.01	.04	n.s.	.00	n.s.	.01	n.s.
INT	.01	n.s.	.03	n.s.	.00	n.s.	.01	n.s.	.06	.05	.02	n.s.

Note. n.s. = not significant.
[a]In order of entry into regression equation.

are in agreement with the work of Neimeyer and Chapman (4), who found that respondents with high levels of actualization were significantly less fearful of death and less death anxious than respondents with lower levels of actualization. These authors argued, from the perspective of Sartrean existential philosophy, that the closer the individual was to the completion of primary life projects, the more actualized the individual would be and the less death would be seen as a threat to the completion of those life projects. Obviously, these findings have important implications.

On a theoretical level, it would seem important that future research with the TI include the measure of actualization. At a more practical level, it may be of benefit, especially when working with patients whose level of actualization is low, to explore their achievements in the hope that they may become more aware of personal accomplishments and less fearful and apprehensive concerning their ultimate fate.

The final analysis to be performed was concerned with the additive effects of ACT and INT and was intended to test the hypothesis that those respondents who were both highly actualized and highly integrated would be the least death anxious and the least fearful of death when compared with respondents demonstrating lower levels on one or both of these variables. The regression analyses (Table 4) indicated that after the effects of INT had been taken into consideration, ACT still accounted for a significant proportion of the variance associated with the DAS, $F(1, 96) = 10.08$, $p < .01$, the FDS, $F(1, 96) = 8.67$, $p < .01$, and the FDS subscales, DS, $F(1, 96) = 5.19$, $p < .05$, and DYS, $F(1, 96) = 6.49$, $p < .05$.

Except for the DYS subscale, INT contributed essentially nothing to the variance associated with the various measures of death concern and no additive effect was observed. This finding was confirmed when ACT and INT were taken out of the regression equation in the reverse order. When ACT was taken into account first, it was found that INT did not make a significant contribution on any of the measures except DYS, $F(1, 96) = 5.31$, $p < .05$. These findings clearly suggest, with these particular respondents, that virtually nothing can be predicted from both actualization and integration that cannot be predicted from actualization alone.

TABLE 4 Hierarchical Multiple Regression Analyses for Both Actualization (ACT) and Integration (INT) on Various Measures of Death Anxiety and Fear of Death

Criterion	DAS		FDS		DS		DO		DYS		DYO	
Variable[a]	R^2 Change	p	R^2 Change	p	R^2 Change	p	R^2 Change	p	R^2 Change	p	R^2 Change	p
Age	.08	.01	.02	n.s.	.10	.01	.04	n.s.	.00	n.s.	.01	n.s.
ACT	.09	.01	.09	.01	.05	.05	.03	n.s.	.07	.01	.04	.05
INT	.01	n.s.	.02	n.s.	.00	n.s.	.01	n.s.	.05	.01	.01	n.s.
Age	.08	.01	.02	n.s.	.10	.01	.04	n.s.	.00	n.s.	.01	n.s.
INT	.01	n.s.	.03	n.s.	.00	n.s.	.01	n.s.	.06	.05	.02	n.s.
ACT	.09	.01	.08	.01	.05	.05	.02	n.s.	.06	.05	.03	n.s.

Note. n.s. = not significant.
[a]In order of entry into regression equation.

This marked lack of effect associated with integration in the present study was not expected. It is possible that the relative unimportance of this measure of integration in the present study was due to its slight correlation ($r = .10$) with the ACT measure or to some unidentifiable characteristic unique to the samples investigated. The fact that it also does not contribute to the additive model described in previous research (8, 9) makes the lack of integration effects beyond those associated with actualization that much more puzzling.

Summary and Conclusions

The present study found a significant relationship between actualization and orientation toward death, with higher levels of actualization being associated with reduced death anxiety and fear of death. In addition, it was found that physical illness did not influence death anxiety or fear of death in any detectable way. Together, these findings have implications for the management and understanding of seriously ill and dying patients.

Although the relationship between actualization and death orientation was clear-cut in the present investigation, the relative lack of unique effects for integration was troublesome and inconsistent with the past literature. Future research with the TI is needed in order to further investigate the possible independent and additive effects of these two variables in both healthy and ill populations.

References

1. Krieger, S. R., Epting, F. R., & Leitner, L. M. Personal constructs, threat, and attitudes toward death. *Omega*, 1974, *5*, 299–310.
2. Epting, F. R., Rainey, L. C., & Weiss, M. J. Constructions of death and the levels of fear. *Death Education*, 1979, *3*, 21–30.
3. Krieger, S. R. Death orientation and the specialty choice and training of physicians. *Dissertations Abstracts International*, 1977, *37*, 3616-B.
4. Neimeyer, R. A., & Chapman, K. M. Self/ideal discrepancy and fear of death: The test of an existential hypothesis. *Omega*, 1980–1981, *11*, 233–240.

5. Neimeyer, R. A., & Dingemans, P. Death orientation in the suicide intervention worker. *Omega*, 1980-1981, *11*, 17-25.

6. Neimeyer, R. A., Dingemans, P., & Epting, F. R. Convergent validity, situational stability and meaningfulness of the Treat Index. *Omega*, 1977, *8*, 251-265.

7. Kelly, G. A. *The psychology of personal constructs* (Vol. 1). New York: Norton, 1955.

8. Robinson, R. J., & Wood, K. *The Threat Index: An additive approach.* Manuscript submitted for publication, 1982.

9. Wood, K., & Robinson, P. J. Actualization and the fear of death: Retesting an existential hypothesis. *Essence*, 1982, *5*, 235-243.

10. Collett, L., & Lester, D. The fear of death and the fear of dying. *Journal of Psychology*, 1969, *72*, 179-181.

11. Templer, D. I. The construction and validation of a death anxiety scale. *Journal of General Psychology*, 1970, *82*, 165-177.

12. Kimsey, L. R., Roberts, J. L., & Logan, D. L. Death, dying, and denial in the aged. *American Journal of Psychiatry*, 1972, *129*, 161-166.

13. Rhudick, P. J., & Dibner, A. S. Age, personality, and health correlates of death concerns in normal aged individuals. *Journal of Gerontology*, 1961, *16*, 44-49.

14. Lieberman, M. A., & Coplan, A. S. Distance from death as a variable in the study of aging. *Developmental Psychology*, 1970, 2, 71-84.

15. Swenson, W. M. Attitudes toward death in an aged population. *Journal of Gerontology*, 1961, *16*, 49-52.

16. Nehrke, M. F., Bellucci, G., & Gabriel, S. J. Death anxiety, locus of control, and life satisfaction in the elderly: Toward a definition of ego-integrity. *Omega*, 1977-1978, *8*, 359-368.

17. Boyar, J. I. The construction and partial validation of a scale for the measurement of the fear of death. *Dissertation Abstracts International*, 1964, *25*(3), 2041.

18. Shrut, S. D. Attitudes toward old age and death. *Mental Hygiene*, 1958, *42*, 259-266.

19. Templer, D. I. Death anxiety as related to depression and health of retired persons. *Journal of Gerontology*, 1971, *26*, 521-523.

20. Feifel, H. Religious conviction and fear of death among the healthy and the terminally ill. *Journal for the Scientific Study of Religion*, 1974, *13*, 353-360.

21. Feifel, H., & Branscomb, A. B. Who's afraid of death? *Journal of Abnormal Psychology*, 1973, *81*, 282-288.

22. Feifel, H., Freilich, J., & Hermann, L. J. Death fear in dying heart and cancer patients. *Journal of Psychosomatic Research*, 1973, *17*, 161-166.

23. Hinton, J. M. The physical and mental distress of the dying. *Quarterly Journal of Medicine*, 1963, *32*, 1-21.

24. Hinton, J. M. *Dying.* Baltimore: Penguin, 1967.

25. Gibbs, H. W., & Achterberg-Lawlis, J. Spiritual values and death

anxiety: Implications for counseling with terminal cancer patients. *Journal of Counseling Psychology,* 1978, *25,* 563–569.

26. Devins, G. M. Death anxiety and voluntary passive euthanasia: Influences of proximity to death and experiences with death in important other persons. *Journal of Consulting and Clinical Psychology,* 1979, *47,* 301–309.

27. Gielen, A. C., & Roche, K. A. Death anxiety and psychometric studies in Huntington's disease. *Omega,* 1979–1980, *10,* 135–145.

28. Lucas, R. A. A comparative study of general anxiety and death anxiety among three medical groups including patient and wife. *Omega,* 1974, *5,* 233–243.

29. Lester, D. Experimental and correlational studies of the fear of death. *Psychological Bulletin,* 1967, *67,* 27–36.

30. Pollak, G. M. Correlates of death anxiety: A review of empirical studies. *Omega,* 1979–1980, *10,* 97–121.

31. Cohen, J., & Cohen, P. *Applied multiple regression/correlation analysis for the behavioral sciences.* Hillsdale, N.J.: Lawrence Erlbaum Associates, 1975.

CONCERNS ABOUT DEATH AMONG
SEVERELY ILL PEOPLE

LINDA L. VINEY

University of Wollongong

Personal construct psychology was used to generate a set of questions about concerns about death among severely ill people. Answers to these questions were provided by content analyses of the responses of a large group of ill people to an open-ended question about their current experiences. Comparison of their responses with those of a similar group of well people indicated that they expressed more concerns about death. More death-related concerns were reported by those ill people who were facing surgery rather than those who were not, those whose illnesses were acute rather than chronic, and those who were interviewed while in the hospital rather than at home. Gender, age, marital status, and educational attainment were all considered predictors of death-related concerns; but none was found to be significant, nor were concerns about death observed to vary according to illness type. The psychological states found to accompany greater death-related concerns among ill people proved to represent both the adaptive and the dislocative processes of mourning. People who were not ill, but who had greater death-related concerns than other well people, on contrast, showed signs only of the more dislocative processes. Some of the implications of these findings for thanatological counseling of severely ill people are discussed.

It has been established by Viney (1) that people who are severely ill search for meaning in their illness, that is, they try to

Thanks are due to Sue Beattie, Yvonne Benjamin, and Carol Preston for the collection and analyses of the data referred to herein. I also thank the patients of the Bulli and Wollongong hospitals who have shared their experiences with us, together with our other research participants. Our work with them has been funded by the Australian Research Grants Committee and the Commonwealth Department of Health.

229[143]

interpret it in ways that make sense to them. This finding fits well with George Kelly's (2) personal construct psychology, which maintains that all people try to interpret the events they are experiencing in order to anticipate what will happen to them. They anticipate events by using their individually developed systems of personal constructs. Constructs are patterns or templates that they create, on the basis of their unique experiences, and then fit onto current and future events. It also follows from this psychology that people, ill and well, search for meaning in death, that is, try to anticipate it. This is made difficult for people who have experienced few death-related events.

Because most people lack the constructs, based on prior experience, to enable them to make sense of their own death, Kelly (3) notes that it can be very anxiety arousing for them. Kelly also notes that death can constitute a threat to them if it requires a great change in that important part of their construct system that deals with how they relate to other people. For some people this threatened change may be so great that "life" and "death" are for them incompatible constructs (3). Most people, however, can be concerned about both life and death. In fact, it has been suggested by Rowe (4) that people's ways of making sense of their life must also have implications for their death.

Some Questions about Concerns about Death among Severely Ill People

In this paper a personal construct psychology of death has been used to construct some questions about ill peoples' concerns about death. Do severely ill people show more concerns about death than people who are well? Do concerns about death vary according to such personal characteristics as gender, age, marital status, or educational attainment? Do concerns about death differ according to whether those ill people are about to have surgery? Do they differ according to whether peoples' illnesses are acute or chronic? Do people for whom different illnesses have been diagnosed show characteristically different concerns about death? Do their concerns depend on whether they are interviewed during a period of hospitalization or while they are at home? Finally, are people's concerns about death associated with some psychological states rather than others? The answers to all of these questions—but especially to the last—have implications for thanatological counseling.

Concerns about Death: A Pandora's Box

Concerns about death can differ greatly in their content. Schultz (5) has described the range of concerns as running from fear of physical suffering, of humiliation, of punishment, and of not being to a frustrating interference with the achievement of goals. One of the commonly used measures of death anxiety by Templer, Ruff, and Franks (6) proved, when analyzed, to focus on at least four different sources of anxiety: thoughts and feelings about death, physical changes related to death, the rapid passage of time before death, and dealing with pain and other stresses associated with death (7).

These not atypical examples of current work indicate that researchers have been concerned about the more negative aspects of death. It may be that their own death-related anxiety has prompted them to use research instruments ensuring that the Pandora's box of concerns about death is opened only a little and so lets out only the few concerns about death that they were personally anticipating and could therefore handle.

Method

How Can Concerns about Death be Assessed?

Concerns about death can best be assessed by asking people to talk freely about their experiences and listening carefully to their replies. Questionnaires and other structured pencil-and-paper techniques cannot provide as much information as this technique does, because they limit the range of concerns that people can raise and so limit the findings. Careful listening is what takes skill. The method used here is content analysis of the verbalizations of the research participants, a method that ensures relatively unbiased information from the participants while being scientifically acceptable (9). When the interrater reliability of content analysis scales is established and a network of validational information about them is built up, they can be valuable tools.

The content analysis scale used for this work was the Death Anxiety Subscale, which has acceptable reliability and validity (10-13). It involves scoring any references made by the research participants to their own death (e.g., "When I die, the family will be able to manage"), or dying (e.g., "I'm ready to go") or indicating a threat of death (e.g., "The priest was anointing me, as if I were dying") or anxiety about death (e.g., "I worry that I'll never see our children grow up"), death of other people (e.g., "A lot of our friends seem to be dying lately"), or animals (e.g., "My old dog died while I was in hospital"), destruction of objects (e.g., "The car was a write-off"), or denial of death anxiety (e.g., "Death doesn't scare me"). This last content analysis category of denial is a necessary one in western cultures in which death is a taboo topic (14, 15). It is not only well people who can deny death and death-related anxieties. Severely ill people can as well (16, 17), especially during their initial reactions to imminent death (18).

Description of the Participants

The two groups of people whose responses to open-ended instructions were recorded and content analyzed were 496 people who were severely ill and 297 people who were not then troubled by severe illness. In the first large group there were equal numbers of men and women, and their ages ranged from 18 to 90 years. Most of them were married. Some of them had completed only primary school, others had partial high school educations, yet others had earned high school diplomas, and a few had tertiary level qualifications. The other large group was similar, although it contained slightly more younger and better-educated people (but not to the point of statistical significance). Both groups of people were given the same instructions in the course of an interview about lifespan transitions currently relevant to them: "I'd like you to talk to me for a few minutes about your life at the moment—the good things and the bad—what it's like for you."

All of the ill group were suffering from severe and often painful illness or the disabling effects of accidents. Many of those who were diagnosed by their physicians as acutely ill were scheduled for exploratory or corrective surgery for back pain or for gastrointestinal or genitourinary problems. There were also some who were hospitalized for observation and care of respiratory problems such as asthma and pneumonia and for gastrointestinal problems such as ulcers. They were diagnosed as chronically ill if they had a condition that would last at least six months or had caused a permanent disability. The largest group of chronically ill people were those who had had heart attacks or who suffered from other heart problems, such as angina. Victims of strokes were also common. There were also people with specific disorders such as diabetes and progressive diseases of the nervous system such as multiple sclerosis. Paraplegic and quadraplegic accident victims were also considered to be chronically ill, as were cancer victims for whom, even in remission, cancer continued to be an ever-present threat to life.

Results and Discussion

Do Severely Ill People Show More Concerns about Death than People Who Are Well?

Personal construct psychology considers death a greater threat when it is perceived as causing a great change in the core constructs that people use to interpret how they relate to other people. People who are severely ill are more likely to be experiencing such changes, both because of illness-related events and because of the nearness of death, than those who are well. Ill people should then show more concerns about death than well people. Research evidence already available about this question is conflicting. Descriptive accounts of the experiences of ill people agree with the hypothesis (16, 19). Direct comparisons of ill and well groups using traditional measures, however, have found no differences between them (20, 21).

These findings, however, were in support of the hypotheses. Using the measure selected, a statistically significant difference was found between the groups, $F(1,791) = 65.55$, $p < .001$. Ill people were shown to score higher than well people, $\bar{X} = .65$, $SD = .36$ and $\bar{X} = .46$, $SD = .27$, respectively. Severely ill people showed more concerns about death than people who were well.

Do Concerns about Death Vary According to Characteristics Such as Gender, Age, Marital Status, or Education?

Because constructs, including those about death, are developed by people on the basis of their own unique experiences, individual differences in people's views of death are likely. It may be that these differences follow a pattern dictated by the differences in experiences of women and men, of the young and the old, of the married and the not married, of the well educated and the less educated. The research literature has considered the last two characteristics very little. Gender has been considered as a factor, but again with somewhat equivocal results. It is possible to find studies showing that women have more death-related concerns (6, 22) or that men do (23). The findings concerning both gender and age are confusing (5), although age seems a likely predictor of increasing death concerns.

Personal construct psychology, on the basis of its view of death as threatening because of the immediacy of the changes it promises, gives rise to the hypothesis that older people should show more death-related concerns. This may, however, be an oversimplified conceptualization, because it does not take into account the differing effects of maturity as individuals move through the lifespan (24). Some of the available evidence provided by Weisman and Kastem (25) is, in fact, against this hypothesis, with younger and middle-aged people showing more concerns about death than the elderly. In this research, no relationships were found between the number of death references and any of the four factors of gender, age, marital status, and educational attainment. (No Pearson product moment correlation coefficients significant at $p < .01$ were found for either the group of 496 ill or that of 297 well research participants.) Concerns about death were not found to be affected by these personal characteristics in any consistent way.

Do Ill People's Concerns about Death Differ According to Whether They Are Going to Have Surgery?

Personal construct psychology suggests that imminent surgery should make more immediate the threat of change in people's view of themselves through death. Ill people who were to have surgery should therefore have greater concerns about death than those who were not. A statistically significant difference was found between the groups of 211 surgical and 285 nonsurgical patients, using ANOVA, $F(1,494) = 15.83$, $p < .001$. The surgery group was found to have higher scores than the medical group, $\bar{X} = .73$, $SD = .35$ and $\bar{X} = .60$, $SD = .36$, respectively. Ill people facing surgery described more concerns about death than ill people who were not facing surgery.

Do Concerns about Death Differ According to Whether Peoples' Illnesses Are Acute or Chronic?

The same personal construct psychology view concerning the immediacy of the threat of change brought about by death suggests that people with sudden, acute illness should show more death-related concerns than those whose illnesses and disabilities were lingeringly chronic. This hypothesis was tested with the ill people divided into the 228 of them diagnosed as having an acute medical problem and the 268 of them diagnosed as having a chronic medical problem. The results supported the hypothesis. There was a significant difference between the groups, $F(1,494) = 23.35$, $p < .001$, and the acute group had higher scores than the chronic group, $\bar{X} = .74$, $SD = .38$ and $\bar{X} = .58$, $SD = .33$, respectively. People with acute illnesses described more concerns about death than people with chronic illnesses.

Do the Concerns about Death of People Suffering from Heart Conditions Differ from Those of People Suffering from Diabetes?

People suffering from different illnesses and disabilities may differ in their death-related concerns. According to personal construct psychology, each illness experience validates and supports some constructs that the sufferer has developed and invalidates others (3). Illnesses that involve very different experiences should then lead to different kinds of constructs in their sufferers. Heart disease, for example, often subjects its victims to pain, shortness of breath, and the likelihood of sudden death, which could be hard to prevent. Diabetes in its early stages, in contrast, subjects its victims to little pain, but a lack of energy and irritability and the possibility of sudden blackouts, which, although not often fatal, can be debilitating and embarrassing. These two different sets of illness-related experiences should lead to differences in the number of concerns about death.

To test this hypothesis, 102 people with heart conditions were compared with 60 diabetic people selected from the larger group of ill people. They were not found to differ significantly, $F(1,160) = 0.72$, $p > .01$. Their distributions of scores representing death-related concerns were very similar, $\bar{X} = .58$, $SD = .31$ and $\bar{X} = .58$, $SD = .38$ for heart condition and diabetic people, respectively. People with heart conditions did not differ in their concerns about death from people with diabetes. Although many other similar comparisons of disease groups remain to be carried out, this finding supports the view that people who are ill agree in their view of illness-related events and do not necessarily differ because their physical symptoms differ (26).

Do Ill People's Concerns about Death Differ According to Whether They Are Interviewed While in the Hospital or at Home?

Personal construct psychology holds that people's constructs change as the events they experience change (3). Ill people's concerns abut death should therefore change according to the situation in which they find themselves. For people dealing with illness or disabling injury, the hospital is a likely place for them to be interviewed. Hospitalization, however, involves many special events. Some of these are comforting and supportive, but many are isolating and frustrating (27–30). The concerns about death of people who were in the hospital were therefore compared with those held by ill people who were interviewed at home. Death may have seemed a more likely event to those who were hospitalized. If so, the threat during hospitalization should be more immediate. Concerns about death were predicted to be greater for that group of ill people than for those who were not hospitalized.

This hypothesis was tested, using the original group of ill people, 398 of whom were interviewed in the hospital and 98 of whom were interviewed at home. This hypothesis, unlike that about type of illness, was supported, $F(1,494) = 14.95$, $p < .001$. The hospitalized group had higher average scores than the group interviewed at home, $\bar{X} = .68$, $SD = 36$ and $\bar{X} = .53$, $SD = .33$, respectively. Ill people who were hospitalized described more concerns about death than ill people who were not hospitalized.

Are Peoples' Concerns about Death Associated with Certain Psychological States Rather than Others?

People who have many concerns about death, whether they are ill or well, can be thought of as people in mourning. They are prematurely bereaved. Can a personal construct theory of mourning (31) successfully identify the psychological states that are associated with such concerns? The theory has proposed two coexisting processes of mourning: one involving dislocation of the construct system and the other involving adaptation by that system. The psychological states associated with the dislocative processes are uncertainty (the shock and confusion occurring when the construct system is extended beyond the range of meaningful interpretation), sadness (the feelings of loss resulting from invalidation of some of the implications of the constructs dealing with the way people relate to others), anger expressed directly and indirectly (in an effort to find support for old

constructs in the face of invalidating change), and helplessness
(the hopelessness or despair representing awareness that the
events occurring are not open to meaningful anticipation by the
present construct system). The psychological states associated
with adaptation are feelings of mastery (which occur as a result
of active, self-directed exploration of one's world), sociability
(which occurs as a result of those elaborations involving positive
interactions with others), and positive feelings (involving idealiza-
tion in which what is mourned is reflected on in terms of the
positive poles of the relevant bipolar constructs, while the
negative poles are submerged). These personal construct psychology accounts of these common psychological states have been
developed by a number of writers (3, 32, 31).

These states were assessed using a set of content analysis
scales like the one already described. They similarly have
adequate interrater reliability and validity. Uncertainty as
measured by the Cognitive Anxiety Scale (32); sadness by the
Hostility In Scale, (10); anger expressed directly and indirectly
by the Hostility Out and Ambivalent Hostility Scales, respectively (10), and helplessness by the Pawn Scale (33). Mastery
was assessed by the Origin Scale (33), sociability by the
Sociality Scale (34), and good feelings by the Positive Affect
Scale (35). Some of these psychological states have been found
to be more common among ill than well people, for example,
the dislocative feelings of uncertainty (36), sadness and anger
(37, 38) and helplessness (29, 38–40). It was therefore considered appropriate to test the predicted associations between
death-related concerns and other psychological states separately
for the ill and well groups of people.

For ill people, death concerns proved to be significantly
related to seven of the eight psychological states examined. A
regression analysis yielded $R = .32$, with $F(8,549) = 8.32$,
$p < .01$. Only sadness was not found to be related to the
number of death concerns expressed. The largest relationships
were with good feelings ($r = .21$), then uncertainty ($r = .18$),
and anger indirectly expressed ($r = .18$). For well people, the
pattern of relationships was somewhat different. There was no
overall significant association to which other relationships contributed. This regression analysis yielded only $R = .25$, so that

with $F(8,288) = 2.33$, $p > .05$. Some individual significant relationships between death-related concerns and uncertainty, anger expressed directly and indirectly, and helplessness did, however, emerge. The largest of these relationships were with anger expressed directly ($r = .18$) and indirectly ($r = .18$). Mastery, sociability, and positive feelings were not found to be related to death-related concerns in people who were well.

These findings, although they did not confirm all the hypotheses about concerns about death as a premature bereavement, provided some interesting information about such concerns in severely ill people. Certain psychological states—those associated with the dislocative mourning processes—proved to be similarly related to the death-related concerns of both groups. These were uncertainty, anger, and helplessness. The more adaptive processes, represented by emotions such as mastery, sociability, and positive feelings, were related to concerns about death only among those people who were severely ill. The construct systems of well people who were more concerned with death than others who were also well proved to be more at the mercy of dislocative mourning processes. Those who were severely ill and expressing rather than suppressing their concerns about death, which was a likely event for them, were interpreting their experiences with construct systems that were subject to adaptive as well as dislocative processes.

Conclusion

Some Implications of the Answers to the Questions about Concerns about Death for Ill People

Professionals, paraprofessionals, families, and friends who wish to help people who are severely ill need to know more about their concerns about death. It is useful, for example, to know that ill people express more death-related concerns than people who are well. It is also of some benefit to know that death-related concerns do not appear to be the prerogative of women or men, the young or the old, those married or not married, or even of those with certain educational attainments. There is no evidence from this research that they are the prerogative of those suffering from certain types of illness. The findings that support the personal construct theory hypotheses about the immediacy of the threatened changes to be brought about by death are also of interest. Ill people facing surgery described more concerns about death than those not facing surgery. Those with acute illnesses described more concerns than those with chronic illnesses. Those who were hospitalized described more concerns than those who were able to stay at home.

Where personal construct psychology has proved especially useful, however, is in the hypotheses that it has generated about the mourning processes of ill people who are concerned about death. Personal construct psychologists see as essential to any form of counseling, a focusing on the experience of clients and an exploration of that experience to make it more meaningful to them (41-43). In thanatological counseling, these goals remain; but they must be achieved quickly and in terms of the construct system available to the clients at that time (44). The goal of thanatological counseling thus becomes to make the client's dying meaningful to him or her in terms of his or her current view of their world. This task is made easier for counselors by a knowledge of both the dislocative and adaptive processes of mourning. It is also useful for them to be able to recognize the more adaptive processes when they are expressed as feelings of mastery, sociability, and pleasure.

Some researchers in this field may have been afraid of opening up a Pandora's box of feelings associated with death. It is interesting that, in spite of their fears, the findings that have been achieved through the less limiting techniques of this research have had to do with positive emotions. People who were ill and expressing concerns about death also expressed feelings of competence, talked of good relationships with others, and showed pleasure and happiness. It has been suggested that pleasurable dying is a goal that may in western cultures, with luck, be achieved some time in the future (45). This research shows that for some severely ill people that goal has already been achieved.

References

1. Viney, L. L. Experiencing chronic illness: A personal construct commentary. Paper presented at the Fourth International Personal Construct Psychology Congress, Brock University, St. Catharines Canada, August, 1981.
2. Kelly, G. A. A psychology of the optimal man. In A. H. Mahrer (Ed.), *The goals of psychotherapy*. New York: Appleton-Century-Crofts, 1967.
3. Kelly, G. A. *The psychology of personal constructs* (2 vols.). New York: Norton, 1955.
4. Rowe, D. *The construction of life and death*. New York: Wiley, 1981.
5. Schultz, R. *The psychology of death, aging and bereavement*. New York: Addison-Wesley, 1978.
6. Templer, D., Ruff, C., & Franks, C. Death anxiety: Age, sex and parental resemblance in diverse populations. *Psychological Reports*, 1974, *35*, 216–225.
7. Lonetto, R., Fleming, S., & Mercer, G. W. The structure of death anxiety: A factor analytic study. *Journal of Personality Assessment*, 1979, *43*, 388–392.
8. Viney, L. L., & Westbrook, M. T. Measuring patients' experienced quality of life: The application of content analysis scales in health care. *Community Health Studies*, 1981, *5*, 45–52.
9. Viney, L. L. *Rigour with vigour: The assessment of psychological states by content analysis of verbal communications*. Unpublished paper, University of Wollongong, 1982.
10. Gottschalk, L. A., Winget, C. N., & Gleser, G. C. *Manual of instructions for using the Gottschalk-Gleser content analysis scales*. Berkeley: University of California Press, 1969.
11. Gottschalk, L. A., & Gleser, G. C. *The measurement of psychological states from the content analysis of verbal behavior*. Berkeley: University of California Press, 1969.
12. Gottschalk, L. A. *The content analysis of verbal behavior: Further studies*. New York: SP Medical & Scientific Books, 1979.
13. Viney, L. L. *Transitions*. Sydney: Cassell, 1980.
14. Weisman, A. D. *On dying and denying*. New York: Behavioral Publications, 1972.
15. Becker, E. *The denial of death*. New York: Free Press, 1973.
16. Hackett, T. P., & Cassem, N. H. Psychological management of the myocardiac infarction patient. *Journal of Human Stress*, 1976, *6*, 69–101.
17. Sanders, J. B., & Kardinal, C. G. Adaptive coping mechanisms in adult acute leukemia patients in remission. *Journal of American Medical Association*, 1977, *238*, 952–954.

18. Kübler-Ross, E. *On death and dying.* New York: Macmillan, 1969.
19. Mages, N. L., & Mendelsohn, G. A. Effects of cancer on patients' lives: A personalogical approach. In G. C. Stone, F. Cohen, & N. E. Adler (Eds.), *Health Psychology.* San Francisco: Jossey Bass, 1979.
20. Feifel, H. Religious conviction and fear of death among the healthy and terminally ill. *Journal for the Scientific Study of Religion,* 1974, *13,* 353–360.
21. Lucas, R. A comparative study of measures of general anxiety and death anxiety among three medical groups including patient and wife. *Omega,* 1974, *5,* 233.
22. Iammarino, N. K. Relationship between death anxiety and demographic variables. *Psychological Reports,* 1975, *17,* 262–266.
23. Krieger, S., Epting, F., & Leitner, L. M. Personal constructs, threat and attitudes toward death. *Omega,* 1974, *5,* 299–309.
24. Pattison, E. M. *The experience of dying.* New Jersey: Prentice-Hall, 1977.
25. Weisman, A. D., & Kastenbaum, R. *The psychological autopsy: A study of the terminal phase of life.* New York: Behavioral Publications, 1968.
26. Viney, L. L., & Westbrook, M. T. Psychosocial reactions to heart disease: An application of content analysis methodology. In *Proceedings of the Geigy Symposium on Behavioral Medicine.* Melbourne, 1980.
27. Lucente, F. E., & Fleck, S. A study of hospitalization anxiety in 408 medical and surgical patients. *Psychosomatic Medicine,* 1972, *34,* 304–312.
28. Volicer, B. J. Hospital stress and patient reports of pain and physical status. *Journal of Human Stress,* 1978, *4,* 28–37.
29. Taylor, S. E. Hospital patient behavior: Reactance, helplessness or control. *Journal of Social Issues,* 1979, *35,* 156–184.
30. Viney, L. L., & Westbrook, M. T. Psychological reactions to chronic illness-related disability as a function of its severity and type. *Journal of Psychosomatic Research,* in press.
31. Woodfield, R. L., & Viney, L. L. A personal construct approach to bereavement. *Omega,* in press.
32. McCoy, M. Reconstruction of emotion. In D. Bannister (Ed.), *New perspectives in personal construct theory.* New York: Academic Press, 1977.
33. Viney, L. L., & Westbrook, M. T. Cognitive anxiety: A method of content analysis for verbal samples. *Journal of Personality Assessment,* 1976, *40,* 140–150.
34. Westbrook, M. T., & Viney, L. L. Scales of origin and pawn perception using content analysis of speech. *Journal of Personality Assessment,* 1980, *44,* 157–166.
35. Viney, L. L., & Westbrook, M. T. Sociality: A concent analysis for verbalizations. *Social Behavior and Personality,* 1979, *7,* 129–137.

36. Westbrook, M. T. Positive affect: A method of content analysis for verbal samples. *Journal of Consulting and Clinical Psychology*, 1976, *44*, 715–719.
37. Moos, R. H., & Tsu, V. D. The crisis of physical illness: An overview. In R. H. Moss (Ed.), *Coping with physical illness*. New York: Plenum, 1977.
38. Hamburg, D. A. Coping behavior in life threatening circumstances. *Psychotherapy and Psychosomatics*, 1974, *23*, 13–25.
39. Westbrook, M. T., & Viney, L. L. Psychological reaction to the onset of chronic illness. *Social Science and Medicine*, in press.
40. Janis, I. L., & Rodin, J. Attribution, control and decision-making: Social psychology and health. In G. C. Stone, F. Cohen, & E. Adler (Eds.), *Health psychology—A handbook*. San Francisco: Jossey Bass, 1979.
41. Anderson, N. D. Exclusion: A study of depersonalization in health care. *Journal of Humanistic Psychology*, 1981, *21*, 167–178.
42. Kelly, G. Personal construct theory and the psychotherapeutic interview. In B. A. Maher (Ed.), *Clinical psychology and personality: Selected papers of George Kelly*. New York: Wiley, 1969.
43. Landfield, A. W. Personal construct psychotherapy: A personal construction. In A. W. Landfield & L. M. Leitner (Eds.), *Personal construct psychology: Psychotherapy and personality*. New York: Wiley, 1980.
44. Viney, L. L. Experimenting with experience: A psychotherapeutic case study. *Psychotherapy: Research, Theory, and Practice*, 1981, *18*, 271–278.
45. Feigenberg, L., & Shneidman, E. S. Clinical thanatology and psychotherapy: Some reflections on caring for the dying person. *Omega*, 1979, *10*, 1–8.
46. Kastenbaum, R. "Healthy dying": A paradoxical quest continues. *Journal of Social Issues*, 1979, *35*, 185–206.

∞∞∞

CONSTRUCTS AND COPING:
PHYSICIANS' RESPONSES TO PATIENT DEATH

∞∞∞

GREG J. NEIMEYER, MARYLOU BEHNKE, and JOHN REISS

University of Florida, Gainesville

This paper explores the relationship between physicians' personal orientations toward death and their responses to patient death. A group of 25 pediatric residents were asked to complete the Threat Index and to respond to vignettes depicting personal death. Consistent with predictions derived from personal construct theory, particular death orientations were associated with various behavioral and psychophysiological reactions. Residents with high death threat and anxiety were more likely to adopt avoidance and denial strategies and to experience fewer psychophysiological symptoms when faced with a patient's death. Implications of these findings for further research and treatment are discussed.

Physicians are confronted with numerous losses resulting from patient death during the course of their work (1-4). As well as being a personal loss, the death of a patient is often experienced as a failure that challenges the physician's feelings of professional competence (2, 5-8). Some schools provide formal training for their medical students on how to counsel the grieving family, but almost no training is available that is designed to help physicians deal effectively with personal feelings of loss, grief, and self-doubt. A survey of medical schools throughout the United States, for example, found that only 7 of 107 schools offered a full-term course on death and dying (9). In the

The authors wish to express their appreciation to Jill Lehrer and Lisa Santos for their contributions to this project and to thank Johnette Arnold and Oonagh Kater for their editorial assistance.

Data used in this paper are derived in part from a larger project concerning the attitudes of physicians toward patient death (28).

absence of specific training, doctors are left to develop their own personal strategies for coping with patient death (6). Although these strategies vary widely in their effectiveness (3-5), recent research has noted the inadequacy of many of the most common approaches (10-14).

Research indicates that one common strategy used by physicians is avoidance. In an effort to cope with the feelings of anxiety, guilt, and isolation that may accompany the death of a patient, many physicians try to ignore or deny their feelings, adopt a stance of professional detachment, withdraw emotionally, and focus on tasks (10-14). These methods of coping with death can be dysfunctional. By adopting avoidance strategies physicians actually deprive themselves of the successful resolution of personal issues related to patient death (15). As a further consequence, physicians are rendered inaccessable to the patient's family and others who are in need of emotional support and for this reason are often viewed as distant and uncaring. For example, in a recent study of women who had experienced a perinatal death, it was found that more than 50 percent of the mothers perceived their physician as cold and indifferent and felt that their emotional needs were not met during a time of crisis (16). Results of studies such as these suggest that, in the absence of sufficient training, some physicians develop coping strategies that are harmful to themselves and their patients.

On the other hand, by maintaining open communication with the family, facilitating the expression of grief, and involving other social service personnel in the support process, other physicians have been able to deal very effectively with their own and the family's grief issues. These physicians are typically emotionally expressive, seek emotional support, and request professional consultation regarding the issues surrounding patient death (3, 8, 17, 18).

From these studies, it is evident that physicians use a wide variety of coping strategies and exhibit a wide range of counseling skills in dealing with patient death. It is not clear, however, what factors distinguish those physicians who use avoidance strategies in death-related issues from those who do not.

One answer may be found in examining the doctor's own

relationship to death. One's own orientation toward death may influence the way in which one responds to the death of others. This implies that the use of specific coping strategies may be predictable from a physician's particular death orientation. Kelly's psychology of personal constructs (19) provides some grounds for distinguishing various death orientations in a way that allows this theory to be tested.

According to Kelly, in order to understand their environment individuals develop conceptual structures composed of many bipolar bases of discrimination termed "constructs" (e.g., exciting versus boring). Each of these constructs serves as a system for ordering and predicting experience. When confronted with new information or experience, an individual renders the event meaningful by understanding or "construing" it in light of his or her current constructs.

According to this theory, persons are threatened when the events that they seek to understand jeopardize their most central constructions of themselves, that is, when their experience of such events would require a major reconstruction of their self-image. In an elaboration of this concept, Krieger, Epting, and Leitner (20) have developed the concept of death threat. Death threat is defined as the reluctance of an individual to subsume his or her present "self" and "death" as elements under the same pole of a sample of constructs. Thus,

> It is assumed that the person who describes both himself and death with the same pole of a single construct dimension is organizing his world in such a way as to be able to see death as a personal reality. The person who places himself and death on opposite poles of a construct, however, would have to reorganize his system to construe self and death together. (20, p. 301)

In research on physicians, it has often been found that death threat is higher among members of the medical profession than among other professional groups (21). Because the elevated death threat appears at the time of application to medical school (7, 8), it has been argued that people choose the medical profession in an effort to work out their death-related concerns. Thus, the choice to work in the medical field may represent a defense against death for some physicians.

In Kelly's (19) terms it represents a hostile defense against death, in which hostility is understood as an attempt to prove a prediction that has already proved itself a failure. In other words, some physicians may be attracted to the profession in an effort to affirm their own immortality. When confronted repeatedly with patient death, however, it seems likely that highly threatened doctors would redouble their defenses against the reality of death. Here, physicians may adopt a hostile stance by retreating to technology, in which precision and control belies the randomness of death. The following excerpt from White (8) illustrates the operation of hostility as a means of coping with death threat.

> I bent every effort to make sure that at the moment of death my patient had a normal white count, hemoglobin, sodium, potassium, chloride, carbon dioxide, and in fact to make sure that everything I could measure was normal. Only in that way could I convince myself that I had tried, that I had done enough. My patients, when they died, were the least sick dead patients one could imagine. This was really a refusal to face the death of a patient and a retreat to scientism, to technology, and was a means of convincing myself that I was performing important work in preventing death. It convinced me, against the facts, that I retained control. (p. 828)

Other hostile means of coping with death threat might include losing oneself in professional responsibilities or trying to distract oneself in an effort to minimize the effect of patient's death on professional perfomance. In each case the physician attempts to prove, against reality, that the impact of the death was minimal.

For physicians with high death threat, then, particular coping mechanisms are predictable. Because death occasions massive personal reconstruction, the highly threatened physician chooses those mechanisms that help to avoid or deny the reality of patient death. Strategies such as avoiding emotional involvement and minimizing contact with the dying patient's relatives serve to insulate the physician from the reality of death. To the extent that they are effective, such strategies should prevent emotional turmoil. Somewhat paradoxically, high death threat may be associated with less visible emotional and psychophysiological symptomatology.

In contrast to death threat, death anxiety reflects the inability to understand or meaningfully construe death. Kelly (19) regards anxiety as an awareness "that the events with which one is confronted lie outside the range of convenience of one's construct system" (p. 495). In other words, anxiety occurs when an event cannot be understood meaningfully within the existing construct system.

The less meaningful an event, the lower its impact on the system as a whole. Thus, for highly anxious physicians, patient death may create relatively little personal distress because the event lies largely outside the range of convenience of the system. As a result, highly anxious physicians may be better able to distance themselves from the death and thereby minimize the effect on professional performance and psychophysiological functioning.

In sum, we would expect that physicians' personal relationships to death might carry implications for the way in which they deal with patient death. In particular, doctors characterized by high death threat would be expected to adopt coping strategies aimed at denial and avoidance. This is because these strategies prevent the awareness of the major personal reconstruction that death portends. Emotional withdrawal and getting lost in one's work are examples of such coping mechanisms. To the extent that they have some immediate functional value, we would expect physicians with high death threat to display less psychological and physiological turmoil than less threatened and less defended individuals.

High-death-anxiety physicians are characterized by systems that are not structured in such a way as to understand death meaningfully. The impact of a patient's death is therefore minimal, because loss carries few implications for the system as a whole.

Method

Subjects

A group of 25 pediatric residents (14 males, 11 females) involved in postgraduate training at a university teaching hospital were included in the study. Ages ranged from 24 to 37 years (mean age = 29 years; *SD* = 3.4 years). Subjects were sampled across training levels with 7 individuals designated as PL-1s (first-year postgraduate training), 8 as PL-2s (second-year postgraduate training), and 10 as PL-3s (third-year postgraduate training).

Instruments and Procedure

A self-administered three-part questionnaire was completed individually by each of the residents. Part 1 of the questionnaire requested demographic information. Subjects were asked to indicate their age, marital status, level of postgraduate training, previous death education, and religious preference.

Part 2 consisted of the Death Threat Index (20). The 40-item provided-construct form of the Threat Index (TIp 40) was used (see ref. 22 for reliability and validity information) with the modification introduced by Neimeyer (23). Subjects were instructed to rate "self" and "own death" along 40 standardized bipolar constructs. Each construct pole anchored the end of a 13-point Likert-type scale (e.g., predictable 6 5 4 3 2 1 0 1 2 3 4 5 6 random). Two scores were derived from the Threat Index.

Death threat was calculated in standard fashion by summing the number of times that the self and death elements were assigned to opposite poles of the constructs. The number of such "splits" is taken as an index of death threat because it indicates the amount of construct system reconstruction that would be required by the personal anticipation of one's own death. Threat scores could range from 0 to 40.

Death anxiety is viewed as the inability to construe death meaningfully. It was calculated by summing the absolute value of all ratings across the death element. The total of such "extremity" scores is taken to indicate how meaningfully one's own death is construed (22, 23). Higher extremity scores indicate greater meaningfulness and lower death anxiety. Lower extremity scores reflect lower meaningfulness and higher death anxiety. Scores could range from 0 to 240.

Part 3 of the questionnaire consisted of two brief vignettes, each depicting the circumstances surrounding a child's death in a hospital setting. The vignettes were designed to vary the physician's personal level of attachment to the patient by manipulating factors having a demonstrated impact on the physician's feelings (17). A sample of the low-attachment vignette follows:

> At 11:00 p.m. the ER called saying they had just received a call from the paramedics. A mother hand delivered a 1900 gram baby at home, and the baby was having trouble breathing. In spite of emergency measures by the paramedics, the baby was blue and had a low heart rate, but they were on their way to the hospital doing mouth to mouth resuscitation. It would take 20 minutes to get there. At 11:05 p.m. the resident from the emergency room called: "What should I do when the baby arrives in the ER? Should I try to fully resuscitate it, or should I stop all efforts at trying to save the baby? I know if the baby had been born in the hospital it might have lived but what about now? Won't it be badly brain damaged after all this time? I don't want to resuscitate a child who is severely damaged, but I don't want to stand by and do nothing either."
>
> For the next fifteen minutes the two of us paced the floors of the ER, anxiously awaiting the arrival of the baby, still not knowing exactly what we were going to do. Shortly the baby arrived and was extremely cyanotic, pale, bradycardic and having agonal respirations. I made the decision to let the baby die.

In the high-attachment vignette, the physician's length of acquaintance and degree of interaction with the patient were greater than in the low-attachment vignette. Each vignette was followed by 14 possible behavioral responses and 20 psychophysiological reactions (see Table 1) derived from the literature (24) and clinical experience. Subjects were instructed to imagine themselves as the attending physician in each of the vignettes and then to rate how typical each of the responses would be for themselves and for an ideal physician. Ratings were performed on a 5-point Likert-type scale ranging from 1, "very uncommon," to 5, "very common."

Finally, in order to obtain ratings of perceived effectiveness of coping with death concerns, the PL-3s were contacted 3 weeks after completion of the materials and asked to rate each of the residents according to "their effectiveness in helping patients and their families cope with death." These evaluations

TABLE 1   Physicians' Responses to Patient Death

Behavioral responses	Psychophysiologic responses
1. Talk with spouse/close friend	1. Appetite change
2. Lash out at others	2. Sleep pattern change
3. Seek physical exercise	3. Nightmares
4. Talk with peers	4. Body aches
5. Take alcohol/drugs	5. Energy loss
6. Cry	6. Recurring thoughts of dead infant
7. Seek professional help	7. Guilt
8. Blame self	8. Irritability
9. Blame others	9. Anger
10. Review medical records	10. Despair
11. Shake it off	11. Emptiness
12. Become involved in work	12. Poor concentration
13. Attend the funeral	13. Time disturbance
14. Remain unaffected by the death	14. Unreality
	15. Decreased interest in normal activities
	16. Feeling isolated
	17. Anxiety
	18. Worthlessness
	19. Shocked/numb
	20. Loss of interest in sex.

were conducted along a 5-point scale ranging from 5, "very effective," to 1, "very ineffective." A "not applicable" designation was permitted for any individual not known sufficiently to evaluate. PL-3s were chosen to perform the ratings because of their better familiarity with the group as a whole. Five PL-3s returned their assessments, and the degree of concordance between them was moderately high ($W = .86$).

Results

The data were compiled for two sets of analyses. The first addressed the relationship between death threat and the various coping strategies, psychophysiological responses, and ratings of perceived effectiveness. The second set of analyses concerned the relationship of death anxiety to those same variables. A Spearman correlation between death threat and death anxiety was calculated in order to determine the relationship between the variables. The magnitude of the coefficient ($r = .20$) indicated a low, though significant ($p \leqslant .05$), intercorrelation between threat and anxiety scores.

Death Threat

In order to examine the effects of death threat, the 25 subjects were rank ordered according to their Threat Index (TI) scores. A median split was then performed on the distribution, and the data from the centermost subject were discarded. The uppermost ($n = 12$; mean TI $= 30.75$, $SD = 4.80$) and lowermost ($n = 12$; mean TI $= 10.33$; $SD = 9.00$) halves of the distribution were designated as high and low death threat, respectively.

Data were then compiled in a $2 \times 2 \times 2$ mixed factorial design. The factors referred to the level of death threat (high or low), the attachment level of the vignette (high or low), and the target rated (the self or ideal physician). The three-way ANOVA was conducted on each of the 34 dependent variables (14 coping strategies and 20 psychophysiological responses).

Results revealed significant main effects for death threat along 11 of the dependent variables (see Table 2). When

TABLE 2 Means and Standard Deviations for Death Threat Main Effects (across Target and Attachment)

Response	High death threat		Low death threat	
	$\bar{X}$	*SD*	$\bar{X}$	*SD*
Talk with spouse	4.27	0.84	3.53	1.14
Review medical records	3.70	1.09	3.06	1.09
Shake it off	3.72	0.89	3.04	1.15
Become involved in work	3.40	0.89	2.79	1.14
Seek professional help	1.72	0.89	2.20	1.05
Attend the funeral	1.59	0.86	2.23	1.34
Appetite change	2.02	1.02	2.61	1.01
Sleep pattern change	1.80	0.72	2.34	1.12
Energy loss	2.13	0.89	2.57	1.22
Irritability	2.11	0.98	2.53	1.10
Poor concentration	2.08	0.90	2.51	1.13

residents with low death threat were compared to residents with high death threat, the highly threatened residents perceived themselves as more likely to talk with their spouses about the death, $F(1,86) = 11.07$, $p \leqslant .01$, meticulously review the patient's medical record for possible errors in medical management, $F(1,79) = 7.63$, $p \leqslant .01$, try to shake it off, $F(1,79) = 8.82$, $p \leqslant .01$, and become more involved in work, $F(1,79) = 7.10$, $p \leqslant .01$. It was also determined that highly threatened residents were less likely than their peers with low death threat to seek professional help, $F(1,79) = 5.22$, $p \leqslant .05$, and attend the patient's funeral, $F(1,79) = 7.98$, $p \leqslant .01$, as well as to experience such psychophysiological reactions as changes in appetite, $F(1,83) = 7.72$, $p \leqslant .01$, changes in sleep patterns, $F(1,84) = 7.35$, $p \leqslant .01$, loss of energy, $F(1,84) = 3.87$, $p \leqslant .05$, irritability, $F(1,84) = 4.01$, $p \leqslant .05$, and loss of concentration, $F(1,84) = 3.94$, $p \leqslant .05$.

Across levels of death interest, six main effects for target were also observed (see Table 3). Compared with themselves, residents perceived the ideal physician as more likely to seek professional help, $F(1,79) = 5.32$, $p \leqslant .05$, and review medical records, $F(1,79) = 4.81$, $p \leqslant .05$, but less likely to talk with their spouse, $F(1,79) = 3.96$, $p \leqslant .05$, or to experience nightmares, $F(1,84) = 5.66$, $p \leqslant .05$, recurring thoughts of the dead infant, $F(1,84) = 5.88$, $p \leqslant .05$, and guilt, $F(1,84) = 6.90$, $p \leqslant .01$.

TABLE 3 Means and Standard Deviations for Target Main Effects (across Death Threat and Attachment)

Response	Self		Ideal physician	
	$\bar{X}$	SD	$\bar{X}$	SD
Seek professional help	2.14	1.10	2.27	1.03
Review medical records	2.90	0.88	3.84	1.01
Talk with spouse	3.71	1.18	3.36	1.09
Nightmares	2.13	1.25	1.58	0.65
Recurring thoughts of dead infant	2.69	1.22	2.12	1.11
Guilt	3.04	1.22	2.37	1.17

A main effect for attachment level was observed for only one response. Residents were more likely to attend the patient's funeral, $F(1,79) = 4.05$, $p \leqslant .05$, under conditions of high attachment ($\bar{X} = 2.40$) than under conditions of low attachment ($\bar{X} = 1.90$). Attachment and threat levels also interacted significantly for blaming self, $F(1,79) = 5.35$, $p \leqslant .02$, and guilt, $F(1,84) = 4.24$, $p \leqslant .05$. The direction of the differences was such that highly threatened residents were more likely than low-threat residents to blame themselves under conditions of high attachment but not under conditions of low attachment. Under conditions of high but not low attachment, high-threat residents were more likely to blame themselves than low-threat residents. In regard to guilt, low-threat residents felt more guilty than high-threat residents under conditions of low attachment but not under conditions of high attachment. No three-way interaction was observed.

Lastly a Spearman correlation was calculated between TI scores and peer ratings of perceived coping effectiveness. The correlation coefficient ($r = .042$) indicated no significant relationship between death threat and perceived effectiveness in helping others cope with death as judged by peers.

Death Anxiety

In order to determine the effects of death anxiety (DA), the 25 subjects were rank ordered according to their DA scores. A median split was then performed on the distribution, and the data from the centermost subject were discarded. Because higher scores reflect lower death anxiety the uppermost ($n = 12$; mean DA $= 176.72$; $SD = 31.43$) and lowermost ($n = 12$; mean DA $= 80.63$; $SD = 36.12$) halves of the distribution were designated as low and high anxiety, respectively.

Data were then compiled in a 2 X 2 X 2 mixed factorial design. The factors referred to the level of death anxiety (high and low), the attachment level of the vignette (high and low), and the target rated (self or ideal physician). The three-way ANOVA was again performed on each of the 34 variables (14 coping strategies and 20 psychophysiological responses).

Results revealed main effects for death anxiety along eight

of the dependent variables (see Table 4). Compared with low-anxiety residents, high-anxiety subjects were more likely to take tranquilizers or alcohol in response to a patient's death, $F(1,79) = 3.85$, $p \leqslant .05$, try to shake it off, $F(1,79) = 4.64$, $p \leqslant .05$, and become more involved in their work, $F(1,79) = 14.41$, $p \leqslant .001$. High-anxiety residents were less likely than low-anxiety subjects to attend the patient's funeral, $F(1,79) = 7.50$, $p \leqslant .01$, or to experience changes in appetite, $F(1,83) = 6.05$, $p \leqslant .05$, changes in sleep patterns, $F(1,84) = 7.04$, $p \leqslant .01$, loss of energy, $F(1,84) = 5.31$, $p \leqslant .05$, and irritability, $F(1,84) = 3.93$, $p \leqslant .05$.

Main effects for target were also observed (see Table 5). Compared with themselves, residents perceived the ideal physician as more likely to seek professional help, $F(1,79) = 5.96$, $p \leqslant .01$, review the medical records, $F(1,79) = 4.87$, $p \leqslant .05$, and attend the funeral, $F(1,79) = 3.90$, $p \leqslant .05$, but less likely to experience nightmares, $F(1,84) = 4.94$, $p \leqslant .05$, recurring thoughts of the dead infant, $F(1,84) = 5.93$, $p \leqslant .05$, or guilt, $F(1,84) = 5.62$, $p \leqslant .05$.

Main effects for attachment level were observed for crying, $F(1,79) = 3.95$, $p \leqslant .05$, and attending the funeral, $F(1,79) = 4.40$, $p \leqslant .05$. Differences were such that residents were more likely to cry under conditions of high attachment $(\bar{X} = 2.90)$ than under conditions of low attachment $(\bar{X} = 2.18)$. They were

TABLE 4 Means and Standard Deviations for Death Anxiety Main Effects (across Target and Attachment)

Response	High death anxiety		Low death anxiety	
	$\bar{X}$	SD	$\bar{X}$	SD
Take alcohol/drugs	1.85	0.76	1.51	0.80
Shake it off	3.65	0.86	3.12	1.22
Become involved in work	3.57	0.71	2.72	1.19
Attend the funeral	1.52	0.75	2.17	1.35
Appetite change	2.04	1.01	2.59	1.05
Sleep pattern change	1.80	0.84	2.34	1.04
Energy loss	2.08	1.08	2.61	1.05
Irritability	2.13	0.86	2.57	1.21

TABLE 5 Means and Standard Deviations for Target Main Effects (across Death Anxiety and Attachment)

	Self		Ideal physician	
Response	$\bar{X}$	SD	$\bar{X}$	SD
Seek professional help	1.52	0.74	2.05	0.91
Review medical records	2.90	0.88	3.84	1.01
Attend the funeral	1.28	0.46	1.78	0.91
Nightmares	1.77	0.92	1.47	0.51
Recurring thoughts of dead infant	2.54	1.10	1.86	0.75
Guilt	2.68	0.77	2.17	0.77

also more likely to attend the funeral under conditions of high attachment ($\bar{X} = 1.30$) than under conditions of low attachment ($\bar{X} = 1.27$). No significant interactions were observed between attachment level and death anxiety, nor was the three-way interaction significant.

Lastly, a Spearman correlation was computed between DA scores and peer ratings of coping effectiveness. Because higher DA is associated with lower scores, the correlation of $- .46$ ($p \leqslant .001$) indicated that higher death anxiety is related to higher peer ratings of perceived effectiveness in helping others cope with patient death.

Discussion

The results of this exploratory study help clarify the relationship between physician's personal orientations toward death and the use of particular strategies for coping with patient loss. In general, death orientation appears to predict physician response.

Death Threat

High-death-threat orientations were related to denial and avoidance strategies. In response to patient death, highly threatened residents perceived themselves as more likely to reinvolve themselves in work, review the patient's records, and attempt to shake it off in an effort to minimize the impact of a patient's death on other work. These results imply an avoidance or denial orientation, an interpretation supported by the finding that more threatened residents were also less likely to seek professional help or to attend the patient's funeral. These results were qualified by the finding that highly threatened residents viewed themselves as more likely to talk with their spouses about the death. This may indicate a receptivity on the part of the highly threatened residents to available personal support systems.

Despite this hopeful sign, it seems likely that the general image of the physician obstructs support seeking within the medical context. Across levels of death threat, residents seemed to share an image of the ideal physician as a somewhat impervious and omnipotent figure. Compared with themselves, residents viewed the ideal physician as less likely to talk with a spouse or to experience nightmares, guilt, or recurrent thoughts of the dead patient. Admitting human responsiveness appears tantamount to admitting professional inferiority. It seems likely that this conceptualization of the ideal physician covertly reinforces defensive and avoidance strategies and thereby obstructs effective responses.

It is interesting to note, however, that death threat did not correlate significantly with perceived counseling effectiveness as judged by peer ratings. This may indicate the actual insignificant covariation of these variables, or it may reflect the inability of outside persons to assess the effectiveness of peers in facilitating the grieving of the patient's family. It is also possible that the insignificant relationship between death threat and perceived effectiveness reflects a genuine ambivalence within the medical profession. On the one hand, some residents may see the avoidance and denial strategies as cold, insensitive, and destructive. On the other hand, these strategies operate to keep the physician objective, aloof, and detached in a way that approximates perceptions of the ideal physician. Peer ratings may reflect this ambivalence by giving highly threatened persons both lower and higher ratings of effectiveness compared with low-threat residents. This would have the effect of reducing the magnitude of the correlation.

Regardless of its relationship to perceived effectiveness, the functional value of such coping procedures merits mention. From a construct theory viewpoint, highly death-threatened physicians have not organized their understandings in such a way as to be able to anticipate the personal reality of death. To do so would require a major revision of their self-constructions. Therefore, when confronted with death they tend to adopt protective strategies to help insulate themselves from its reality. These coping mechanisms may vary from simple avoidance tactics, such as avoiding the funeral, to more actively "hostile" strategies, such as getting reinvolved in work as a distraction. The function of such hostile approaches is to prove that the death has had a minimal personal impact. By shaking it off or becoming reinvolved in work, the highly threatened physician demonstrates the need to actively deny the personal impact of patient loss. Avoidance and denial strategies, to the extent that they are effective, should help insulate and protect the physician from emotional turmoil. The findings that high-death-threat residents were less likely than low-death-threat residents to experience sleep changes, irritability, loss of energy, and lapses of concentration, supports this interpretation.

Because they may provide short-term protection, these strategies are retained and perhaps fortified over time. From the standpoint of intervention, removing these defenses may necessitate providing alternative means of coping. The highly threatened physician needs these avoidance and denial strategies to prevent the immobilization that might otherwise follow from repeated confrontation with death. Ideally, intervention should focus on means of helping the high-death-threat physician reconstrue death in such a way as to recognize its personal reality; to realize its compatability with aspects of the self. In this regard, perhaps a reconstruction in professional identity from that of a healer to a helper would be useful. The physician's self-image as a healer necessarily pits him or her against death as the enemy. The two are difficult to reconcile within a single system. According to this view, threat is in part compelled by the professional image. If the image were to be construed as that of a helper, the self and death would no longer, of necessity, be antithetical. As White (8) notes:

> With this new set of values, success can be an internal thing, measured by one's feeling that he has tried, with all his skills, and technique and love, to help a patient through a trying time. If the patient improves and may live longer, this is in part a success and in part a bonus; if the patient has worsened or died, this may still be a success, although a sad one. Under these new values, death becomes a reality and not a defeat. (p. 830)

One way to effect such a change could be through educational interventions. Death education courses that focus on one's personal relationship to death may be especially effective in reducing death threat. Tobacyk and Eckstein (25) have compared the threat scores of 30 students in a death education course with scores derived from a comparable control group. Their results indicated that the experimental group showed lower levels of death threat before and after the death education course. Controlling for pretest differences, however, the death education course resulted in a significantly greater decrease in death threat than the change that occurred in the control group. This finding is supported by other research (26) that suggests that death threat can be modified through educational interventions.

Death Anxiety

Personal construct theory (20) clearly distinguishes between threat and anxiety. In contrast to threat, anxiety represents an underdimensionalized or inadequate understanding of the experience one wishes to interpret. Rather than fearing the fundamental reconstruction of the self that threat would imply, the highly anxious person cannot quite comprehend or make sense of the event. Death is not fully meaningful. Accordingly, the high-death-anxiety physician should show a less pronounced reaction to patient death.

Consistent with this reasoning, high-anxiety residents saw themselves as less affected by a patient's death than did low-anxiety residents. Low-anxiety residents perceived themselves as experiencing greater change in appetite and sleep patterns and suffering greater irritability and energy loss. Because the death was more meaningful for them, the low-anxiety residents also were more likely to attend the patient's funeral. They viewed themselves as less likely, however, to become more involved with their work, to take alcohol or drugs, or to simply shake it off.

By rendering the loss more meaningful, the impact of the death is registered more clearly in low-anxiety residents. The psychophysiological symptoms may not only be produced by, but may themselves reinforce, the salience of the death. Rather than moderating the personal impact of patient death on low-anxiety physicians, intervention might better be aimed at helping the individual to anticipate and accept the loss.

The useful role of anticipatory grieving is already well documented (27). By anticipating the death, the individual begins to deal with the issues of loss prior to the death and thereby elaborates a system of understanding to rely on when the death actually occurs. The physician is less affected at the time of death, because the loss has been anticipated and dealt with gradually during the time preceding the death.

In addition to anticipation, efforts to accept the loss and its impact may be helpful. Across levels of anxiety there appeared to be a general belief that the ideal physician should remain relatively unaffected by patient death. In particular, they were perceived as experiencing fewer nightmares, less guilt, and less preoccupation with thoughts of the dead infant. It seems likely that these expectations concerning the ideal responses themselves exacerbate anxiety. Rather than experiencing their psychophysiological reactions as "part of what it means to be human," they are interpreted as liabilities to professional competence. This is consistent with the finding that those residents who were perceived as being more effective in helping others cope with loss were those for whom patient death was less meaningful. This belief that physicians are more effective to the extent that they are more detached persists despite evidence to the contrary (15, 16). Strategies aimed at legitimizing both the experience and the expression of emotion may be useful interventions in this regard.

Finally, methods that would help infuse death with either personal or professional meaning could help alleviate death anxiety. Strategies such as follow-up contact with the family, staff ventilation and support sessions, and case review meetings may assist the physician in experiencing the loss within a supportive professional context.

Summary

The results of this exploratory study help clarify the relationship between personal death orientation and responses to patient death. High death threat was related to the use of avoidance and denial strategies. These methods help the individual defend against the need to massively revise the construct system to include death as a personal reality. Their functional value was seen in the lower emotional turmoil associated with high death threat. Rather than tearing down these defenses, intervention might aim at helping high-threat personnel to reconstrue their identities in such a way as to include death as a part of that image.

The results concerning death anxiety closely resembled those of death threat. In contrast to high-death-anxiety residents, low-anxiety individuals were more affected by patient loss. Perhaps because the death was more meaningful for them, they showed greater vulnerability to emotional impact as indicated by the higher incidence of psychophysiological reactions. Intervention aimed at anticipating and accepting patient death and its emotional impact might be useful for such physicians.

Although suggestive, these findings are limited by the number of possibly interdependent variables examined, as well as by the nature of the design. The present findings failed to adequately distinguish between the effects of death threat and death anxiety, in part because small sample size prevented the use of a more powerful between-subjects design. Such a method would involve assigning each subject to only one cell of a 2 X 2 matrix defined by levels of death threat and death anxiety (high threat/high anxiety; high threat/low anxiety; low threat/high anxiety; low threat/low anxiety). This design would define more precisely the effects of these variables on reactions to patient death. If further work supports the current suggestion that death orientations predict particular coping responses and reflect specific psychological needs, then work in this area could profit by considering the physician's personal relationship to death. Research could address the impact of various interventions on individuals who differ in their personal death orientations. Experiential interventions aimed at reconstruing the self-image, didactic presentations aimed at increasing conceptual understanding, and skill-based programs aimed at improving communication and coping may show markedly different effects on physicians of different death orientations. By determining such differences, work can advance toward developing personalized intervention based on the unique needs of the individual.

References

1. Barton, D. An approach to caring for dying persons. In D. Barton (Ed.), *Dying and death: A clinical guide for caregivers*. Baltimore: Williams and Wilkins, 1977.
2. Knapp, R. J., & Peppers, L. G. Doctor-patient relationships in fetal/infant death encounters. *Journal of Medical Education*, 1979, *54*, 775–780.
3. Rothenberg, M. B. Reactions of those who treat children with cancer. *Pediatrics*, 1967, *40*, 507–519.
4. Shanfield, S. B. *Professionalism in medical students and residents of issues concerning illness and death*. Unpublished manuscript, University of Arizona, 1979.
5. Barton, D. The need for continuing instruction on death and dying in the medical curriculum. *Journal of Medical Education*, 1972, *47*, 169–175.
6. Easson, W. M. The family of the dying child. *Pediatric Clinics of North America*, 1972, *19*, 1157–1165.
7. Wahl, C. W. The physicians' treatment of the dying patient. *Annals of the New York Academy of Science*, 1969, *164*, 759–766.
8. White, L. P. The self-image of the physician and the care of dying patients. *Annals of the New York Academy of Science*, 1969, *164*, 822–831.
9. Dickinson, G. E. Death education in U.S. medical schools. *Journal of Medical Education*, 1976, *51*, 134–136.

10. Shoenberg, B., & Carr, A. C. Educating the health professional in the psychosocial care of the terminally ill. In B. Schoenberg, A. C. Carr, D. Peretz, & A. H. Kutscher (Eds.), *Psychosocial aspects of terminal care.* New York: Columbia University Press, 1972.
11. Menzies, I. E. A case study in the function of social systems as a defense against anxiety: A report of a study of the nursing service of a general hospital. *Human Relations,* 1960, *13,* 95–121.
12. Quint, J. Awareness of death and the nurse's composure. *Nursing Research,* 1966, *15,* 449–455.
13. Quint, J. *The nurse and the dying patient.* New York: Macmillan, 1967.
14. Sobel, D. E. Personalization on the coronary care unit. *American Journal of Nursing,* 1969, *69,* 1439–1442.
15. Mauksch, H. O. The organizational context of dying. In E. Kübler-Ross (Ed.), *Death: The final stage of growth.* Englewood Cliffs: Prentice-Hall, 1975.
16. Peppers, L. G., & Knapp, R. J. Maternal reactions to involuntary fetal/infant death. *Psychiatry,* 1980, *43,* 155–159.
17. Sahler, O. J. Z., McAnasfrey, E. R., & Friedman, S. B. Factors influencing pediatric interns' relationships with dying children and their parents. *Pediatrics,* 1981, *67,* 207–216.
18. Schowalter, J. E. The reactions of caregivers dealing with fatally children and their families. In O. J. Z. Sahler (Ed.), *The child and death.* St. Louis: C. V. Mosby, 1978.
19. Kelly, G. A. *The psychology of personal constructs* (2 vols). New York: Norton, 1955.
20. Kreiger, S. R. L., Epting, F. R., & Leitner, L. M. Personal constructs, threat, and attitudes toward death. *Omega,* 1974, *5,* 299–310.
21. Feifel, H. The function of attitudes toward death. *Group for the Advancement of Psychiatry, Symposium,* 1965, *5,* 633–641.
22. Rigdon, M. A., Epting, F. R., Neimeyer, R. A., & Krieger, S. R. The threat index: A research report. *Death Education,* 1979, *3,* 245–270.
23. Neimeyer, R. A. Death anxiety and the threat index: An addendum. *Death Education,* 1978, *1,* 464–467.
24. Kirkley-Best, E. Grief in response to prenatal loss: An argument for the earliest maternal attachment. *Dissertation Abstracts International.* In press.
25. Tobacyk, J., & Eckstein, D. Death threat and death concerns in the college student. *Omega,* 1980–1981, *11,* 139–155.
26. Miles, M. S. The effects of a course on death and grief on nurses' attitudes toward dying patients and death. *Death Education,* 1980, *4,* 245–260.
27. Stillion, J., and Wass, H. Children and death. In H. Wass (Ed.), *Dying: Facing the facts.* Washington: Hemisphere, 1979.
28. Behnke, M., Neimeyer, G. J., Reiss, J., & Setzer, E. S. Psychophysiologic and behavioral effects of patient death on pediatric houseofficers. *Pediatric Research,* 1982, *16,* pt. 2, 183A.

∞∞

DEATH EDUCATION

∞∞

PERSONAL CONSTRUCT PSYCHOLOGY: BROADENING DEATH RESEARCH AND DEATH EDUCATION

W. G. WARREN

University of Newcastle, New South Wales

This paper is concerned with some theoretical aspects of death education and how these are illuminated and accommodated by the perspective of personal construct psychology. As death education emerged essentially from a psychological interest in death, rather than, say, a philosophical, sociological, or, indeed, educational interest, matters long under discussion by philosophers and theorists of education have generally been passed over. Equally, matters that have been subjected to significant criticism in philosophy of education emerge in positive terms, or terms of "advocacy," in the death education literature. For example, there is little concern for the nature of education or for what concept of education is embedded in the very expression "death education"; and there are papers calling for a "taxonomic approach" (1) or for a statement of "behavioral objectives" (2) in the face of some significant criticisms of these notions (e.g., 3, 4). It is therefore of value to consider a number of theoretical aspects and this paper addresses four: the nature of education, the "type" of psychology that informs death education, alternative theoretical models, and the manner in which personal construct psychology provides a more useful and perhaps timely perspective.

Approaches to Education

A perennial question that has plagued reflective educationists is just what education "is"; and an examination of the literature since the classical Greeks discloses numerous definitions, conceptions, and criteria of the activity labelled "education." This question may in fact be too difficult to answer, or it may be inappropriate, an example of an "essentialist methodology" that according to Karl Popper retards the social sciences (5). Without engaging this last argument, however, a useful response to the question bypasses the various specific definitions to summarize them into two or three types of approach to (or construals of) what education is. Fortunately for present purposes this response has been documented in at least two papers that can be outlined to indicate the general idea that is to be made use of here: Richard Brumbough's "Education and Reality: Two Revolutions" (6), and W. V. Doniela's "The University: Sophistic or Socratic?" (7).

Brumbough's analysis of education refers to three competing conceptions that subsume the various definitions: education as fantasy, education as simple technology, education as understanding. Doniela's discussion identifies a Sophistic approach to education (which parallels Brumbough's fantasy and, more clearly, his technology) and a Socratic approach (which parallels Brumbough's understanding). The idea of education as fantasy is now outmoded and referred essentially to the education that provided the young with "guidance by good example" and "a book" (Homer, the Bible) on the belief that certain attitudes, habits of mind, and behavior would develop. Except for rare cases of extreme religious cults or moral positions this is not a particularly useful notion for analyzing contemporary education, but the other two are.

Brumbough's wider thesis is that what is required in education is a major revolution in the way we see, regard, or construe the activity and that this will occur only if there is a prior or concurrent revolution in the way we view "reality." This last involved a shift from a "metaphysic of limitation" to a "metaphysic of plenitude," from seeing things in terms of their "sameness," "form," or as being "of a type" to seeing them in terms of their difference from type when taken individually, their complexity, and their aesthetic quality.

This wider thesis is quite compatible with personal construct psychology, and in turn both are consistent with a number of radical educational theorists. Paulo Freire, for example, writes of how education is never a neutral act and how one's "political background choice" will reflect one's educational practices. In our terms, if a construction system revolves around constructs of human nature as essentially bad or evil and people needing to be guided and controlled for their own sake, conservative or even authoritarian educational practices might be seen to be essential and more democratic or radical alternatives not countenanced. Equally, in death education a teacher's whole orientation to death and to life will reflect on whether and how death education is advocated and conducted.

Aside from Brumbough's wider thesis, however, this characterization of attitudes to that activity called "education" is of value in clarifying what the expression "death education" does, could, or has come to, mean. Is death education involved with a concept of education as mere technology, knowledge for its instrumental value ("getting on," solving practical problems, getting a job, being able to live a comfortable life), or is it more related to education concerned with knowledge for its own sake—in Doniela's (7) terms motivated by "a sense of wonder . . . and an interest in trying to understand things as they are or how they work regardless of whether such knowledge can be made use of?"

Of course, the dichotomy between education as mere technology and education as understanding, like all dichotomies, is problematic. Taken as devices, however, methodological tools for clearing the ground, or ideal types to which practices, attitudes, or beliefs can be seen to approximate, they provide a useful way of ordering a dicussion. It is in this sense that they are taken here, and the suggestion is that death education, for the most part, has to be located at the technology or Sophistic or instrumental end of a continuum formed by treating the two positions as opposite ends. This is apparent, for example, from both the conception of education as a transmission of knowledge (Freire's "banking concept" of education) that underpins death education, from the rejection of radical positions on death, and indeed from the fact of our limited understanding of death in life.

The assertion that death education is essentially instrumental in orientation has been discussed elsewhere (8) but needs to be given a brief sketch here. Take, for example, an early paper that outlined the scope of death education and in which a definition and a set of goals were given (9). The definition was clearly in terms of transmission of knowledge: death education "transmits to individuals and society valid death-related knowledge" (9); and the goals emphasized "other-determined" aspects: anxiety reduction (anxiety increase might be equally as valid, as will be indicated), appropriate or valid death orientations (the problems of "who determines?" and "on what criteria?" remain), rational discussion (can we rationally discuss death?; is rage and anger not permitted?). In addition, the problems of "knowledge of death" and "who are the experts?" loom large, as does the consequent institutionalization that other radicals like Illich and Reimer suggest flows from conservative construals of what education is really about.

Again, the perspective provided by existentialism is basically ignored in death education, suggesting again how the general orientation is conservative. An examination of the existentialist position, by no means a uniform position, indicates that death education pursued along lines consistent with it would be a potentially radical exercise both individually and socially. This alternative is taken up later and has also been discussed more fully in a previous paper (8). What is significant at this point, however, is to note a further way in which death education can be characterized as falling more to the technology than to the understanding end of the continuum. This, of course, is not meant to reflect on proponents who construe the value of death education in instrumental terms, terms that are as legitimate as any other. What could be the case, however, is that such construal is not conscious, but rather reflects the general ethos in the major underpinning of death education: psychology itself and, in turn, in educational psychology and educational thought generally. Some attention to this ethos is of value.

Death Research and Traditional Psychology

To understand what has happened in psychology and in education over the last century or so, an excursion into developments in philosophy is of value.

Perhaps the most significant single development in philosophy since the mid-1950s has been in philosophy of science. Two general, related lines of development can in fact be discerned. On one hand has been a concern to examine science internally, to reconsider old notions that science was explanation, prediction, and control and to analyze different models, and indeed to accept that models play a very significant role in the activity of science as such. The second line of development attacked the asocial and apolitical pretensions of science and argued, most forcefully in Paul Feyerabend, that science was significantly a social activity. This second line argues that what was accepted as "scientific" and thus as "knowledge" was significantly influenced, if not determined, by extrascientific sources, and moreover such forces determined that only science could provide knowledge.

What is in fact represented in these two general lines of development is a significant attack on the dominance of positivism in science, positivism defined in terms of two central notions: the idea that science has its basis in the certainty of its observations and the idea that one can deduce from these observations. In psychology, moreover, positivism means that the human must be seen as continuous with the nonhuman, and it finds its expression in behaviorism, information processing theory, cybernetics, and more generally in empirical and experimental methodology that makes inferential judgments in disregard of the problems of induction and resorts to reductions.

The next step in these matters is in process of its own development at this time and a strong claim is made by realism. Roy Bhaskar in England (10) and Cliff Hooker in North America (11) have both made strong cases for a realist position in science, a position that comes down relatively more strongly on the role of the activity of science qua science. By contrast, Marxist epistemologies give relatively greater significance to the social dimensions and the way in which power elites structure the world such that "knowledge" is really "desirable" or "acceptable" knowledge. A forceful statement of this last position, including an indication of how it occurs through schooling, is given by Kevin Harris, the title of whose book carries the message here: *Education and Knowledge: The Structured Misrepresentation of Reality* (12).

A wave of criticism is now apparent, and it has come significantly from the philosophers of science and the philosophers of society who turned to certain forces and unexamined assumptions that had outlawed certain modes of proceeding and raised science, as conceived by positivism, to pride of place. In psychology, the hope of a scientific psychology was replaced by the fact of a scientific psychology, and variety in approaches to examining human behaving was substituted by a single, acceptable approach ("human behaving" is Sigmund Koch's phrase; see 13). In education, "relevance" became a slogan, (relevance to a given scheme of social arrangements that thus went unquestioned) and gadgets, technology, and technological mentality (focused on organization, management, and efficiency) came to dominate.

Now, from these observations it is not difficult to understand how death education emerges as instrumental in orientation and how psychology itself proceeds in relation to death. Thus, one major focus has been the assessment, usually quantitative, of death orientation. This has resulted in numerous scales focused on one or other of a number of not always clearly defined or differentiated concepts. For the most part the scales that developed were interesting but of doubtful validity and sometimes trivial when placed against the domain they were supposed to address. When used in "before and after" models with a death education course representing an intervening variable, these scales often showed mixed or unexpected results that probably indicated their relative coarseness in connection with a phenomenon that is exceedingly complex. Again, some research has focussed on comparing this group with that group—for example, the death involved with those at a greater distance—to indicate that, rather than how or why, death fear, anxiety, acceptance, or concern differ between groups. Sometimes this research indicates significant quantitative differences and sometimes there are differences within a group: Livingston and Zimet (14), for example, found different medical specialists-in-training expressing different levels of anxiety.

This last type of approach with its long history and good pedigree in psychology might be of interest and value, but it generates many problems. If, in general, psychiatrists are more death anxious than pediatricians, we cannot assume that this particular psychiatrist is more death anxious than this particular pediatrician. That, of course, is obvious and usually granted; but more important we cannot assume that either "death" or "anxiety" mean the same thing to each person. For one person death and anxiety might be abstractions that the work of Heidegger illuminates; for another a sense of deep yearning for a lost loved one might be signified by both of these same words. In education that movement of the early part of this century called progressivism generated a notion of education as a science and the cult of management and efficiency in education. Thus, neat, standardized tests emerged, ostensibly to help answer neutral questions but in reality serving particular interests with particular construals of what education was about. In this way psychology itself is subverted and in turn predetermines the way in which questions are asked and answered. Traditional psychology might be at best irrelevant, at worst mischievious, in education.

What is observed then is psychology being turned to yet another area of human behaving (an area that is perhaps the most complex, with the greatest number of links to other social and individual factors, and yet remains mysterious) and adopting the same methods as have been adopted historically for about the last century, methods that are taken over relatively uncritically from the physical sciences and that in recent years have come under some significant criticism. The extent of the way in which psychology is locked into certain ways of proceeding and how this penetrates death education emerges again in a consideration of other ways in which death education might be regarded.

Alternative Postures towards Death and Death Education

A major alternative from which death education might be approached has been noted: the perspective, or, better, perspectives, provided by existentialism. If one substituted the goal of anxiety reduction, proposed in most concepts of death education, for that of anxiety increase one might approach a position

that the existentialist would applaud. Of course, different exis-
tentialists might take different attitudes. Sartre, for example,
who accords death relatively little importance, might want death
seen as a simple background factor in our lives, a factor we
should note and recognize to be sure, but otherwise something
that cannot enter into that choosing by or through which we
achieve authenticity. By contrast, Heidegger might see death
education as the vital element in the preparation for and living
of one's life: standing before the nothingness of our own
personal death and tolerating the dread confers a sense of
wholeness or totality and gives one the sense of individuality.
For Heidegger, too, the group, the "they," is the enemy who
attempt to allay fears and try to seduce one away from the
consciousness of personal mortality by encouraging a concern
for things in the world: commodities, cares, possessions.

What emerges from this major alternative posture from the
standpoint of Heidegger is a concept of death education
approaching the understanding or Socratic end of our continuum. For Heidegger we must get above the conforming
influences of the group and confront the fundamental question
of why there is Being rather than non-Being. In posing this
question and confronting one's own mortality consciously and
constantly keeping this in the forefront of consciousness, we
achieve the most fundamental understanding, which understanding has the additional social consequences of significantly and
critically examining the given situation. This indeed is what
Socrates preached, and in fact that critical exercise led to his
death on the intervention of the protecters of the given scheme
of things.

Sartre's position, on the other hand, approaches from a
different angle another alternative attitude to death education:
that of traditional philosophy. Since Socrates himself at least
death was a matter of little importance, to be regarded with
indifference. Indeed, in the *Apology* Socrates asks whether in
fact death might be a good thing—a sleep that is undisturbed or
a chance to meet and talk to all of the great people who have
gone on before us. Equally, Spinoza was led to advise that the
wise man thought of life not of death, and Choron (15)
indicates, summarizing these and other attitudes, that when one

considers western thought on death the question is not how different thinkers treat the topic but whether it is treated at all. Clearly then an attitude of indifference to death has been the main western stance, and although Sartre's position does not suggest the fact of death be denied it does suggest that other things are important. From these perspectives some puzzlement might be expected that death education emerges at all. More positively perhaps, there might be a concern to think carefully about the desirabilities and possibilities of death education lest a relatively insignificant fact of life be inflated to a prominence it did not deserve. Yet, again, it may be this very indifference that generates a need for death education in societies now removed and different from those that generated the attitude in indifference.

These last suggestions are beyond the scope of present interests, but they do indicate something of the complexity of standpoints that one might take in relation to death education. Moreover, this sketch of the existentialist positions enlarges previous comments to indicate further how death education, as it has emerged and from a psychological perspective that is itself sociohistorically bound, might be locked into a particular mode that is limited and limiting.

Personal Construct Psychology, Death and Death Education

Personal construct psychology provides an approach to death research and death education that avoids the problems now being pointed up for positivist-empiricist-dominated psychology and allows to be captured something of the complexity in the way individuals deal with the phenomenon of death. In general terms, and despite a rather casual attempt in Kelly's original formulation to relate the theory to the dominant empiricist approach, personal construct psychology provides rather a phenomenological perspective. Phenomenology is, of course, a notoriously difficult position to pin down, but in general terms it represents a reaction to the reductionism of positivism, a rejection of explanatory hypotheses, and an attempt to recapture the qualitative richness of experiences and focus the meaning given to experience, situations, or events. The specific directions in which personal construct psychology might take death research are quite open—indeed, as this last methodology encourages—and this is well illustrated in the present volume and in other published work (e.g., 16-18). In addition, it is worth noting that personal construct psychology provides a position that might form part of a realist position being developed against positivism, in that in this psychology the individual is accorded a creative, active role in ascribing a meaning to that "outside world" accepted by the realist as object of study. Equally, personal construct theory is not at variance with that strand of reaction to positivism that emphasizes the social dimension of knowledge (significantly the Marxist reaction): personal construct theory emphasizes the way we operate with constructs and the role of "reality" in thier formulation and operation, not this or that origin of them—whether their origin is in child-rearing practices or pressures of class, sex, or race is not central to, though perhaps explicable in terms of, this theory. In fact Louis Althusser, when he wrote epistemoloy, emphasized that the ultimate locus of hegemony is in a cognitive structure transmitted by a system and this is accommodated by a notion of a shared construct system (sociality corollary).

There is a final point of interest concerning the relationship of personal construct psychology to that movement against positivism that came from psychologists themselves: radical psychology. This was a reaction to the way in which psychology both regarded (construed as object) and treated (construed as being in need of "cure") the person. Four strands in fact merged into this reaction: existentialism, Marxism, consideration of race and of sex; and it was consequently a confused reaction, but one that uncovered some of the consequences of the dominance of positivist-empiricist approaches in psychology and potentially taught a great deal. Now, it is clear that personal construct psychology escapes the thrust of the reaction and emerges as a position that did not in the first place make these errors in regarding and treating the person. Personal construct psychology has as its model "man the scientist-psychologist," there is an acceptance that values are implicit and inescapable in psychological method and theory, and there is the insistence on liberating the person, including psychologists themselves, from restrictive constructs of their, and the, world. The charges brought by radical psychology are not well founded here. Personal construct psychology, then, offers a radically different perspective for death research, one with a sound tradition that has not succumbed to the temptations of the dominant mode of psychology that is now under so much and varied attack.

What of death education? A number of specific aspects emerge in relation to personal construct psychology and death education. A first point is that personal construct psychology avoids a notion that educational goals or objectives, and common concepts like death anxiety or fear, must be imposed or pressed onto programs and people. As has been indicated elsewhere (18) a more useful strategy to that of simply imposing a notion of "death anxiety decrease" on persons in courses—presuming already that they are death anxious—might be to determine just what meanings do attach to death for a particular person, how "functional" or comfortable these leave the person, and then decide on whether and how a death education program might proceed. This is something of a "methodological" contribution perhaps, but more generally such an approach could form the very basis of a course and become an organizing principle of a curriculum.

A second contribution of personal construct psychology is more theoretical and allows a recapture of the concept of education as understanding. Few phenomena invite the puzzlement, awe, and deep personal questioning as does the fact of death in our lives. This very motivation of questioning underpins the search for understanding and meaning, and personal construct psychology is well placed, both theoretically and in terms of its methodology, for providing the basis of an approach to death education sketched previously and labeled "education as understanding." Again, this is not to deny the place of instrumental approaches; but it does allow a recognition of the manner in which the instrumental has come to dominate in advanced technological societies. It allows also the preservation of an equally important alternative (and perhaps antidote) that can be swamped by the more expansionist instrumental approach and its seductive appeal to "relevance."

Arising from this last point is a third: the manner in which the area of death education might be rescued from approaches that are "scientific" and replaced as a "humanity." Tests and measures using imposed concepts, technical gadgetry, and even contrived experiential situations (however well-intentioned and properly conducted) can generate superficial, passing sensations that trivialize a very complex dimension of human life. There is evidence and much critical literature in education that indicates how the "cult of efficiency" overarches educational thinking and manifests in notions like objectives, accountability, and effectiveness that may well be appropriate to a field of training but have limited application to that of education. By its very orientation, its way of regarding and treating people, personal construct psychology avoids these excesses and this problem.

Related to the humanizing aspect is the individualizing aspect of personal construct psychology for death education. As has been shown elsewhere (18) individuals at the same "distance" from death have quite different patterns of meaning in relation to death. An approach that allows these structures of meaning to be derived with an individual preserves death education at the level of the individual. It also provides the basis for individualized, and thereby personalized and humanized, education.

Finally, personal construct psychology approaches are timely. Death education is a relatively recent phenomenon, and it is apparent that the directions taken to date reflect origins in a particular dominant mode of psychology. As this mode is under significant and justified attack, personal construct approaches can serve as a counter to that dominant mode. In this way it serves a useful critical function, much lacking in educational discourse, and thereby again preserves the proper questioning approach that is a feature of the notion of education as understanding.

There is a chance, then, to recognize and counter Hardison's assessment in his lament for the humanities in American education (19), and there could be few better phenomena in life in connection with which to correct the error of our ways than that of death:

the short-term signs point toward vocationalism, accountability, and the rise of gadgetry in public education . . . . The point is that if the concept of education represented by Summerhill is even partially valid, we are moving in the wrong direction. We are moving in the wrong direction in terms of our present responsibilities and we are moving in the wrong direction in terms of our responsibilities to the future. (p. 109)

Conclusion

Personal construct psychology is well placed to provide an approach to one of the most complex aspects of human life: our reaction to the phenomenon of death. It is hoped that this paper indicates how personal construct psychology in breaking with the positivist-empiricist tradition widens the scope of death education at the same time as it allows accommodation of a broader spectrum of thought on death, avoids imposition of other-determined goals and standards, and allows death education as a concept to be seen as noninstrumental, noninterest serving, and properly a "humanity."

References

1. Stillion, J. M. Rediscovering the taxonomies: A structural framework of death education courses. *Death Education,* 1979, *3,* 157–164.
2. Crase, D. The need to assess the impact of death education. *Death Education,* 1978, *1,* 423–431.
3. Atkin, J. M. Behavioral objectives in curriculum design: A cautionary note. In J. R. Martin (Ed.), *Readings in the philosophy of education: A study of curriculum.* Boston: Allyn and Bacon, Inc., 1970.
4. Holly, D. *Society schools and humanity.* Granada Publishing Co. (Paladin), 1971.
5. Popper, K. *The open society and its enemies.* London: Routledge and Kegan Paul, 1945.
6. Brumbough, R. Education and reality: Two revolutions. *Thought,* 1973, *48,* 5–18.
7. Doniela, W. V. The university: Sophistic or socratic? *Dialectic* (University of Newcastle, Australia) 1972, *7,* 34–45.
8. Warren, W. G. Death education: An outline and some critical observations. *British Journal of Educational Studies,* 1981, *29,* 29–41.

9. Leviton, D. The scope of death education. *Death Education*, 1977, *1*, 41-56.
10. Bhaskar, R. *A realist theory of science.* Leeds: Leeds Books Ltd., 1975.
11. Hooker, C. A. Philosophy and meta-philosophy of science: Empiricism, Popperianism and realism. *Synthese*, 1975, *32*, 177-231.
12. Harris, K., Education and knowledge: The structured misrepresentation of reality. London: Routledge and Kegan Paul, 1979.
13. Koch, S. The image of man in encounter group. *American Scholar*, 1973, 636-652.
14. Livingston, P. B., & Zimet, C. N. Death anxiety, authoritarianism and choice of specialty in medical students. *Journal of Nervous and Mental Disease*, 1965, *140*, 222-230.
15. Choron, J. *Death and western thought.* New York: Collier, 1963.
16. Krieger, S. R., Epting, F. R., & Leitner, L. M., Personal constructs, threat and attitudes toward death. *Omega*, 1974, *5*, 299-310.
17. Rigdon, M. A., Epting, F. R., Neimeyer, R., & Krieger, S. R. The Threat Index: A research report. *Death Education*, 1979, *3*, 245-270.
18. Warren, W. G. Personal construction of death and death education. *Death Education*, 1981, *5*, 291-310.
19. Hardison, O. B., Jr. *Toward freedom and dignity: The humanities and the idea of humanity.* Baltimore: Johns Hopkins University Press, 1972.

∞∞

DEATH EDUCATION FOR ONCOLOGY PROFESSIONALS:
A PERSONAL CONSTRUCT THEORY PERSPECTIVE

∞∞

LAWRENCE C. RAINEY

UCLA Jonsson Comprehensive Cancer Center

Using observations from a psychosocial training program for oncology professionals, this article illustrates how one can model, while training the student, the very methods he or she can adopt in working with patients and families. One starts with an elicitation of the student's (patient's) operative personal constructs and then devises strategies to elaborate, integrate, loosen, tighten, preempt, or take other action, as needed. The very means used to promote movement within the student's own death-related constructs can be adopted for use by him or her in the clinical situation. As the helper's pathways of action and thought with regard to this domain become more comprehensive and as the helper becomes more skilled at moving freely along them, he or she becomes more perceptive and resourceful to those in need.

Introduction

George Kelly had relatively little to say about death; for that matter, he did not concern himself extensively with pedagogy. This might leave the commentator on "The Kellian Approach to Death Education" with remarkably little to explicate. What Kelly's work has provided, however, is a heuristically valuable approach to thinking about persons, how they encounter and process their experiences, and how they change. The more formal, as opposed to content-laden, nature of Kelly's theory probably has contributed to the lasting interest it has enjoyed and has prevented it going the way of tail fins, sockhops, and other products of the 1950s. This general framework has been taken by Kelly's followers and productively applied to diverse domains within and outside the traditional concerns of psychology. Among illustrations of the latter is the attempt, amply illustrated in this volume, to construe death-related phenomena in personal construct theory terms.

This paper discusses selected aspects of death education from the perspective of personal construct theory. The focus here is not on the whole of death education, but instead on death education as shaped by a particular context: namely, continuing education for oncology health care professionals, which includes thanatological concerns as well as many other psychosocial issues.[1] Thus, the death education efforts described here are: (*a*) shaped by the concerns and patient management issues peculiar to cancer; (*b*) couched in the context of psychosocial and rehabilitational issues broader than thanatology per se; (*c*) targeted for experienced, practicing health professionals from several disciplines (nursing, social work, medicine, pharmacy, physical therapy, pastoral care, etc.); and (*d*) especially concerned with pragmatic issues of patient care. These characteristics make this a rather specialized case of death education, very different, for instance, from teaching "Death and Dying" to college students or from addressing death concerns of seriously ill patients of bereaved individuals. I am speaking only about a small portion or the broad and multifaceted endeavor that death education, in the best sense of the phrase, can entail.

Goals

Thanatological education does not lend itself easily to creating a list of specific objectives, although the challenge for any of a number of reasons is often met. Learning about death should not and cannot be reduced to a simple checklist of procedures, as can, for instance, learning to do a technical procedures such as cardiopulmonary resuscitation. On the other hand, thanatologi-

---

[1] A full description of the entire training program alluded to above is contained in L. Rainey and D. Wellisch, "Training Health Professionals in Psychosocial Aspects of Cancer," a paper presented at the 1981 annual convention of the American Psychological Association, Los Angeles. This paper is available on request from the author.

cal education, if it is to be accepted and tolerated by health care professionals, cannot err in the opposite direction, seeking nothing more concrete than "increased sensitivity" or developing a philosophic mindedness that has no direct ties to clinical practice. A middle course, avoiding extremes of oversimplified technique and irrelevant theorizing, is to be recommended.

From a personal construct theory point of view, a pragmatic overarching goal can be stated. It is to stimulate elaboration and integration of the trainee's death-related constructs. With constructs seen as "pathways of action and thought," the goal is to enrich the network of pathways along which the health professional can move in thought and action as death-related events are encountered. As greater articulation in the construct system is achieved, students will be better able to perceive death-related phenomena, and their options for intervention will be enhanced.

Although the oncology physician, nurse, social worker, or other allied health care professional is surrounded by death (at current rates approximately 60 percent of all cancer patients, across sites, eventually die of the disease), the professional may not attend specifically to death-related phenomena. Previous training may not have provided preparation to do so, and the current medical care system does not usually provide much validation for such activity. Dozens of other issues and tasks, each very important in its own right, vie for time and attention. Into this fray comes the death educator, saying, in effect, "Attend to these events (i.e., death-related feelings, thoughts, behaviors), in addition to all else you are doing; and consider doing these acts (i.e., any of a number of possible interventions) over and beyond your present clinical responsibilities." Realistically, one does not expect these concerns—that is, this portion of the professional's overall construct system—to be engaged at all times. (Who would want nurses stalking the hallways thinking "death and dying" all the time?) But one would hope that when the occasion calls for it (be the call overt or, as it so often is, rather subtle) that such death-related constructs and related response capabilities would be available.

Implied in what has already been said is the position that the goal is not to prepare "thanatologists," "death and dying counselors," nor any other such "death specialists." Instead, the intent is to prepare those professionals who are already indigenous to the health delivery system to be able to be appropriately responsive to their patient's death-related concerns. Several factors suggest this orientation, including the following: (*a*) in most clinical situations budgetary constraints make it highly unlikely that additional personnel (e.g., thanatologists) would be added to the staff; (*b*) many death-related concerns are intimately related to and intertwined with medical, nursing, and social factors already being addressed by members of the primary health team and as such are best treated in that context, not as a separate issue; and (*c*) having an "expert" invites the other staff to abandon any responsibilities to deal with the whole topic—"that's that thanatologist's turf, after all." It is usually more efficient and practical to have death-related concerns included routinely as part of the normal patterns of care provided by health care team members.

Returning to the basic goal of elaborating and integrating the trainee's death-related construct system, there are two major domains that can be immediately identified. They are constructs pertaining to assessment of the patient, family member, or other person being assisted (assessment) and constructs with regard to available courses of action (intervention). Both domains, assessment and intervention, need attention in a well-rounded course. An adequate death education course for health professionals must steer a course that honors, at all times, knowing and doing. The ultimate objective would be to have professionals who can think insightfully and broadly about their clients' death concerns and be able to act efficiently and flexibly in response to those concerns.

Comments on Pedagogic Approach

A personal construct theory perspective to education must begin by attending closely to the conceptual grid that the student/helper employs. What are the trainee's operative constructs? How are his or her experiences, at least those related to death, psychologically channelized? In what directions is he or she free to move in thought and action? Where are there lacunae? What are the "submerged poles" of the constructs most prominent in the student's repertoire?

In my experience, the answers to such queries reveal any of a number of problems or deficiencies in the novice caregiver's death-related constructs. Sometimes the trainee simply has an inadequate repertoire of constructs for this domain (e.g., the medical professional who simply is not "psychologically minded"). Other times the student is well equipped with constructs but needs a stimulus to apply them to elements in this field (e.g., a social worker who has quite a repertoire of assessment and intervention capacities but has not previously applied them to situations related to seriously ill persons). Often there is a lack of complexity in the construct system; an adequate array of constructs can be elicited (for instance, when the student is discussing a clinical case), but the interrelationships between constructs are simple or largely subsumed by one dominant theme (e.g., "good patients" versus "crocks" or "doing something" versus "just talking"). Unnecessary limits in the range of convenience of constructs may also have to be addressed (e.g., assessment constructs sensitively applied to patients and families but not to self and other staff). Occasionally, excessively tight construing and/or constellatory constructs will be manifested and must be altered.

In a sense, these types of problems set the agenda for the death education course. Where there is a paucity of constructs the objective is to stimulate further elaboration; where there is simplicity, to promote complexity; where there is a narrow range of convenience, to encourage a broader scope of construct application; and so on.

The pedagogic approach is, in the spirit of personal construct theory, quite individualistic. Methods can be varied but usually involve some form of active involvement with actual case material (that is, the actual "elements" to be construed in the professional's practice). The attentive instructor can quickly ascertain the trainee's dominant constructs by having him or her describe a case, for instance, or interview a patient and recommend a treatment plan. A few probing questions will illuminate relationships between operative constructs, the hierarchical structure, and the breadth of application. Attempts to strengthen,

alter, enrich, loosen, or tighten part of the construct system are
also best done in the context of dealing with case material. As
in therapy done from a personal construct theory perspective,
the student is encouraged to "try on" new ways of thinking and
acting. New roles may be prescribed (e.g., "While hanging this
IV interact with the patient as if you were a social worker, as
opposed to a registered nurse"). Care should be taken to have
the student actually elaborate constructs rather than just slot
rattle along already well established dimensions. And a gradient
of activities should be planned, beginning with experiments in
imagination, graduating to active role plays in safe situations,
proceeding to interventions with simpler cases, or situations with
a high probability of success, and culminating in applications to
problematical cases with which one is actually struggling in the
real clinical setting.

In the paragraphs that follow, I use the familiar scheme
alluded to above—construing the other and construing one's role
(assessment and intervention)—as a framework through which to
illustrate some of the specific problems and inadequacies revealed in trainees' death-related constructs and to show how
they can be dealt with in a death education course.

Construing the Other: Issues of Assessment

Let us consider the issue of assessing the "dying patient," the
obvious "element" to be dealt with. Most students begin with
the assumption that it is the dying patient who is the primary
object of concern. Obviously, it is the patient and his or her
situation that concerns us primarily (but not solely). To begin
the process of elaboration, however, one can confront the use of
this label ("dying patient") and its related constructs. Various
means can be used to stress that the dying patient is not just a
patient and that he or she is not just dying. The patient is, after
all, a person (and all that that implies) who, at this moment, in
this setting, as the object of the health care professional's
perception, is occupying a patient role. There are numerous
dimensions of his or her being (at other times, in other settings,
in relation to other people) that lie beyond the patient role.

Furthermore, the patient is not just dying. Within the realm of patienthood, the patient has needs over and beyond those strictly related to the process of dying. (Although these points are seemingly obvious, it has been my experience that many health care staff are genuinely surprised that seriously ill patients have interests and involvements in other matters, such as sexuality, finances, the fate of the local baseball team, or any number of other trivial to serious concerns. Of course, reifying patients has a certain utility to those who must administer distressing medical regimens and tolerate so many deaths among those served.)

In personal construct theory terms what we are talking about here is overcoming constellatory notions of dying—that is, dying does not subsume everything about the person as a living being. Although construed as dying, the patient still has a personality (complete with idiosyncratic needs), a personal history (including social roles more elevated and interesting than the current patient role), and a social network (including family, friends, and colleagues, who may or may not be present in the medical setting). Neither dying nor the more general status of patienthood necessarily becomes the core construct controlling all else in the individual's life. Even within the circumscribed domain of trying to understand and empathize with the patient's psychological state, the would-be helper must use other constructs. These would include constructs related to the patient's diagnosis and disease history, the current treatment regimen, and the constraints and demands of the current medical treatment setting, any or all of which may be more closely tied to the patient's emotional state than the fact that the patient is dying. It has been my experience that many students coming from the psychosocial disciplines (e.g., social workers, psychologists, marriage and family counselors, and pastoral counselors) can benefit by expanding constructs related to disease and treatment variables. Although they often are attuned to the role that factors such as socioeconomic status, ethnicity, and religious orientation may play in shaping the attitudes, behavior, and affect of the patient, they may be blind to the effects that a particular chemotherapy regimen or central nervous system metastases have on psychological status. An embarrassing and all too frequent occurrence in the medical setting is to see psycho-social personnel naively jumping to any one of a variety of psychological constructions of phenomena that are much more readily and accurately explained in terms of disease or treat-ment-related effects.

Another way in which the construct system of the helper can often be usefully expanded is to include more elements. Although the patient will always remain the prime focus in the clinical setting, he or she can nonetheless be better understood and served if seen contextually—that is, in the context of the "family" (primary social unit). An interesting issue is the helper's understanding of "family." In urban America today, traditional definitions of family (married couple living together with offspring) are limiting and misleading. Unmarried single persons, unmarried couples, persons in various states of separa-tion or divorce, gay and bisexual individuals, and persons from a variety of ethnic groups, races, and nationalities (varying widely in the number of relatives included in the "immediate" family) can be regularly found on our wards and present, of course, a multiplicity of family constellations. In some instances, other social groupings—the neighborhood, church, school, class, work colleagues, club, or voluntary organization—take on particular significance as well. The helper who construes only the patient, oblivious to the person as situated in social contexts, is extremely handicapped. In practical management terms, this means assessing and working with the family (or other important social group).

Particular assessment construct dimensions need "loosening": Certain assessment-related constructs are frequently invoked by the novice helper of the dying. Often these dimensions, while useful, need to be made more permeable or the lines of association to other constructs need to be loosened. Let me cite just a few examples:

Denial versus Acceptance. These two notions, often used in this fashion as alternative poles of one construct, have crept into the working vocabulary of even the most nonpsychologically minded of medical personnel. Though a useful dimension, it is used inappropriately, or at least too broadly, by many. Sometimes this is the only psychological construct employed by the medical professional. In somewhat less extreme instances, this dimension will play a central role in the construct system, and all other psychological constructs will be subsumed by it. In its most naive and potentially harmful expression, denial versus acceptance is seen as a good versus bad issue. The good patient accepts death; the bad patient denies impending terminality. It is not uncommon for the psychological consultant to receive a consult request that says, in essence, "the patient is denying; do something about it." Or, in similar fashion, the unexperienced helper might construe the helper's task as finding a means to undermine denial and promote death acceptance. The seasoned clinician, of course, appreciates the value of denial for the patient or family caught in horrendous medical situations. The student must be helped to understand the value of denial and furthermore to appreciate gradations of denial and acceptance. To promote such understanding it is useful to address this issue not in terms of defensive processes, but rather under the rubric of "coping mechanisms" (a more appropriately neutral designation). Further, many trainees benefit by simple relabeling of the construct dimension. For instance, one could see this as an issue of vigilant focusing versus minimization. Simple relabeling may change the connotative value of a construct (in this case, the negative evaluative connotation of the denial pole) and enable the student to employ the construct in a more productive fashion.

Dealing with It versus Not Dealing with It. This construct (similar to, but not identical with denial versus acceptance) is one that arrays patients or family members as dealing with it or not dealing with it ("it" being an imprecise way of referring to some ill-defined, death-related task). This is an example of a construct with which it may be productive to have the student ladder down—that is, to be specific, objective, and concrete in delineating the construct. What one often discovers is that dealing with it, that is, dealing with death, connotes that the patient or family member adopts a certain emotional style (for example, a frank, self-disclosing, affectively aroused manner, or some other style personally favored by the evaluator/student), whereas not dealing with it consists of being reserved, quiet, introverted, decorous, or some other attribute not preferred by the evaluator. For many students, the very process of laddering is sufficient to reveal what may be a rather arbitrary assumptive structure in the construct system and to suggest a need to loosen or redefine the lines of association between this and other evaluative constructs. The student can be led to see that dealing with it (that is, accomplishing any of a number of spiritual, emotional, legal, financial, interpersonal, and other tasks associated with the process of dying) can be achieved in a wide variety of ways. Encountering this construct also provides a convenient occasion to have the students elaborate what the tasks associated with dying are for each of the parties (patient, family, friends, staff) who are involved. Many times this will encourage expansion of the construct system to include concerns beyond one's immediate area of professional expertise.

Terminal Patients versus Nonterminal Patients. Exactly who is designated as "terminal" in the trainee's construct system and the network of associations related to terminality are worthy of exploration in any death education course. Here again, it has been my experience that many students use the construct preemptively and have overly tight associations between terminality and other constructs. In some instances, for instance, one finds students (particularly those who describe themselves as "interested in death and dying") who will use the terminal pole to designate all persons with serious chronic illness, such as cancer. Although some trainees (for instance, those working in a tertiary care setting) will see a large number of patients who are in fact destined to die from their disease, even in this instance patients are probably better construed as terminal not for the entire duration of their illness, but at some point closer to the actual event of death. It is helpful to separate the construct of terminality from that of life-threatening illness. One can certainly have a potentially life-threatening illness without, at any given time, being terminal. Such matters are not mere semantic quibbles. If one explores a student's construct hierarchy it may be found that the notion of terminality preempts all other tasks of living now. Thus the student who construes a patient as terminal cannot be attentive to other important domains of the patient's life worthy of attention. Sometimes the patient's placement on the terminal versus nonterminal dimension has direct implications for treatment, including psychosocial and medical management. Any of a number of possibilities may reveal themselves here: for instance, those who are terminal may be offered psychosocial ministrations of various sorts while those who are nonterminal may not; those who are terminal may be eligible for certain palliative measures, such as higher doses or more frequent administration of pain medications, while those who are nonterminal do not receive such treatment; or those who are judged to be terminal may be moved to a special facility, for instance, a hospice, convalescent facility, or other alternative to an acute care hospital. A very frequent and unfortunate association that one discovers in many health professional's construct systems is that being terminal is a condition for having death-related concerns. It is very important to dislodge this association and assist the student to appreciate that the degree to which one is concerned about death-related matters bears no necessary relationship to one's present medical status or prognosis. For instance, many recently diagnosed patients with localized tumors, which have high probabilities of being successfully treated, are nonetheless highly anxious about death. Conversely, some patients who are in fact terminal have dealt extensively with their own impending death at an earlier point in their illness trajectory and are no longer explicitly concerned about death-related matters.

Further Assessment Issues. Space does not allow us to deal fully with all the issues involved in a comprehensive psychosocial assessment of the terminal patient, but a few broader concerns might be cited in addition to the particular issues discussed above. A general rule is that adequate psychosocial assessment of the terminal patient and the patient's family is not unlike psychosocial assessment of any other individual under stress. From a pedagogic point of view this usually entails expanding the student's construct system to include a number of more general assessment issues. To understand the person who is dying entails understanding more than just death-related feelings,

292[206]   *L. C. Rainey*

beliefs, and attitudes of the patient. Among the broader issues that must be considered by the helper is the patient's history, particularly his or her experiences in dealing with other significant stressors. Tied to this is an understanding of the coping processes (affective, cognitive, and behavioral) used by the patient. Also especially critical are those constructs dealing with "normal" versus "abnormal" behavior. Care must be taken to differentiate psychiatric disturbances from common, but intense, psychosocial response patterns of individuals under stress. The student's understanding of developmental stages and age-appropriate behavior is yet another subset of constructs that will come into play, particularly if the health care professional works with patients or family members across a wide range of ages. Both a 10-year-old and a 40-year-old who are anticipating a bone marrow aspiration may manifest considerable anxiety, but the manifestations might be very different in each case. Or the pattern of grief in a 15-year-old child of a dying parent may be very different from that of a 60-year-old who is losing a parent. Though obvious to the experienced clinician, the health care professional new to psychosocial care may not realize that the task is not to learn about "anticipatory anxiety prior to a medical procedure" or about "grief reactions" but to learn about these issues as they interact with more general factors such as developmental stage, ethnicity, socioeconomic status, coping style, and a number of other psychosocial factors.

From a Kellian perspective, one would teach the care provider to take an idiographic approach to assessment. One would not perhaps expect formal psychodiagnostic assessment to be conducted, but an attentive thoughtful approach to understanding the individual should be promoted. The trainee can be taught to try to understand the patient or family member's own construct system. This can be achieved by teaching the trainee to listen for the frequently used core constructs that emerge as the patient or family member reviews his or her disease history and coping processes, to take a credulous approach to understanding the meaning given to these constructs, and to ask about such issues as how constructs are grounded (opposite pole) and their relationships to each other (that is, structural relationships). The general point is to teach the would-be helper to take a phenomenological approach to understanding the other. The helper should be asking himself or herself, "What is the nature of the conceptual grid through which this individual (patient, family member, other health team member) is viewing this situation?" "What are his or her possible pathways of action?" "What are the limitations and gaps that appear?" "What are the particularly developed areas?" "In what ways is this person's construct system consistent or divergent from my own?"

These types of questions and concerns can form the backdrop whether the assessment is taking place through a brief, informal conversation between professional and patient while another treatment task is being performed or whether the assessment is done more formally and at greater length. The essential task is to understand the other person, his or her concerns and needs, background and current status, and to resist confining one's construal of the other to some predetermined, narrowly focused set of constructs supposedly pertinent only to "the dying patient."

Constructs Related to Intervention

Just as with assessment, the overarching goal with regard to intervention is to expand the trainee's construct network. As with any clinical endeavor, adequate intervention must be built on a base of adequate assessment. One cannot ascertain what to do until one has clarified exactly what the problems are, what the helpee is requesting, and so on. This point is worthy of note because the novice psychosocial caregiver, struggling with a great degree of anticipatory insecurity, is often eager to rush to perform some intervention. The well-meaning but naive question frequently posed by the novice helper is, "What can I do?" or "What does one say to someone who's dying?" A well-rounded training program must resist pressures to rush to a premature specification of intervention techniques (the notorious "how to do it" weekend seminar featuring this year's gimmick), while at the same time respecting the legitimate need for appropriate and practical intervention strategies.

Again, the focus here must be restricted to looking at a few of the more common concerns and issues that arise as health care team members are prepared to provide psychosocial care to dying persons. We begin by looking at several constellatory constructs that must be challenged.

The first such mistaken notion that one often encounters is that terminal care is coterminous with psychosocial counseling or, in somewhat more attenuated form, that psychosocial counseling is the major component of terminal care. The fact is that comprehensive care for terminal illness entails a variety of medical, nursing, pharmaceutical, rehabilitational, spiritual, and social service interventions, as well as psychological care. At various junctures each of these disciplines and its contributions will be needed, and at any given time one may be more critical than others. One must begin with the understanding that terminal care is an endeavor with multiple foci, requiring a multidisciplinary effort. Counseling plays an important but limited role.

Once the role of psychosocial counseling has been placed in perspective, a second constellatory notion to be confronted is that psychosocial counseling necessarily entails sitting and talking at length with the patient or family member. Although there is no doubt that formal face-to-face psychosocial counseling over several sessions will in fact take place in some instances, it is not the most frequent form in which psychosocial care will actually be delivered in most medical settings. If caregivers construe counseling in this limited and stereotyped fashion, the very real result is that very little counseling will get done. Too many health care professionals polarize counseling with their other professional duties—nursing duties versus counseling, physical therapy versus counseling, medical care versus counseling, and so on. It is my experience that if the health care team is to attend to and deal with the psychosocial dimensions of terminal illness, they must do so in the context of performing their other duties and responsibilities.

Some settings, particularly large university hospitals, may have specialized counseling personnel available who can play an important role on the multidisciplinary health care team. This, however, is the exception rather than the rule. Even in such instances it is important for all members of the health care team to be attuned to and responsive to the psychosocial needs of patients and families. With regard to the roles of the team members, it is important to overcome rigid boundaries and role definitions, particularly as these pertain to psychosocial care. Attentiveness to the emotional, interpersonal, and behavioral needs of patients and family members is no one's special turf. Good communication cannot be reserved as a quality for the psychosocial "expert" alone.

We have begun with the notions that terminal care does not equal psychosocial care, that psychosocial care is not equivalent to formal, lengthy counseling, and that psychosocial care is not the exclusive province of the mental health professional. Moving down one more level in the direction of constructs pertaining to actual patterns of practice, one could clarify that psychosocial responsiveness is not equivalent to frank verbal responses to every question posed or every need expressed by the patient or family. It has been my experience that many novice helpers have somehow acquired the notion that to be a good psychosocial caregiver in the medical setting entails a nearly brutal frankness and a total neglect of discrimination, diplomacy, and nuance in communications. Comparable to appreciating the value of denial in the patient's repertoire of coping responses, the student must appreciate the use of silence, indirect language, and innuendo when approaching delicate and sometimes traumatic areas of the individual's experience. "Helping the patient and family" cannot be reduced merely to frank talk. In construing a professional role, the student must understand that helping does not necessarily entail doing anything proactive at all. (This may be extraordinarily difficult for the health care student who has been socialized into a very active, instrumental, problem-solving, authoritative professional style.)

Another danger that one must avoid is that of having the helper-in-training merely slot rattle. For instance, one may discover that the trainee thinks of helping characteristics in terms of constructs such as avoiding versus approaching, cold versus warm, and inattentive versus attentive, to cite but a few commonly expressed dimensions. The goal should not be to have the trainee simply try to move from being avoidant to more approaching, from colder to warmer, from inattentive to more empathic; instead the objective would be to have the trainee elaborate his or her role. With regard to these particular role constructs, one would want to help the trainee be able to adopt a position at either pole of the construct, as the situation demands. (A common mistake is to value only an approaching, warm, emotionally empathic style. Trainees locked into this stance will soon find themselves pulverized in the crucible of caring for the catastrophically ill person.) Obviously, if these were the only helping constructs the trainee had in his repertoire, there would be an additional need to elaborate the system, that is, to expand the construct system to include other helping possibilities.

Many students can substantially increase their network of helping alternatives by adopting strategies intended to accomplish limited ends associated with special problems encountered by the terminally ill. These may be circumscribed interventions not focused on profound existential issues of death but nonetheless of import to the seriously ill individual. For example, the helper can suggest and support new role enactments for the patient—such as relaxing in the presence of formerly anxiety-provoking stimuli such as a chemotherapy procedure. Or the confused, ill-informed family member might be helped to respond more assertively when asking questions of the medical staff. Or a lonely patient might be instructed about how to provide validation to friends and staff when they are attending to him, thereby increasing the probability of such interactions. These types of "behavioral" intervention (for example, desensitization, assertive training, and shaping) are often neglected by those who want to help the dying, but they can be of great utility.

∞∞

RESOURCES FOR FURTHER RESEARCH

∞∞

∞∞

A MANUAL FOR CONTENT ANALYSIS
OF DEATH CONSTRUCTS

∞∞

ROBERT A. NEIMEYER
Memphis State University

DEBORAH J. FONTANA and KENNETH GOLD
University of Rochester

This paper details a system for analyzing the content of constructs that persons employ to conceptualize situations involving death and dying. The development of the content coding manual is reviewed, and the interjudge reliability of the scoring system is presented. The paper outlines instructions for using the manual and discusses potential areas for its application.

As personal construct researchers have moved into the domain of thanatology over the last decade, their primary contribution has been the development of instruments to assess the individual's personal orientations toward death. Not surprisingly, these instruments represent adaptations of Kelly's original Role Construct Repertory Test or Repertory Grid (1). Thus, both the interview form of the Threat Index (TI) (2, 3) and more elaborate grid procedures (4) require respondents to compare and contrast a specific set of elements (in this case, situations involving death and dying) in order to elicit the personal constructs used to interpret that domain of their experience. Typically, ratings of elements on these construct dimensions are analyzed to yield any of a number of quantitative scores that reflect the respondent's cognitive structure regarding death. In the Threat Index (3) procedure, for example, the number of instances in which the individual rates "self" and "death" on opposite poles of a construct (e.g., meaningful versus empty) is tallied to yield a measure of the threat implied by one's personal mortality. Similarly, other repertory grid techniques (4) yield mathematical indices of the subjective distance that the respondent interposes between "self" and "death," and so on. Both scores are structural in the sense that they represent the relative placement of particular elements within the construct system; they are independent of the actual meanings of the constructs themselves.

This preference for structural over content analysis is not unique to personal construct work in thanatology. Duck (5), surveying research in interpersonal construing, notes that "The emphasis falls so heavily on structure that content often appears relegated to the status of an epiphenomenon" (p. 55). Nonetheless, some investigators have attempted to study the meaning of interpersonal constructs more systematically. Both Duck (5) and Landfield (6) have developed reliable systems for analyzing the content of constructs used to describe other persons and have found that content variables are predictive of friendship development and psychotherapy outcome, respectively. This suggests not only that content analyses are feasible, but also that they may be valuable adjuncts to extant structural methods for scoring grid data.

Development of the Death Construct
Coding Manual

The present paper reports preliminary work in constructing a manual for the content analysis of death-relevant constructs. It was thought that such a system, once developed, could be used to address a broad range of research questions: Do the terms in which individuals conceptualize death vary as a function of their religious affiliation? Their age? Their nearness to death? Do courses in death and dying change the way students construe their mortality? Do people interpret their own deaths in different terms from those in which they interpret the deaths of others? How does the meaning one attributes to dying relate to one's experience of death threat, fear, and anxiety? Do the ways that more actualized individuals perceive death differ from the ways in which less actualized persons do so? Are health care professionals with a particular understanding of death more humane or effective than those with other orientations? Are there detectable differences in the content of death constructions employed by particular cultural or subcultural groups? Answering these and similar questions requires the development of some means of consistently classifying the idiosyncratic meanings that individuals attach to situations involving death and dying.

In a first attempt to develop a manual for the content analysis of death constructs, the first author examined 1,140 constructs previously elicited by administering the TI to 38 introductory psychology students (7). Nineteen content categories were inductively derived from trial groupings of these dimensions (e.g., descriptions such as "good," "favorable," and "pleasant" were grouped together as "positive evaluation"). Subsequent attempts to have three independent judges reliably code several hundred of these constructs into the 19 categories led to certain revisions in the coding system. For example, judges frequently disagreed with one another about whether a particular construct (e.g., "sick") connoted physical or psychological disturbance associated with a death, but had little difficulty identifying constructs pertaining to the pain associated with dying. Thus, the broader category of "physical health" was replaced by a new code emphasizing "suffering." Similarly, several other categories were broadened, narrowed, or dropped altogether, and a number of new categories were added as a result of these efforts. The revised 25-category coding system is presented in Appendix 1.

Final Interjudge Reliability Study

In order to test formally the adequacy of the revised coding system, two independent judges coded a second set of 1,025 construct poles using the new categories. The judges were undergraduate psychology students who received approximately four hours of training in the use of the manual before undertaking the coding task. Constructs were drawn from Death Attitude Repertory Tests (DARTs) administered to a heterogeneous sample of 31 adults enrolled in a university continuing education course in the psychology of death and dying and a sample of 12 nurses and allied health professionals taking a similar course for certification purposes. Like the elicited form of the Threat Index or TI/e (2, 3), the DART requires respondents to compare and contrast a standard set of situations pertaining to death.[1] Unlike the TI/e, which involves a lengthy individualized structured interview, the DART was administered to the death education classes as a paper-and-pencil instrument. The descriptions used to differentiate each set of three death-relevant situations (e.g., "These two deaths were avoidable whereas this one was inevitable") became the constructs subjected to content coding.

Table 1 presents data on interjudge agreement for each of the 25 categories that comprise the revised coding system (for definitions and examples of each category, see Appendix 1).

Three categories (3a, positive emotion; 4a, high acceptance; and 9b, low certainty) were eliminated from the manual because judges failed to attain at least 70 percent agreement concerning their application. The remaining categories had a mean agree-

---

[1] In the DART procedure, the respondent is presented different sorts of 3 of the following situations, printed on index cards, and is asked to describe "some important way in which two of the situations are alike each other and different from the third." Given situations a, d, and g, for example, the respondent might describe a and d as "affecting me personally" whereas g might seem "more distant." Once 15 such constructs are elicited, they are used to anchor 13-point rating scales on which all 15 of the original situations are then placed. This permits a number of quantitative structural scores to be derived from the data, including indices of the degree of death threat and anxiety associated with each of the particular situations, in addition to the content analysis described in this paper. For a fuller discussion of a similar "ratings grid" measures, see Neimeyer and Neimeyer (8).

The 15 situations used in the DART procedure include the following: (a) You discover you have leukemia and have only a few weeks to live. (b) Your closest friend is killed in a plane crash. (c) Your grandmother dies in her sleep. (d) A homicidal maniac is on the loose and has already viciously mutilated six people in your town. (e) Your father drowns while trying to save another person from drowning. (f) A divorced mother of two dies of an overdose. (g) A genetically deformed baby is allowed to die in the hospital. (h) A terminal patient dies after months of unrelievable pain. (i) Three children die when a tornado hits their elementary school. (j) An old man becoming senile starves himself to death in order not to burden his family. (k) Medical staff at a hospital decide to allow a patient to die rather than employ "extraordinary means" to preserve his life. (l) Your own death, as you would expect it to occur if it happened at this time in your life. (m) Your own life, as it currently is. (n) Your own life, as you would ideally like it to be.

TABLE 1 Percentage of Interjudge Agreement by Content Category

Category	Percentage of agreement	Category	Percentage of agreement
1. Purposefulness		**8. Temporal expectation**	
a. purposeful	100.00	a. long range	93.54
b. purposeless	94.10	b. short range	90.30
2. Evaluation		**9. Certainty**	
a. positive	84.6	a. high	85.71
b. negative	73.2	**10. Existence**	
3. Emotional state		a. existence	76.47
b. negative	78.8	b. nonexistence	78.94
4. Acceptance		**11. Choice**	
b. low	81.4	a. high	91.30
5. Understanding		b. low	87.50
a. high	80.95	**12. Specificity**	
b. low	82.35	a. specific	88.88
6. Suffering		b. general	92.30
a. high	78.26	**13. Impact**	
b. low	93.33	a. high	100.00
7. Personal involvement		b. low	93.75
a. high	80.55	**14. Causality**	
b. low	87.50	a. known	82.60
		b. unknown	100.00

ment of 87.05 percent. This level of interjudge reliability was deemed sufficient to justify the use of the coding system in research.

Use of the Death Construct Coding Manual

The manual can be used to perform content analysis of constructs derived from any of a number of sources, including the elicited form of the Threat Index, the Death Attitude Repertory Test, or other forms of repertory grid designed to bring to light dimensions that the respondent uses to conceptualize death and dying. Alternatively, the manual could be used to code descriptions drawn from personal essays, journals, or transcribed interviews that bear on the subject's interpretation of death. The only restriction placed upon the use of the manual is that it be applied to constructs that are clearly death-relevant; constructs that apply to the dying person but not to the death itself (e.g., young versus old) are usually not codable within the present system.

Before using the manual, a rater should read carefully the definitions and examples provided for each category, as well as the alphabetized list of constructs and their appropriate codes as presented in Appendix 2. The rater should then attempt to code several dozen of the descriptions in the alphabetized list by referring only to the definitions and examples of the categories appearing in Appendix 1, taking care to resolve any discrepancies that arise between his or her own scoring and that presented in the appended list.

Because any given construct (e.g., "humane") may be scored under more than one category (e.g., as "positive evaluation" and "low suffering"), problems with overscoring and underscoring may arise. Experience suggests that the former occurs more frequently. For this reason, the rater should adopt parsimony as a rule of thumb when deciding whether multiple scoring is indicated.

In scoring any particular construct, the rater should first check the alphabetized list for appropriate codes, scanning the list for synonyms as well as exact descriptions. It should be kept in mind that not all constructs can be scored within the given categories. When the rater is in doubt as to whether a construct can be coded, no score should be given.

References

1. Kelly, G. A. *The psychology of personal constructs* (2 vols.) New York: Norton, 1955.
2. Krieger, S. R., Epting, F. R., & Leitner, L. M. Personal constructs, threat, and attitudes toward death. *Omega*, 1974, *5*, 299–310.
3. Rigdon, M. A., Epting, F. R., Neimeyer, R. A., & Krieger, S. R. The Threat Index: A research report. *Death Education*, 1979, *3*, 245–270.
4. Warren, W. G., & Parry, G. Personal constructs and death: Some clinical refinements. In H. Bonarius, R. Holland, & S. Rosenberg (Eds.), *Personal construct psychology: Recent advances in theory and practice*. London: Macmillan, 1981.
5. Duck, S. W. *Personal relationships and personal constructs*. London: Wiley, 1973.
6. Landfield, A. W. *Personal construct systems in psychotherapy*. Chicago: Rand McNally, 1971.
7. Neimeyer, R. A., Dingemans, P., & Epting, F. R. Convergent validity, situational stability and meaningfulness of the Threat Index. *Omega*, 1977, *8*, 251–265.
8. Neimeyer, G. J., & Neimeyer, R. A. Personal construct perspectives on cognitive assessment. In T. Merluzzi, C. Glass, & M. Genest (Eds.), *Cognitive assessment*. New York: Guilford, 1981.

Appendix 1:
Death Construct Coding Manual

1. *Purposefulness*
   a. purposeful: constructs dealing with meaningfulness of the death, its having some justification ethically, psychologically, or naturally.
      examples: useful, fulfillment, necessary, a blessing, having a reason, has purpose, contributes to society, punishment, reward, moral.
   b. purposeless: constructs suggesting the meaninglessness of the death, its being unjustified or unnecessary.
      examples: having no cause, having no reason, useless, uncalled for, has no purpose, chance, unnatural.
2. *Evaluation*
   a. positive: constructs expressing an evaluation of death as "good" or valued.

examples: favorable, good, not horrible, desirable, kind, pleasant, reasonable, reward, fair, normal, moral.
  b. negative: constructs having to do with an evaluation of the death as nonvalued or "bad."
     examples: undesirable, unfavorable, horrible, bad, tragic, cruel, punishment, unfair, abnormal, sinful, immoral.
3. *Emotional State*
  b. negative: constructs suggesting negative emotional state.
     examples: despair, sad, sorrow, guilty, grief, ashamed.
4. *Acceptance*
  b. low: constructs depicting the death as something to be rejected or resisted.
     examples: unacceptable, avoiding death, loss, upsetting, a shame, disturbing, traumatic, resentful, bothers people, murder, hard to take.
5. *Understanding*
  a. high: constructs indicating achievement of some understanding of the death.
     examples: familiar, understandable, known, concrete, can relate to it, reasonable, has a known cause.
  b. low: constructs expressing lack of understanding of the death.
     examples: unfamiliar, not known, incomprehensible, beyond the human mind, cannot relate to it.
6. *Suffering*
  a. high: constructs suggesting that the death is painful or induces suffering.
     examples: hurt, painful, viscious, sickening, inhumane, unhealthy, torturous.
  b. low: constructs implying that death is painless or produces minimal suffering.
     examples: painless, well, not hurt, gentle, peaceful, humane, healthy.
7. *Personal Involvement*
  a. high: constructs connoting personal involvement in the death.
     examples: close to me, near, self loss, personal, close to home, relates to a friend, I care about it, relates to me personally, caused by me.
  b. low: constructs depicting the death as remote or not pertaining to the self.
     examples: distant from me, far, not self, impersonal, merely factual, stranger to me, unlikely to affect me.
8. *Temporal Expectation*
  a. long range: constructs suggesting that death is anticipated.
     examples: long, has warning, time to ponder, having time to think, lingering, prepared, happening later.

b. short range: constructs implying that the death is unanticipated.
   examples: no warning, unexpected, sudden, short, no time left, instantaneous, unprepared, surprising, happening now.

9. *Certainty*
   a. high: constructs having to do with certain death.
      examples: eventual, certain, just a matter of time, no hope, not preventable, unavoidable, inevitable.

10. *Existence*
    a. existence: constructs having to do with continued life.
       examples: continuation, not dead, experiencing, still living, changing, existing, saved, life-giving.
    b. nonexistence: constructs having to do with finality of the death.
       examples: dead, the end, no experience, nonbeing, static, stationary, total loss of thought, destroyed, termination.

11. *Choice*
    a. high: constructs emphasizing a degree of personal choice involved in the death.
       examples: responsible, chosen, seeking death, preventable, control, avoidable, suicide.
    b. low: constructs stressing absence of personal choice.
       examples: no choice, chance, not responsible, unprepared, no control, unavoidable, fate, going to die, accidental, not suicide.

12. *Specificity*
    a. specific: constructs pertaining to the uniqueness of death.
       examples: concrete, happening to me, individual, unique, few deaths, singular, rare.
    b. general: constructs suggesting the generality of death.
       examples: general, abstract, common, happens to everyone, frequent, many deaths, not specific, plural.

13. *Impact*
    a. high: constructs dealing with the impact of death.
       examples: stark reality, serious, shocking, severe, grievous, likely to affect me, important.
    b. low: constructs implying that death has minimal impact.
       examples: acceptable, abstract, trivial, unimportant, no shock, unlikely to affect me, doesn't matter.

14. *Causality*
    a. known: constructs suggesting that the physical cause of death is known or explained.
       examples: caused, has a concrete cause, brought about mechanically, heart attack, cancer, suicide, caused by me.
    b. unknown: constructs implying that the physical cause of death is nonspecific or unknown.
       examples: no known cause, not mechanically caused, not caused by action.

Appendix 2:
Death Construct Coding Dictionary

A			
		angry	3b
		animal, like an	no score
abandonment	11a	anguish, deep	2b, 6a
able to find me	7a, 12a	anonymous	12b
abnormal	2b	answer, no	5b
abstract	12b	answerable	5a
accelerated	8b	anticipated	8a
acceptable	no score	anticipated, not	8b
accepted	no score	anxiety	2b, 6a
accident	1b, 11b	anxiety, no	2a, 6b
accidental	1b, 11b	anyone can deal with it	13b
acquainted	5a, 7a	apart	no score
action	no score	appreciate	no score
active	no score	artificial	1b
acts of nature	11b, 14a	ashamed	3b
adaptable	no score	at once	8b
admirable	2a	attached	no score
adult	no score	attempted death	11a
affect others, does not	13b	attempted prevention	no score
affect people around me,		attractive	2a
does not	13b, 7b	aversive	2b
affected mildly	6b, 13b	avoidable	11a
affected with sadness	3b	avoiding death	4b, 11a
affecting	no score	avoiding death, not	no score
affecting me just on the		awareness in advance	8a
surface	13b, 7b	awareness	8a
affecting you more	13a		
affects me	7a, 13a	B	
affects me less	13b, 7b		
affects me more	7a, 13a	bad	2b
affects my lifestyle	7a	bad death	2b
affects others	13a	bad for me	2b, 7a
affects people around me	13a	bad, not	2a
afraid of happening to you	3b	bearable	6a
age	no score	beautiful	2a
age has made unhealthy	6a	beginning	no score
aggravating	3b	being of use	1a
agitated	3b, 6a	being one who is left	7a
agonizing	6a	better	2a
alive	10a	better, for the	2a
already dead	10b	better for person	
anger	3b	involved	2a

better off	2a	chance, by	11b
better off, not	2b	chance, no	9a
biological	no score	chance, has a	no score
blessed	1a, 2a	chance, not having a	9a
blessing	1a, 2a	chance, sudden	8b
bother people, does not	13b	chance, no to survive	9a
bothering people	13a, 4b	cheerful	no score
brave	no score	chemical	14a
bravery	no score	choice	11a
brutal	6a	choice, having	11a
		choice, no	11b
C		choosing	11a
		choosing, not	11b
calculating	11a	circumstance, matter of	11b
calm	no score	clean	no score
can't be helped	11b	close	no score
can't cope	4b	close to home	7a
careful	no score	close to me	7a
careless	no score	close to you	7a
caring	7a	cold	no score
caring, not	no score	comes unknowingly	8b
caring about life	no score	common	12b
caring about life, not	no score	commonplace, not	12a
cause	14a	compassion	no score
cause, having	14a	complacent	no score
cause, no	14b	complicated	no score
cause, having no	14b	concerned	7a
cause, no apparent	14b	concrete	5a
caused by action	14a	condemned	2a, 9a
caused by action, not	14b	conscious	no score
caused by humans	14a	conscious suffering	6a
caused by humans, not	14b	constructive	2a
caused by me	7a, 14a	contented	no score
caused by nature	14a	continuation	10a
caused by someone else	14a	contribute to society,	
caused, mechanically	14a	does not	1b
caused, not mechanically	14b	contributes to society	1a
cause death, I did not	7b	control	11a
cause death, you	14a	control, no	11b
cause, internal	14a	controlable	11a
cause, outside	14a	controlled death	11a
cautions	no score	cope	no score
cautions, not	no score	coping, not	4b
certainty	9a	could have been helped	no score
certain, less	no score	couldn't happen to me	7b
chance	11b	courage	no score

cowardly	no score	difference between life	
crazy	no score	and death	10b
cruel	2a, 6a	different	no score
curse	2a	disaster	13a
		disastrous	13a
D		discriminate	no score
		disease	6a, 14a
dark	2b	disease, no	6b
dead	10b	disgracing	2b
dead, not	10a	disgusting	2b
death	10b	disinterested	13b
death for me	7a, 10b,	dismal	2b
	12a	distant	7b
death is far away	7b	distress	6a
death, less	12a	distressing, very	6a
death, more	12b	disturbing	3b, 4b,
death is paramount	13a		6a, 13a
death is not paramount	13b	disturbing, not	13b
deciding in advance	no score	doesn't apply to me	7b
decision	11a	doing nothing	no score
deeply crushed	3b	doomed	9a
defensive	4b	doubting God	1b
definite	9a	dramatic	13a
deliberate	11a	drawn out	8a
demands personal coping	7a	dreadful	2b
depressed	3b	dream, having a	no score
depressing	2b, 3b	dying	9a, 10b
dependent	no score		
deprived, being	6a	**E**	
depth, having no	1b		
descriptive	no score	easier	2a
descriptive, not	no score	easier to bear	no score
deserving	1a	easier to take	no score
desirable	2a	elating	no score
desired	2a	elements	no score
desired, not	2b	elimination of pain	6b
despair	3b	emotional	13a
despair, no	no score	emptiness	10b
destined	1a	empty	1b
destroy	10b	end	10b
destruction	10b	end, can see ___ coming	8a
destructive	no score	end, can't see ___ coming	8b
detached	13b	end of life	10b
devastating	13a	enemy	2b
deviant	2b	escape	1a
deviance	no score	escape, not	no score

escapism	no score	feelings, inner	13a
ethical	2a	few	12a
euphoric	no score	fighter	4b
euthanasia	11a	final	10b
eventual	9a	fitting	2a
existence, after a short	no score	flow of awareness	10a
existing	10a	forgivable	no score
existing, not	10b	foreign	5b
expected	8a	forseeable	8a
expected, not	8b	forseeable, not	8b
experience	10a	for the best	2a
extended pain	6a	fortuitous	11b
external	no score	fortunate	2a
		fortunate, not	2b

F

		freak accident	11b
		friend, death of	7a
facing death	no score	fright	3b
failure, mechanical	14a	frightening	3b
fair	2a	fulfilled	no score
fair, not	2b	fulfilled, not	3b
faith, having	no score	full	1a
familiar	5a	fuller life	2a
familiar, not	5b	future consequences,	
family	7a	having	13a
family knows	no score		

G

family, not	7b		
family shocked	13a		
far	8a, 7b	gain	2a
fast	9b	gain for you	2a
fast, too ___ to feel pain	6b, 8b	general	12b
fatalistic	9a	gentle	6b
fate	11b	getting everything in order	8a
fated	9a, 11b	getting it over with	no score
father's death	7a, 12a	gift	2a
fault	no score	glad	no score
fault, my	14a	gloomy	3b
fault, no	no score	good	2a
favorable	2a	good, for a ___ cause	1a
favorable, not	2b	good, not for a ___ cause	1b
fear	3b	good idea	2a
fear, no	no score	good, not	2b
fearful	3b	goodness	2a
feeling	13a	granted, taken for	13b
feeling, not ___ it	6b	grateful	no score
feeling, personal	7a	grateful, not	3b
feeling sorrow	3b	gratifying	2a

greater	no score	helped, could not have	
grief	3b	been	9a
grief, no	no score	helpful	2a
grieve	3b	helpless	11b
grieve, not	no score	here, being	10a
grievous	13a	here, not being	10b
group	12b	hero	no score
guilt	3b	hidden	no score
guilt, no	no score	hit home, doesn't	13b, 7b
guilty	3b	hits home	7a, 13a
guilty, not	no score	hollow	1b
guilty death	2b	hope	no score
		hope for the better	9b
H		hope, lack of	9a
		hope, no	9a
handle, anyone can __ it	no score	hopeful	no score
happen to me, couldn't	7b	hopeless	9a
happen, might	no score	horror	3b
happen, will	9a	horror, not	2a
happen, won't	no score	horrible	2b
happened, already	9a	horrible, not	2a
happened, just	9a	horrifying	2b
happening all at once	8b	horrifying, not	2a
happening to me	7a	human	no score
happens, just	11b	human intervention	14a
happy	no score	human intervention,	
happy, not	3b	non	no score
happy being alive	10a	humane	2a, 6b
happy, not __ with life	3b	humane, not	2b, 6a
hard to accept	4b	humanitarian	no score
hard to adapt to	4b	humanity, shock to	13a
harder	2b	humanity's sake, for	1a
harder to bear	4b	humorous	no score
harder to take	4b	hurt	6a
harm	2b	hurt, not	6b
harsh	2b, 6a	hurting	6a
hate	3b	hypothetical	13b
hateful	3b		
hate, no	no score	**I**	
having meaning	1a		
having time	8a	identity, having	12a
health	6b	illness	6a
hectic	13b	imagined	13b
help, able to	no score	imbalance, no severe	13b
helped, can't be	9a	immediate	8b
helped, could have been	no score	impact, less	13b

impact, much	13a	involved, not	no score
impersonal	7b	involved, personally	7a
importance	13a	involvement	7a, 13a
importance, less	13b	involves children	13a
impressing	13a	involves courage	no score
impressing, not	13b	involves fear	3b
improper	2b	involves others	12b
incidental	13b	involves pain	6a
incomprehensible	5b	involves parents	13a
inconceivable	5b	ironic	no score
inconvenient	13a	irrational	1b
incorrect	2b	irresponsible	2b
independent	no score	irrelevant	13b
indifferent	13b	irreversible	10b
indiscriminant	12b		
individual	12a	**J**	
inescapable	9a, 11b		
inevitable	9a	joy	no score
inflicted	no score	joyful	no score
inflicting pain	6a	just	1a, 2a
influenced death	14a	just happened	8b
inhumane	6a, 2b	just one	2a
innocent	2a	justified	1a
insane action	no score	justified, not	1b
insecure	3b		
instant	8b	**K**	
instantaneous	8b		
intellectual	5a	keep on going	10a, 8a
intelligent	no score	killing	14a
intense	13a	killing oneself	11a
intensely emotional	3b	killing others	14a
intent, less	11b	kind	2a
intent, much	11a	kind, not	2b
intent, no	11b	know it is coming	8a
intent, with	11a	know it is coming,	
intention, good	2a	do not	8b
intentional	11a	knowing of facts	
intentional, not	1b, 11b	before death	5a, 8a
interested in an impersonal		knowing of facts after	
way	no score	death, not	5b
interested in a personal way	7a	knowing the people,	
interesting	2a	not	no score
interesting, not	2b	knowing the person	7a
internal	no score	knowing what it is about	5a
involve me, does not	7b	knowing what it is about,	
involves only me	7a, 12a	not	5b

knowing when	9a	loss, less of a	2a, 13b
knowing when, not	8b	loss, more of a	13a
knowledgable	5a	loss, no	2a, 13b
knowledgable, not	5b	loss, personal	7a
knowledge of death, no	5b	loss, self	7a
known	5a	lot of life left	10a
known possibility of		loved	no score
death occurring	5a, 8a	loved on leaving you	7a, 13a
		loved ones, having	no score
L		loves	no score
		loving	no score
lasting	6a, 8a	lucky	2a
lasting idea of death	no score	ludicrous	2b
leaving	10b	lunatic	2b
legal	2a		
legal, not	2b	**M**	
life	10a		
life experienced	10a	man	no score
life not experienced	10b	man causes	14a
life, fearing for my	3b	man made	14a
life giving	10a	manipulator	no score
life, jeopardizes	no score	masochistic	6a
life, lacking	10b	mass	12b
life, risking one's	11a	matters	13a
life saving	10a	mature	8a
life, shortening of	10b	mature, not	8b
life, terminates	10b	may be	no score
light	no score	may not be	no score
like an animal	no score	maybe better off dead	2a
lingering	8a	me	7a
lingering death	8a, 6a	me, close to	7a
live with it, not having to	13b	me, part of	7a
lived, hasn't yet	no score	me, not part of	13b, 7b
lives her life	10a	me, pertaining to	7a
living	10a	meaningful	1a
logical	2a, 5a	meaningless	1b
logical, not	1b, 2b, 5b	memory, brutal	6a
lonely	3b	mental	no score
lonely, not	2a	mentally prepared	5a, 8a
long	8a	mentally prepared, not	5b, 8b
long after	no score	merciful	1a, 2a
long time	8a	merciful, not	2b
losing	2b	mercy killing	1a
loss	2b, 13a	mercy killing, not	1b
loss for you	7a	minutes thinking	no score
loss, great	13a	mistake	2b

peaceful	2a, 6b	preventable, not	9a
peaceful, not	2b	pride	no score
people killed	12b	problem	2b
people, less	12a	process, death as	8a
people to care for	no score	prolonged	8a, 6a
person, one	12a	proud	no score
personal	7a	proud, not	3b
personal, not	7b	publicized	13a
personal hurt	7a, 3b	punishment	1a
personal loss	7a, 2b	purpose	1a
personal loss, no	7b	purpose, having a	
personal suffering	7a, 6a	definite	1a
personally, could relate to	7a, 5a	purposeful	1a
personally involved	7a	purposeless	1b
pertaining to others	7b	put off	8a
phenomenon, natural	14a		
physical	9a	**Q**	
physical death	9a, 10b		
physically inactive	no score	question why his death	4b
pity	3b	questionable	4b
pity myself	3b	questionable, not	no score
planned	11a	quiet	no score
planned, not	11b	quick	8b
pleasant	2a		
pleasurable	2a	**R**	
pleasurable, not	2b		
pleasure	no score	rare	12a
plural	12b	ready to accept	no score
pointed	no score	ready to accept, not	4b
positive	2a	real	13a
positive, not	2b	real, not	13b
potential, full	no score	realistic	no score
potential, had __ but		realistic, not	4b
were killed	no score	realization of death's	
powerful	no score	possibility	8a
predestiny	9a, 11b	reason	1a
predetermined	14a, 9a	reason, having a	1a
predetermined, not	no score	reason, no	1b
predictable	8a, 9a	reasonable	2a, 5a
predictable, not	8b	reasonable, not	2b, 1b
preparations	8a	reckless	2b
prepared	8a	rediscovering life	10a
prepared, not	8b	regrettable	2b
present	9a	regretted	2b
pretty good life	2a	regretted, not	2a
preventable	no score	relate	5a

relate, can __ to it	5a	saved	10a
relate, can't __ to it	5b	saved, could be	no score
related	7a	saved, could not be	9a
related, not	no score	saving, not	11a
related to me	7a	scared	3b
relating to a loved one	7a, 13a	scary	2b
relating to someone		second chance, no	10b, 9a
unknown	13b, 7b	secure	2a
relatives	7a	see, can __ myself	
relaxing	2a, 6b	dying	7a
relief	no score	see, can't __ myself	
relief, no	3b	dying	7b
relieved	no score	see, you can __ the	
reluctant	4b	end coming	8a
reluctant, not	no score	see, you can't __ the	
remorse	3b	end coming	8b
remorse, no	13b	seeking death	11a
remorseful	2b, 13a	seen	8a
remorseful, not	2a, 13b	seen, not	8b
removed	13b	self	7a
representation of future	no score	self-anger	3b
repulsive	2b	self-determined	11a
respectable	2a	self-hate	3b
responsible	11a	self-inflicted	11a
responsible, not	11b	self-life	10a
responsibility	11a	self, not	no score
responsibility, no	11b	self-sacrifice	11a
restful	6b, 2a	selfish	2b
reward	1a	sensational	13a
rewarded	1a	sensational, not	13b
rewarded, not	1b	senseless	1b
right	2a	sensible	2a
routine	12b	sensible, not	1b, 2b
		serene	2a, 6b
S		serious	13a
		severe	13a
sad	3b	severe consequences	13a
sad, not	no score	severe consequences,	
sad, real	3b	less	13b
sad situation	2b, 3b	shame	3b
sadness, impersonal	3b, 7b	shameful	2b, 3b
sadness, personal	7a, 3b	shocking	13a
sadistic	6a, 2b	shocking, not	13b
safe	2a	short life left	8b
safety, feeling of	2a	short pain	6b
sane	2a	should be alive	2b

timely	2a	unfair, not	2a
togetherness	no score	unfamiliar	5b
torturous	2b, 6a, 13a	unforgivable	2b, 4b
		unforseeable	8b, 9a
total loss of thought	10b	unfortunate	2b
touch, in __ with reality	5a	unfulfillment	2b
touchable	5a	unhappiness	3b
tragedy	13a	unhealthy	6a
tragic	2b, 13a	universal	12b
tragic, less	13b	unjust	2b
traumatic	2b, 13b	unknowing	5b
trustworthy	2a	unknowledgable	5b
trying to save	11a	unknown	5b
trying, not __ to save	11a	unlucky	2b
trying to help someone	11a	unregretted	13a
typical	12b	unrelated	no score
typical, cultural	12b	unremorseful	no score
		unstable	4b

U

		untimely	2b
		upsetting	2b, 3b
ugly	2b	useful	1a
unaffected	7b, 13b	useless	1b
unappreciative	3b, 4b		
unacquainted	4b, 5b		
unattached	7b, 13b	**V**	
unavoidable	9a	vicious	2b, 6a
unaware	5b	vicious, not	2a, 6b
unbearable	4b, 6a, 13a	victory	1a, 2a
		vile	2b
uncalled for	1b, 2b	violent	2b, 6a
uncalm	3b, 4b	violent, less	no score
uncertainty	no score	violent, not	6b
unchosen	11b	violent, sickeningly	2b, 6a, 13a
uncomplicated	2a		
unconscious happening	6b	violent, slightly	no score
uncontrol	9a, 11b	vulgar	2b
understandable	5a		
understandable, not	5b	**W**	
undeserving	1b, 2b		
undesirable	2b	waiting	8a
undisturbing	13b	waiting for death	8a
unexpected	8b	wanting	2a, 11a
unexpected nature	8b	wanting, not	2b
unexpected people	8b	wanted, not	2b
unfair	2b	wanting to live	no score

wanting to die	2a	worry that it will	
wanting to die, not	2b	happen	3b, 4b
warm	no score	worse	2b
warning	8a	wrong	1b, 2b
warning, no	8b	wrong for another	1b, 2b
waste	2b	wrong for me	1b, 2b,
waste, not a	2a		7a
weak	3b	wrong, something went	2b
weird	2b		
welcomed	2a	Y	
welcomed, not	2b		
well	6b	you guilty	3b
will happen	9a	you killed someone	14a
willed	11a	you saw happen	9a, 13a
willed, not	11b	young	no score
willing to die	11a	young is healthy	10a
winning	no score	young promising life	no score
worried	3b	youthful	no score

∞∞∞

A PROCEDURE MANUAL FOR THE THREAT INDEX

∞∞∞

ROBERT A. NEIMEYER

Memphis State University

FRANZ R. EPTING

University of Florida

MICHAEL A. RIGDON

University of Utah

Several of the foregoing papers have used versions of the Threat Index (1) as a means of exploring the personal meanings that individuals attribute to their own mortality. For the convenience of the interested clinician and researcher, the procedures for administering and scoring the most commonly used forms of the instrument are presented here. A detailed review of studies examining the psychometric properties of the TI has been provided elsewhere (2). Several additional publications (noted below) address the theoretical rationale underpinning the instrument, guidelines for interpretation of the scores derivable from it, and examples of the instrument's application.

The Threat Index: Elicited Form (TIe)

Format: Structured interview; individual administration only.

Time required: 60-90 minutes.

Advantages: Provides clinically rich and personally relevant depiction of interviewee's construal of death; may facilitate psychotherapeutic exploration of client's death concern.

Disadvantages: Lengthy; requires relatively articulate interviewee.

Special notes: Because of the potential sensitivity of the issues raised, a professional counselor always has been available on a standby basis during the administration of the TIe.

Procedure: A large portion of the threat-assessment interview is devoted to the elicitation of death-relevant constructs (1). This is accomplished by the use of 10 element cards, presented in groups of 3, termed a triad. The first of the element cards simply has the word "death" printed on it. The other 9 situations involving death are as follows:

2. You discover that you have leukemia and only a few weeks to live.
3. Your closest friend is killed in a plane crash.
4. Your grandmother dies in her sleep.
5. President Kennedy's assassination.
6. A Buddhist monk burns himself to protest the war in Indochina.
7. You run over and kill a young child.
8. A baby dies of lead poisoning from eating chips of paint.
9. Capital punishment.
10. A homicidal maniac is on the loose and has already viciously mutilated six people in your community.

The following 11 elements were used in a later study (3): Elements 1, 2, 3, 4, 7, and 10 above (now elements 1-6) plus 5 others:

7. Your father dies while trying to save another person from drowning.
8. A divorced mother of two dies from an overdose.
9. A genetically deformed baby is allowed to die in the hospital.
10. A terminal patient dies after months of unrelievable pain.
11. Three children die when a tornado hits their elementary school.

The actual procedure begins with the interviewer providing an introduction to brief the subject on the nature of the procedure and to help put her or him at ease. The interviewer then lays out the first triad of cards in front of the subject. The "death" card is presented in each triad to help focus the subject on death-relevant constructs. The subject is asked, "how are two alike and different from the third?" The interviewer enters the response and obtains the contrast pole by asking, "What is the opposite of that?"

The construct dimensions produced by the triad procedure are referred to as subordinate constructs. Using the laddering technique, the interviewer elicits a set of superordinate constructs from the subject's responses to the triad procedure. Laddering is accomplished by asking the subject, "Do you prefer to associate your self more closely with _____ (construct pole) or with _____ (contrast pole)?" The interviewer enters the subject's response and asks, "Why do you prefer to see yourself this way as opposed to the other?" If the subject has trouble answering, an additional question is asked: "What are the advantages of this one (the preferred pole) as opposed to the disadvantages of that one (the nonpreferred pole)?" Or the subject is prompted with the incomplete sentence, "I prefer to see myself as _____ (the preferred pole) because . . . ." This response is entered as a pole of a second construct; an opposite is called for; a preference is obtained; and "Why?" again asked. This cycle is continued until the subject can no longer respond to "Why?" At this point she or he is presented with a new triad of cards and the procedure is begun again, continuing until 30 constructs have been collected. The interviewer also begins a new triad whenever the subject begins to repeat constructs previously given. Because it is important that 30 different constructs be obtained, the subject is consulted whenever there is any doubt about the difference between two constructs. If the subject says that she or he means the same thing by the two phrases in question, it is assumed that they are the same construct, and one is discarded.

Once 30 different constructs are recorded along with a pole preference for each, the interviewer directs the subject's attention back to the first construct and asks, "Do you, in fact, more closely associate yourself with _____ (construct pole) or with _____ (contrast pole)?" This placement of the self element is entered, unless the subject says, "Neither." The same procedure is followed for the death element: "Do you more closely associate your own death with _____ (construct pole) or with _____ (contrast pole)?" This placement is also recorded. The interviewer continues in this way for all 30 constructs.

Scoring: Originally, the total threat score was calculated by tallying the number of instances in which the subject subsumed the "self" (S) and "preferred self" (P) elements under one pole of a construct, and "death" (D) under the other. Recent adaptations of the TI have excluded placement of the P element, since preliminary research indicates that the number of S/D "splits" alone provides a valid measure of the respondent's death threat.

The personal format of the TIe also permits the scoring of death construct content, using the manual developed by Neimeyer, Fontana, and Gold (4).

Research using the method: 1, 5, 6.

The Threat Index: Provided Forms (TIp)

Format: Paper-and-pencil test; individual or large group administration.

Time required: 15–30 minutes.

Advantages: Easily administered; permits standardization and between-subject comparison.

Disadvantages: May not assess adequately idiosyncratic construals of death; relatively impersonal format may be objectionable to some respondents.

Special notes: Some subjects have difficulty completing the TIp because no conversational context exists to clarify the meaning of the construct dimensions it utilizes.

Procedure: The following instructions are stated on a separate page for each of the three elements:

1. Self element. Below is a list of dimensions, each of which is made up of a pair of opposites. For each dimension, please circle the side with which you see yourself or your

present life more closely associated. In some cases, you may feel as if both sides describe you to some degree, but please circle only one side of each dimension: the one that describes you better. For example, do you see yourself as more predictable or random?

2. Preferred self element. For each of the dimensions below, please circle the side with which you more closely associate your ideal self or the way you would prefer to be living. For example, would you prefer to be more predictable or random?

3. Death element. For each of the dimensions below, please circle the side with which you more closely associate your own death, thinking of your own death as if it were to occur at this time in your life.

For the bipolar TI, the following dimensions are simply listed immediately following each set of instructions. For the scalar TI, the two poles lie at each end of a 7-point scale.

Dimensions for the TIp40

predictable–random
empty–meaningful
lackof control–control
satisfied–dissatisfied
relating to others–not relating to others
pleasure–pain
feels bad–feels good
objective–subjective
alive–dead
helping others–being selfish
specific–general
kind–cruel
incompetent–competent
insecure–secure
static–changing
unnatural–natural
calm–anxious
easy–hard
productive–unproductive
learning–not learning

sad–happy
personal–impersonal
purposeful–not purposeful
responsible–not responsible
bad–good
not caring–caring
crazy–healthy
conforming–not conforming
animate–inanimate
weak–strong
useful–useless
closed–open
peaceful–violent
freedom–restriction
nonexistence–existence
understanding–not understanding
sick–healthy
stagnation–growth
abstract–concrete
hope–no hope

Dimensions for the TIp30

predictable–random	not caring–caring
empty–meaningful	satisfied–dissatisfied
sad–happy	relating to others–not relating to others
personal–impersonal	feels bad–feels good
lack of control–control	objective–subjective
specific–general	animate–inanimate
kind–cruel	weak–strong
static–changing	closed–open
unnatural–natural	peaceful–violent
calm–anxious	freedom–restriction
easy–hard	nonexistence–existence
learning–not learning	understanding–not understanding
purposeful–not purposeful	sick–healthy
responsible–not responsible	abstract–concrete
bad–good	hope–no hope

Scoring: As with the elicited from of the TI, the TIp may be scored by calculating the absolute number of *SP/D* splits, or more simply *S/D* splits.

In addition, investigators have experimented with deriving two other scores from the TIp. One method (see 7, 8) requires presenting the construct poles in such a way that they flank 7-point Likert scales on which the respondent rates the *D* element (e.g., random 1 2 3 4 5 6 7 predictable). A rating extremity score is then computed by summing the absolute values of the deviations of these ratings from 4. The lower the extremity score, the more death anxiety (as opposed to death threat) the respondent is likely to experience.

A second scoring procedure involves tabulating the number of self/preferred self splits, that is the number of instances in which the *S* and *P* elements are placed on opposite poles of a construct dimension. Theoretically, this score has been interpreted as a measure of self/ideal discrepancy (9) (or inversely, actualization, 10), and it has been found to correlate negatively with death anxiety as indexed by a variety of questionnaires.

Research using the method: 3, 5, 6, 7, 8, 9, 10, 11, 12, 13.

References

1. Krieger, S. R., Epting, F. R., & Leitner, L. M. Personal constructs, threat and attitudes toward death. *Omega*, 1974, *5*, 299-310.
2. Rigdon, M. A., Epting, F. R., Neimeyer, R. A., & Krieger. S. R. The Threat Index: A research report. *Death Education*, 1979, *3*, 245-270.
3. Rainey, L. C., & Epting, F. R. Death threat constructions in the student and the prudent. *Omega*, 1977, *8*, 19-28.
4. Neimeyer, R. A., Fontana, D., & Gold, K. M. A death construct coding manual. In F. R. Epting & R. A. Neimeyer (Eds.), *Personal meanings of death*. New York: Hemisphere/McGraw-Hill, 1983.
5. Krieger, S. R., Epting, F. R., & Hays, C. H. Validity and reliability of provided constructs in assessing death threat: A self-administered form. *Omega*, 1979, *10*, 87-95.
6. Neimeyer, R. A., Dingemans, P. M., & Epting, F. R. Convergent validity, situational stability and meaningfulness of the Threat Index. *Omega*, 1977, *8*, 251-265.
7. Neimeyer, R. A. Death anxiety and the Threat Index: An addendum. *Death Education*, 1978, *1*, 464-476.
8. Neimeyer, G. J., Behnke, M., & Reis, J. Constructs and coping: Physicians' responses to patient death. In F. R. Epting & R. A. Neimeyer (Eds.), *Personal meanings of death*. New York: Hemisphere/McGraw-Hill, 1983.
9. Neimeyer, R. A., & Chapman, K. M. Self-ideal discrepancy and fear of death: The test of an existential hypothesis. *Omega*, 1981, *11*, 233-240.
10. Robinson, P. J., & Wood, K. Fear of death and physical illness: A personal construct approach. In F. R. Epting & R. A. Neimeyer (Eds.), *Personal meanings of death*. New York: Hemisphere/McGraw-Hill, 1983.
11. Durlak, J. A., & Kass, R. A. Clarifying the measurement of death attitudes: factor-analytic evaluation of fifteen self-report death scales. *Omega*, 1981, *12*, 129-141.
12. Neimeyer, R. A., & Dingemans, P. M. Death orientation in the suicide intervention worker. *Omega*, 1980, *11*, 17-25.
13. Epting, F. R., Rainey, L. C., & Weiss, M. J. Constructions of death and levels of death fear. *Death Education*, 1979, *3*, 21-30.